# Dividends of Kinship

This collection reaffirms the importance of kinship, and of studying kinship, within the framework of social anthropology.

The contributors examine both the benefits and the burdens of kinship across cultures and explore how 'relatedness' is inextricably linked with other concepts which define people's identities, such as gender, power and history. With examples from a wide range of areas including Austria, Greenland, Portugal, Turkey and the Amazon, the book covers themes such as:

- how people choose and activate kin
- leadership, spiritual power and kinship
- inheritance, marriage and social inequality
- familial sentiment and economic interest
- the role of kinship in Utopian communes

*Dividends of Kinship* provides a timely and critical reappraisal of the place of familial relations in the contemporary world. It will be of interest to undergraduates, postgraduates and academics in anthropology, and across the social sciences.

**Peter P. Schweitzer** is Associate Professor of Anthropology at the University of Alaska Fairbanks and Lecturer at the University of Vienna.

# European Association of Social Anthropologists

Series facilitator: Jon P. Mitchell
*University of Sussex*

The European Association of Social Anthropologists (EASA) was inaugurated in January 1989, in response to a widely felt need for a professional association that would represent social anthropologists in Europe and foster co-operation and interchange in teaching and research. As Europe transforms itself in the 1990s, the EASA is dedicated to the renewal of the distinctive European tradition in social anthropology.

Other titles in the series:

# Dividends of Kinship

## Meanings and uses of social relatedness

## Edited by Peter P. Schweitzer

London and New York

First published 2000
by Routledge
11 New Fetter Lane, London EC4P 4EE

Simultaneously published in the USA and Canada
by Routledge
29 West 35th Street, New York, NY 10001

*Routledge is an imprint of the Taylor & Francis Group*

© 2000 selection and editorial matter, EASA; individual chapters
© the contributors

Typeset in Galliard by Taylor & Francis Books Ltd
Printed and bound in Great Britain by St Edmundsbury Press,
Bury St Edmunds, Suffolk

*British Library Cataloguing in Publication Data*
A catalogue record for this book is available from the British
Library

*Library of Congress Cataloging in Publication Data*
Dividends of kinship: meanings and uses of social relatedness /
edited by Peter P. Schweitzer. p.cm. – (European Association of
Social Anthropologists) Includes bibliographical references and
index.
1. Kinship–Cross cultural studies. 2. Family–Cross cultural
studies. I. Schweitzer, Peter P. II. European Association of Social
Anthropologists (Series)
GN480.2 .D58 2000
306.85–dc21                          99–047551

ISBN 0–415–18283–2 (hbk)
ISBN 0–415–18284–0 (pbk)

# Contents

# Contributors

**Christoph Brumann** is Lecturer at the Institute of Ethnology, University of Cologne. Other than on Utopian communes in Japan and elsewhere, he has written on gift exchange in Tokyo, globalisation and the concept of culture. Currently, he is analysing fieldwork data on tradition, democracy and the urban landscape in Kyoto, Japan. He has published *Die Kunst des Teilens: Eine vergleichende Untersuchung zu den Überlebensbedingungen kommunitärer Gruppen* (Lit, 1998).

**Richard Gippelhauser** is Lecturer at the Institute of Ethnology, Cultural and Social Anthropology, University of Vienna. He has conducted extensive research on social and political organisation in the Peruvian Amazon region. Currently, he is engaged in archaeological research in Austria and Peru.

**Elke Mader** is Associate Professor at the Institute of Ethnology, Cultural and Social Anthropology, University of Vienna, where she defended her '*venia docendi* thesis' in 1997. Her current research focuses on myth, shamanism and social change in the Ecuadorian Oriente. Her most recent book is *Metamorfosis del poder. Persona, mito y visión en la sociedad de Shuar y Achuar* (Abya Yala, 1999).

**Mark Nuttall** is Senior Lecturer in Anthropology and Sociology at the University of Aberdeen. He has carried out research in Greenland, Scotland and Alaska, and his publications include *Arctic Homeland: Kinship, Community and Development in Northwest Greenland* (University of Toronto Press, 1992), *White Settlers: The Impact of Rural Repopulation in Scotland* (Harwood Academic Publishers, 1996, with Charles Jedrej) and *Protecting the Arctic: Indigenous Peoples and Cultural Survival* (Harwood Academic Publishers, 1998).

**Antónia Pedroso de Lima** is Assistant Professor of Social Anthropology at the Department of Anthropology in ISCTE (University of Lisbon), specialising in kinship theory and contemporary family relations. She has published on Portuguese urban families, focusing both on the working-class neighbourhoods of Lisbon and on the Portuguese economic élite. She is currently working on a project about dynastic families and their major enterprises.

**Peter P. Schweitzer** received his Ph.D. from the University of Vienna and is currently Associate Professor of Anthropology at the University of Alaska Fairbanks and Lecturer at the Institute of Ethnology, Cultural and Social Anthropology, University of Vienna. He has conducted extensive fieldwork in north-eastern Siberia and western Alaska. As well as kinship, his areas of interest include politics, history, and hunter-gatherer studies. He has published widely on northern issues and is co-editor of *Hunters and Gatherers in the Modern World: Conflict, Resistance, and Self-determination* (Berghahn Books, 2000).

**Gertraud Seiser** is currently – after ten years of public service – a member of the scientific staff at the Institute of Ethnology, Cultural and Social Anthropology, University of Vienna. She is conducting research on European peasant societies and on the impact of the European Community on economic concepts of marginalised rural areas.

**Jenny B. White** is Associate Professor of Anthropology at Boston University. She is the author of *Money Makes Us Relatives: Women's Labor in Urban Turkey* (University of Texas Press, 1994). She has written extensively on the informal sector, civil society, as well as on Turkish identity in Germany after reunification and family life in Turkey. At present she is writing a book on Islamist politics in Turkey.

# Preface

This is the first volume on kinship to appear in the European Association of Social Anthropologists (EASA) series. It is based on papers delivered at 'The Dividends of Kinship' workshop at the fourth EASA conference, in Barcelona (July 1996), which was held with the overall theme of 'Culture and Economy: Conflicting Interests, Divided Loyalties'. While kinship-related workshops were notably absent at the first two EASA meetings, in Coimbra (1990) and Prague (1992), the third conference, in Oslo (1994), featured three workshops under the umbrella topic of 'A New Agenda for Kinship Studies'. However, none of the workshops resulted in an edited volume in the EASA Routledge series.

In 1993, in a first call for papers for the Oslo kinship workshops, the conveners Adam Kuper and Gerd Baumann countered the decline of kinship studies during the 1970s and 1980s with a defensive 'but in the field we are still confronted with kinship – or "kinship". Indeed our informants talk endlessly about marriage and marriage strategies, inheritance and succession, parents and children, siblings, cousins, and family history' (Kuper, A. and Baumann, G. (1993) 'A fresh agenda for kinship studies', *EASA Newsletter* 10: 7). Since then, publishers' catalogues and the tables of contents of anthropological journals are filled with signs of a new 'kinship vogue'. Even the 1998 Annual Meeting of the American Anthropological Association featured a decadal high score of five panels devoted to kinship in one way or another.

The Barcelona workshop on which this volume is based was convened to go beyond approaches to kinship that seemed too narrowly 'cultural relativist', but without retreating to earlier biological or genealogical models of kinship. The abstract called for 'a renewed comparative approach to material and symbolic gains that can be secured through cultural constructs of relatedness', and urged potential applicants 'to explore the plurality of (culturally defined) interests pursued through different notions of kinship'. This call for papers resulted in a large number of applicants; unfortunately, several excellent proposals had to be excluded due to rather stringent time and space constraints. After presenting the papers in the pleasant atmosphere of a lively Barcelona summer, further discussions about the topics and about potential revisions of the papers commenced, which are herewith brought to a preliminary conclusion. All but one of the papers presented in Barcelona are included in this volume.

First, I want to thank the organisers of the Barcelona meeting for their hospitality and the participants of the workshop for their intellectual input, as well as the audience members for their critical questions. Further thanks go to Jon Mitchell, the EASA series facilitator, and Victoria Peters and Fintan Power, the Routledge editors, who – despite lengthy delays – never withdrew their support for the project. The Department of Anthropology at the University of Alaska Fairbanks provided its facilities and the labour of two graduate students, James O'Brien and Stacie McIntosh, for the preparation of this volume. Special recognition must go to the latter, without whose editorial skills this book could not have been published in its present form.

PPS
Fairbanks
1999

# Chapter 1

# Introduction

*Peter P. Schweitzer*

At the end of the twentieth century, the complex career path of one of anthropology's most famous domains of inquiry – kinship – is about to take another unexpected turn. Just sixteen years ago, when David Schneider proclaimed his final verdict in *A Critique of the Study of Kinship* (Schneider 1984), the once cherished 'basic discipline of the subject' (Fox 1983: 10) seemed more like an endangered species. By the late 1990s, however, monographs (e.g. Carsten 1997; Sabean 1998; Weston 1997), edited volumes (e.g. Franklin and Ragoné 1998; Godelier *et al*. 1998; Gullestad and Segalen 1997), textbooks (e.g. Holy 1996; Parkin 1997; Stone 1997) and review articles (e.g. Faubion 1996; Gingrich 1995; Peletz 1995) carrying 'kinship' or 'marriage' in their titles abound.[1]

While the present volume joins this 'rediscovery' of kinship as a legitimate field of anthropological inquiries, we are not interested in a melancholic return to pre-Schneiderian kinship studies. Thus, one objective of this introductory chapter is to probe whether this resurgence is more than the cyclical reoccurrence of a past vogue. Such a perspective is bolstered by the conviction that any so-called 'crisis' of a particular approach, discipline or sub-discipline becomes virulent if the critical questions raised exceed the analytical capacity of the field under attack, no matter how violently its defenders may deny the 'crisis'. Crisis, thus, contains – at least – the potential for refinement and advance.

*Dividends of Kinship* is not intended to provide a well-rounded spectrum of the various possible ways of approaching kinship. Instead, it proposes the further elaboration of one particular perspective that has received little attention lately: namely, the functional aspects of kinship. This entails a shift of emphasis from 'meaning' to 'function' without ignoring the former. The question 'what is kinship' is, thus, reinforced by 'what is done through kinship'. Such a perspective pays particular attention to the tactical dimensions of individual strategies, without ignoring their social contexts. Thematically, this approach refers to the material, symbolic and emotional gains that can be secured through cultural constructs of relatedness.

This introduction will first critically question the above-mentioned 'revival' of kinship studies. In order to understand this phenomenon, however, it is necessary to take a brief look at what led kinship studies into 'crisis' in the first place. Then, innovative contributions of the last twenty-five years will be examined to see whether they are able to overcome the limitations of previous approaches. This will set the stage for an exposition of the perspectives employed in the present volume. Finally, a short preview of the chapters to come will complete the introduction.

## The revival of kinship studies: nostalgia or advancement?

An abbreviated history of the field might contain the following sound-bites: after kinship was 'invented' by Bachofen, Fustel de Coulanges, Maine, McLennan and Morgan in the 1860s (Trautmann 1987), 'doing kinship' became one of the defining aspects of anthropological practices in the inter-war years. Especially in the hands of British structural-functionalism and Lévi-Straussian structuralism, kinship studies were destined to uncover the logic of 'primitive society'. As J.A. Barnes (1971) has pointed out, 1949 marked the climax of that phase: three important books on the subject appeared simultaneously (Fortes 1949; Lévi-Strauss 1949; Murdock 1949). During the 1950s and 1960s, anthropological kinship studies continued to thrive, partly because of continuing discussions about the impact of books published in 1949 (e.g. 'descent' versus 'alliance' theory), and partly because of novel attempts to 'formalise' the confusing subject matter referred to as kinship (e.g. componential analysis etc.).

However, attack was under way. After Schneider (1965a: 73) had criticised both descent and alliance theories[2] for creating over-simplified typologies, he published *American Kinship* in which he analysed 'kinship as a cultural system ... as a system of symbols' (Schneider 1968: 1). Without implicating kinship studies as such (although certain critical strands were already visible in Schneider 1965b), he nevertheless was about to revolutionise how they were to be conducted: 'meaning' was to replace social roles, rules and actions. In a subsequent delivery Schneider added that 'kinship ... is a non-subject since it does not exist in any culture known to man' (Schneider 1972: 59). At the same time, Rodney Needham – one of the foremost British experts on kinship at the time – declared that 'there is no such thing as kinship and it follows that there can be no such thing as kinship theory' (Needham 1971: 5).

While it might seem ironic that Needham and Schneider, who had battled each other savagely over the interpretation of 'prescription' during the 1950s (Homans and Schneider 1955; Needham 1962), entered the 1970s with so similar sounding refusals of kinship, it is relevant to note that both authors arrived at those statements through rather different lines of argumentation, as well as drawing quite distinct lessons from them. Schneider came from a position of 'symbolic anthropology' – which is, other than in his own writings, best exemplified by Clifford Geertz's *œuvre* – taking up the Parsonian distinction between 'social system' and 'cultural system', and focusing entirely on the latter. Despite the unquestionable benefit of bringing 'culture' into the realm of kinship studies, his views ultimately led to a form of cultural relativism, where there was little room for comparative concepts or research strategies. As Schneider himself put it:

> Anthropology, then, is the study of particular cultures. The first task of anthropology, *prerequisite to all others* [emphasis in the original], is to understand and formulate the symbols and meanings and their configuration that a particular culture consists of.
>
> (Schneider 1984: 196)

It is not surprising, then, that a vague term such as kinship – originating from European local meanings and oftentimes ill fit to properly designate other cultural notions of 'kinship' – has no place in Schneider's vocabulary of anthropology. However, what is remarkable is that his intervention, while succeeding at drastically diminishing the American anthropological production of kinship studies, did not have comparable effects in the field of 'religion', 'politics' or 'economy'.[3] After all, his *Critique* ended with the statement that:

> The case I have presented can be generalized to any anthropology which invokes universals on functionalist grounds or which employs any or all of the four privileged institutions of kinship, economics, religion, and politics.
>
> (Schneider 1984: 201)

Needham's sceptical position was triggered by a quite different philo-sophical position from Schneider's cultural relativism. Without ever abandoning the comparative project, Needham felt that much of anthropology's 'comparative sociology' was based on epistemologically shaky ground. Thus, the issue at hand was not to do away with kinship studies (or anthropology, for that matter), but to probe for better fitted conceptual tools rather than 'monothetic' classifications. It also needs to be mentioned that despite his 1971 dictum that there is no such thing as kinship (and, thus, no kinship theory), Needham himself never entirely abandoned the field of kinship studies. For example, the very same essay that contains the above-mentioned quote also features an innovative classification of kinship (or relationship) terminologies (Needham 1971: 13–24). His distinction between 'lineal' and 'non-lineal' terminologies, and his insistence on comparing 'principles' (an idea he traces back to Kroeber (1909) and Lowie (1917)) instead of 'systems', has been taken up by recent writers on the subject (e.g. Parkin 1997). Similarly, Needham's (1973) distinction between 'rules', 'behaviour' and 'terminology' (or classification) has been endorsed by other scholars in the field of kinship studies (e.g. Barnard and Good 1984). Finally, his frequently quoted article about 'polythetic classifica-tion' (Needham 1975) not only uses a variety of examples from the domain of kinship, but has provided a conceptual tool for others in formulating a broad, 'polythetic' definition of kinship (Barnard and Good 1984: 187–9).

It is evident that the 'crisis' and 'revisionism' in kinship studies affected particular national anthropological traditions in distinct ways. If we just limit ourselves to the dominant paradigms of Western anthropology (US American, British and French), these differences are rather obvious.[4] American anthropology was clearly most affected by Schneider's critique, where it really seemed that 'the study of kinship is dead or moribund' (Peletz 1995: 345). However, many of the scholars most influenced by Schneider were also actively involved in reconsti-tuting kinship studies, albeit as a very different domain. For example, Sylvia Yanagisako – who has been strongly influenced by Schneider – has contributed enormously to the revitalisation of kinship studies by introducing issues of ethnicity and gender to the discourse (see, for example, Yanagisako 1978, 1985; Yanagisako and Collier 1987; Yanagisako and Delaney 1995). Nevertheless, throughout the 1980s, the label 'kinship' was avoided by authors who wanted to reach an attentive audience. A case in point is Ann Fienup-Riordan's (1983) excellent monograph about the Nelson Island Yup'ik of south-western

Alaska. While the book is full of references to kinship, the term is rarely used. The key term she uses – 'ritual distribution' – addresses networks that are primarily constituted by kinship links.[5] Works that remained closer to mainstream treatments of kinship (e.g. Goodenough 1970; Scheffler 1978; Scheffler and Lounsbury 1971; Spiro 1977) did not succeed in defending kinship studies against Schneider's attack.

British anthropology has experienced a much less dramatic decline of kinship studies than American anthropology. The 'Cambridge tradition' was forcefully continued through the works of Jack Goody (e.g. 1973, 1976, 1983, 1990), while neo-Marxist interest in kinship was exemplified in the works of Maurice Bloch (e.g. 1971, 1973, 1975, 1978). Nevertheless, when J.A. Barnes wrote in 1980 about the 'current state of the play', he noticed that 'kinship no longer occupies so prominent a place in anthropological studies' (Barnes 1980: 294). Still, his diagnosis was not entirely bleak, because he acknowledged the input of feminism, Marxism, symbolic anthropology, sociobiology and other approaches and research agendas, and hoped for a 'new synthesis' of micro-sociology and structuralism (Barnes 1980: 294, 302). The works of Marilyn Strathern deserve particular attention in this context. While she has undoubtedly contributed to the fact that British anthropology never abandoned kinship studies (see, for example, Strathern 1981, 1984, 1985, 1987), she was among the first in Britain to endorse some of Schneider's heretic approaches to the study of kinship. For example, her *After Nature* includes the acknowledgement that 'David Schneider is the anthropological father of this book, since it is both with and against his ideas on kinship that it is written' (Strathern 1992a: xviii). Despite this caveat, Strathern echoes Schneider in providing a cultural account of English kinship, as well as in exploring the folk concepts of social anthropology that are intricately bound to the field. Throughout the 1990s, this trend to infuse British anthropology with Schneiderian notions has been present in social anthropology's most innovative kinship studies (e.g. Bouquet 1993; Carsten 1997; Nuttall 1992).

French anthropology was obviously least affected by any signs of 'crisis'. The Lévi-Straussian project was continued by himself and many others, while new approaches were added. Most notably, Françoise Héritier (1981; Héritier-Augé and Copet-Rougier 1991–4) has developed the analysis of Crow–Omaha, or semi-complex, systems far beyond Lévi-Strauss's dictum that they combine the principles of restricted and generalised exchange (Lévi-Strauss 1969: 465). Similarly, she has published on incest of the 'second type' (Héritier 1994) and – through her analyses of the cultural ideologies of the 'body' – has attempted to combine structuralist and symbolic approaches. Lévi-Strauss himself has continued to deal with kinship (see, for example, Lévi-Strauss 1985) and his 'The social organization of the Kwakiutl' (in Lévi-Strauss 1982) has triggered a debate about 'house-societies' (see, for example, Carsten and Hugh-Jones 1995; Macdonald 1987). Closer to the interests of the current volume are Pierre Bourdieu's applications of 'practice theory', which will be discussed more fully below. The investigations by Martine Segalen deserve special mention (see, for example, Segalen 1983, 1986 and Gullestad and Segalen 1997 for books available in English). Her work, situated at the interstices between anthropology, history and sociology, has served as a powerful reminder 'that [European] kinship relations that had supposedly been overstretched by the effects of incipient industrialisation were in fact maintained and that certain forms were even strengthened' (Segalen 1986: 5). Finally, the relatively uninterrupted course of French kinship studies is illustrated by the conduct of a major international conference in Paris on transformations of kinship terminologies (Godelier *et al.* 1998), a topic that has received very little attention in other countries in recent times.

The most interesting question, however, is which developments in anthropology/kinship studies have contributed to the sudden revival of kinship studies? Co-occurring with the decline of classic kinship studies, a number of new (and old) perspectives have come to the fore during the last two or three decades. I will mention five of them here, without suggesting that they represent a comprehensive list of achievements.[6] Rather, they are those that are most relevant within the framework of the current volume.

### Local meaning and symbols

It might seem contradictory that (local) meaning, one of the key words of symbolic anthropology, figures among the approaches leading to a renewed interest in kinship. Was not Schneider's culturalist project the cause, or at least the most visible symptom, of the crisis? Whatever the answer to this question might be, I believe it is necessary to point out the achievements to which this approach has led. First and foremost, once a universalistic notion of biological kinship is abandoned, it becomes necessary to inquire locally what particular rules, practices and terms 'mean' before we can assume that we are dealing with 'kinship'. The earliest and most famous prototype of this kind of study is Schneider's *American Kinship* (1968). The study was conducted among white middle-class families of Chicago and was, primarily, based on extensive interviews. The result, an investigation of the 'culture of American kinship', neither deals with kinship rules or with kinship practices. Instead, he elicits 'the symbols which are American kinship' (Schneider 1968: 18). However, his generalisations about American kinship across gender, ethnic and class lines have triggered critical responses (e.g. Yanagisako 1978, 1985; see also Schneider and Smith 1973 and Schneider 1980 for corrections of his view). In any case, Schneider's work has served as a necessary reminder that kinship is a Western concept. He demonstrated that American kinship is based on cultural constructs of biological facts, which made it impossible to pretend that kinship is self-evident or 'natural' (i.e. biological). This view, most explicitly stated in Schneider 1984, turns the analytical usefulness of kinship into a question that has to be answered empirically.

It should come as no surprise that within the context of American anthropology this way of approaching kinship was carried out primarily by anthropologists with an affinity for 'symbolic anthropology' (see, for example, Boon 1977; Blu 1977; Geertz and Geertz 1975; Witherspoon 1975). Less to be expected, however, was the impact that Schneider's approach had on US American feminist anthropologists (see below). Outside of the United States the addition of 'symbol' and 'meaning' to kinship studies took considerably longer. As was mentioned above, it has only been since the 1990s that British kinship studies have made extensive use of Schneider's views on the subject (e.g. Bouquet 1993; Carsten 1997; Nuttall 1992; Strathern 1992a). All of the ethnographies mentioned in this section testify to the viability of this approach. At the same time, their conclusions do not necessarily coincide with Schneider's rejection of kinship. As Janet Carsten put it, although 'we accept that both the definition and the meaning of kinship are culturally variable ... this does not mean that we cannot compare both how people conceive of relatedness and the meaning they attribute it in different cultures' (Carsten 1997: 290).

### Gender, reproduction and sexuality

Since its inception in the early 1970s, feminist anthropology came, by necessity, up against concepts and definitions that were close to the heart of kinship studies (such as 'family', 'exchange of women', etc.). In 1975, Gayle Rubin stated that 'kinship systems ... are made up of, and reproduce, concrete forms of socially organized sexuality. Kinship systems are observable and empirical forms of sex/gender systems' (Rubin 1975: 169). The most outspoken treatment of this connection was provided in an edited volume with the programmatic title of *Gender and Kinship: Essays Toward a Unified Analysis* (Collier and Yanagisako 1987). Its opening lines contain the following statement:

> Our goal is at once to revitalize the study of kinship and to situate the study of gender at the theoretical core of anthropology by calling into question the boundary between these two fields. In challenging the view that kinship and gender are distinct, albeit closely linked, domains of analysis, we hope to renew the intellectual promise of these two fields while reconstituting them as a whole.
>
> (Collier and Yanagisako 1987: 1)

Collier and Yanagisako (1987: 4–6) note that one of the most urgent tasks of feminists facing mainstream kinship theory was to overcome the analytical dichotomy between 'domestic' and 'political-jural' domains of kinship set up by Meyer Fortes. In addition, they interrogate other dichotomies – such as nature/culture and reproduction/production – and call for the eviction of 'biological facts' from the explanatory arsenal of gender and kinship studies (Yanagisako and Collier 1987: 48–50).[7] In a subsequent article Howell and Melhuus (1993) challenge Collier's and Yanagisako's optimism regarding a 'unified analysis' by highlighting the androcentrism of most kinship studies, as well as of most studies of personhood.

A specific field of inquiry emerging in recent years at the intersection between kinship and gender studies is the study of 'reproduction'. This field includes studies of 'new reproductive technologies' (and services) (e.g. Strathern 1992b; Franklin 1997), abortion and adoption debates (e.g. Ginsburg 1989; Modell 1994), as well as the cultural politics of reproduction (e.g. Ginsburg and Rapp 1995; Franklin and Ragoné 1998). They all touch on the 'biological core' of Western kinship studies by evaluating the role of non-biological means in the reproduction of ourselves. By focusing predominantly on developments in Western societies, they have also contributed to the ongoing 'repatriation' of kinship studies. Similarly, the anthropological study of sexuality (e.g. Ortner and Whitehead 1981; Peletz 1996), with its increasing attention to gay and lesbian issues (e.g. Weston 1997, 1998), has contributed to an enlarged understanding of kinship by overcoming hegemonic notions of family, sexuality and kinship bonds.

### Practice, agency and personhood

During the 1980s, 'practice' became one of the most prominent concepts in anthropology (Ortner 1984). Instead of focusing on anonymous and supra-individual entities, the attention shifted to individual actors and their strategies within and against structuring structures (e.g. Bourdieu 1977; Giddens 1984). Agency, as the active input of individuals into the conduct of their lives (with often unconscious motives and unintended consequences), took precedence over the structural constraints of society. Although none of the so-called 'practice approaches' have developed specific methods of dealing with kinship, they have reoriented the focus from kinship systems and corporate groups to individual practices and strategies within these domains. Some of Pierre Bourdieu's contributions to kinship studies can serve as examples of such an approach.[8]

In his famous discussion of patrilateral parallel cousin marriages, Bourdieu (1990b) criticises anthropology for uncritically repeating native official accounts. In Kabylia, parallel patrilateral cousin marriages are rare and 'extra-ordinary', but they hold a privileged place in native discourse as near perfect representations of male ideals of gender relations. Bourdieu demonstrates that this celebrated form of marriage is also its cheapest variant (regarding expenditures for negotiations, bridewealth and the wedding ceremony), a forced choice most often found in the poorest lineages. If put into the context of other marriages, parallel cousin marriage appears as a distinguished way of making a virtue of necessity. Bourdieu (1990a) makes a similar point in his analysis of Bearn (France) inheritance patterns (Bourdieu 1990b). The actual implementation of the official rule of 'complete primogeniture' – with required compensations for the younger siblings – would have led to the break-up of patrimonies. However, by exploiting every possible way of perpetuating the official rule the farmers were generally successful in perpetuating the estate. Again, individual strategies for reaching this goal (including not only inheritance, but also marriage, fertility and educational strategies) can only be understood within the network of possibilities and choices made before and after; or, as Bourdieu has formulated, in the context of matrimonial strategies:

> If the marrying of each of a family's children is seen as the equivalent of playing a card, then it is clear that the value of this move (measured by the criteria of the system) depends both on the quality of its 'hand' – the strength of the cards it has been dealt, as

defined by the rules of the game – and on the skill with which it plays its hand.

(Bourdieu 1990a: 148)

Here, Bourdieu provides a possible road-map for incorporating individual strategies into social analysis without reducing agency to Hobbes's notion of the individual or to rational choice assumptions. Still, his emphasis is on the supra-individual framework and on the effects of practices and not on 'persons' as such. The anthropological interest in 'personhood' developed somewhat independently from the contributions of Bourdieu and Giddens to social theory. Nevertheless, since the 1980s the analytical category of 'person' has become an important element in the revitalisation of kinship studies, as Marilyn Strathern (1997: 7–8) has recently remarked.

The study of personhood seemed, at times, to replace the struggling field of kinship studies. In some cases the problematic status of kinship studies was used as prime motivation to focus on 'concepts of persons' (e.g. Östör et al. 1982). Another strand in the study of personhood (e.g. Carrithers et al. 1985) critically questioned Marcel Mauss's (1979 [1938]) notion that modern concepts of the person or self are specific to Western societies. More recently, a number of anthropologists have vigorously insisted upon making the notion of the self, or self-consciousness, a central concern of the discipline (see, first and foremost, the writings of A.P. Cohen – e.g. 1994). However, as Strathern has demonstrated with Melanesian materials (e.g. Strathern 1988), the concept of 'persons' as individual entities is no less ethno-centric than certain outdated assumptions from the vocabulary of kinship studies. Together with the charge of androcentrism (Howell and Melhuus 1993), the study of personhood no longer appears as an alternative to the study of kinship; rather, both fields seem to address inseparable topics and to face comparable epistemological obstacles. Still, the different approaches that put individual lives and cultural notions of self and personhood at centre stage have added a necessary component to the field of kinship studies, which had been neglected in previous studies that were driven by a Durkheimian totalisation of 'society'.

## Kinship 'at home'

There is no question that the popular stereotype that only the 'other' (i.e. non-Euroamericans) has kinship was prominent as one of the factors that led to the decline of kinship studies. Maine's dictum that 'the movement of the progressive societies has hitherto been a movement *from Status to Contract* [emphasis in the original]' (Maine 1880 [1861]: 170) has provided a blueprint for subsequent conceptualisations of 'us' versus 'them' in regard of kinship. Without denying merit to Maine's original statement, the anthropological deduction that kinship does not play a role in industrial (or modern) societies had become a road-block to a comprehensive understanding of kinship. In addition, the disciplinary division of labour between sociology and anthropology – with sociology responsible for the 'domestic family relations' of Western society and with anthropology in charge of the 'corporate kin groups' and 'prescribed marriages' of non-Western societies – has perpetuated anthropology's expatriation of kinship.

While it is possible to find a few early exceptions to these generalisations,[9] Schneider's Chicago kinship project became the first large-scale investigation to challenge anthropological orthodoxy in this regard.[10] The main monograph (Schneider 1968) and a large number of publications resulting from, or triggered by, the project (e.g. Farber 1981; Schneider and Smith 1973; Yanagisako 1978, 1985, 1987) put 'American kinship' on the map of anthropological topics, where it seems to have solidified its position in recent years (see, for example, McKinnon 1995; Modell 1994; Roschelle 1997). Less known but similar in scope to the Chicago project (see note 8) was the London kinship study initiated by Raymond Firth (see, for example, Firth *et al.* 1969; Hubert *et al.* 1968). A further milestone in that direction was the publication of *Kinship at the Core* (Strathern 1981). This in-depth study of kinship relations in Elmdon, Essex, started in 1962 as a student project supervised by Audrey Richards and Edmund Leach. After a few preliminary publications (e.g. Robin 1980), Marilyn Strathern took on the monumental task of combining the field-notes and insights, compiled by many individuals over almost twenty years, into a single framework. Since then, anthropological studies of English kinship have become a veritable genre (see e.g. Wolfram 1987; Strathern 1992a; Bouquet 1993; Baumann 1995; Finch 1997). Likewise, kinship studies in other parts of Europe have flourished (see, for example, Bestard-Camps 1991; Borneman 1992; Gullestad and Segalen 1997; Pina-Cabral 1989; Pine 1996; Sabean 1998).

The insights flowing from these diverse investigations have been manifold. They demonstrate similarities as well as differences in kinship in non-industrial societies. They delineate the differences between rural and urban kinship settings, regardless of the 'type' of society. They sharpen our awareness of the ethnocentric roots of kinship discourse by putting these roots under the magnifying glass. However, for our purposes the most relevant aspect is the recognition that kinship, however limited its functions may be in certain societies, is a social and cultural construct every social group makes use of. By highlighting the pervasiveness of social constructions of relatedness, kinship lost its stigma of being solely a characteristic of past or pre-modern societies. Several chapters of the present volume testify to the vitality of European kinship studies.

## Power, history and the 'big picture'

Finally, a number of Marxist, materialist and historical analyses have widened the concept of kinship, by treating the social relations normally referred to as kinship within a larger framework of relations of equality and inequality. Feminist scholars joined Marxists and social historians in investigating the diachronic aspects of social inequality, and kinship became one of the factors to be reckoned with.

On the one hand, (predominantly) French neo-Marxist debates of the 1970s made kinship a central matter of contention. While debates over whether kinship can be part of the 'infrastructure' (e.g. by serving as 'relations of production') might sound rather sophistic today (e.g. Bloch 1975; Godelier 1975; Meillassoux 1981; Terray 1972), they nevertheless contributed to making kinship a concern of social analysis at large. Kinship studies were thereby 'often carried out under other rubrics and aliases' (Peletz 1995: 367), as Peletz has stated in connection with Modjeska's (1982) observation that Marxist attempts to focus on (relations of) production inevitably led to kinship relations. A related issue highlighted by these Marxist approaches was to direct attention to the 'ideological' aspects of kinship; under conditions of social exploitation 'kinship is transformed ... into an ideology whose *raison d'être* is not so much to express the relationships generated from the growth and organisation of the society as to justify and even support a domination imposed from outside' (Meillassoux 1978: 167). On the other hand, early feminist approaches within anthropology made use of Engels's (1972 [1884]) conceptualisation of gender inequality, by linking it to the emergence of class relations, private property and the State (see, for example, Leacock 1981; O'Laughlin 1974; Sacks 1974, 1982).

However, Marxism quickly lost its 'monopoly' over the treatment of such subjects. After the 1970s many scholars turned to other analytical models to explain gender and social inequalities. For example, Jane Collier's (1988) ambitious model of how forms of marriage contribute to the creation and maintenance of gender inequality in classless societies had a direct impact on making kinship more relevant to broader issues of social analysis. Similarly, Raymond Kelly's (1993) penetrating critique of Collier's model – arguing that the cosmological system, and not marriage, generates inequality in classless societies – deals extensively with social relations that constitute kinship and gender.[11] Another example is Jack Goody's *œuvre*, which – although anchored in the 'descent theory' tradition of post-Second World War Cambridge anthropology – has demonstrated the usefulness of bold comparativism in a diachronic framework. His comparative 'trilogy' on kinship practices in Asia, Africa and Europe (Goody 1976, 1983, 1990) can be considered a milestone in expanding and, thus, reviving the notion of kinship.

For historians kinship became a 'new topic' during the 1980s and 1990s (e.g. Maynes *et al.* 1996). Ironically, this happened at a time when anthropologists turned away from kinship and when 'history' received increased attention within the discipline (see Medick and Sabean 1984).[12] Even the field of biblical studies 'discovered' kinship (see, for example, Steinberg 1993) and anthropologists have begun to question the social relevance of biblical myths and their underlying kinship constructs (Delaney 1998). By incorporating issues of social and gender inequality, production, reproduction and historical change, the approaches discussed in this section have extended our definition of kinship, as well as our understanding of its relevance.

## From meaning to function (and back): an 'instrumentalist' agenda

All of the above-mentioned developments (and others that have not been mentioned) have contributed to a renewal of kinship studies. The fact that this process of renewal was – to a large degree – couched in critical statements does not make the process less valuable. On the contrary, it can be argued that the (sometimes overdrawn) criticism has forced the field of kinship studies to incorporate more critical perspectives than comparable fields have.

While all of the perspectives discussed above are, in varying degrees, utilised in the case studies of this volume, the immediate concern out of which these papers arose was more narrow. We felt that certain issues (such as 'symbols' and 'meanings') had received their fair share of attention during the last thirty years and that it was necessary to turn to perspectives that have been applied less frequently in recent years.

One example of such neglect is the issue of 'what kinship does' (or, more precisely, 'what people do with or against kinship'). This means that the question of 'what is kinship' had to be shelved for the time being. Of course, neither do we pretend that the question 'what is kinship' has been answered (or even that it ever can be answered universally),[13] nor that these two questions should be considered as mutually exclusive. On the contrary, we believe that in order to investigate what is 'done' through a particular notion of kinship, at least a preliminary understanding of 'what kinship is (locally)' is necessary. At the same time, through a sustained inquiry of 'what kinship does' a better understanding of its cultural meanings can be achieved. The particular agenda of this volume is, thus, to probe the functional aspects of kinship.

In this context, I have chosen the label 'instrumentalist' in direct analogy to debates within the field of ethnicity studies. It is common to conceptualise the different approaches to the subject as a dichotomy (or, alternatively, as a continuum) between 'primordial' and 'instrumentalist' perspectives. Instrumentalist approaches[14] focus in particular on the 'benefits' that individuals and groups draw from employing 'ethnicity' in particular instances. Fredrik Barth's (1969) notion of ethnicity – situated somewhere between the two extremes – reminds us that ethnicity is not the 'property' of a group but denotes a relationship between groups. Instrumentalist approaches become an obstacle to understanding, if the instrumental uses of ethnicity (or kinship) are misconstrued for the conscious and cynical motivations of individual practices. Neither the persistence of ethnicity or of kinship can be explained in that way. Thus, the 'instrumental' view employed here uses a one-sided perspective – 'mellowed', though, by Barth's interactional perspective – in the full consciousness that it is one-sided.

Obviously, our agenda sounds plainly 'functionalist'. However, this does not mean that we subscribe to any brand of 'functionalism'. Actually, I would describe it as a 'functional perspective without functionalism'. The important difference is that we do not hold that 'the *raison d'être* of an institution or custom is to be found in its social function' (Radcliffe-Brown 1950: 62). Instead, we believe that social facts are not caused by their social functions (Bloch 1973: 75). By limiting the scope of functional analysis, functions are less likely to be misunderstood as explaining the phenomena under consideration;

however, only through a functional investigation can everyday practices be situated in a relational context.

Despite a long tradition of 'functionalism' in anthropology there have been few kinship studies that probe the functional questions outlined above. Malinowski's functionalism was seemingly too preoccupied with the supposed procreative roots of kinship (Malinowski 1930), and later with the individual 'needs' it seemed to fulfil (Malinowski 1944), than to probe the issues deeper. Radcliffe-Brownian approaches, which provided the basis for most British kinship studies at mid-century, saw kinship too much at the core of society: thus, its single most important function became societal integration. We, instead, believe that the functions of kinship are much more varied and include, among other things, 'societal disintegration'.

Among 'functionalists', Raymond Firth could best serve as a starting point for our perspectives. In particular, his distinction between 'social organisation' and 'social structure' (Firth 1961 [1951]) continues to be useful and can be viewed as a forerunner to Bourdieu's more elaborate treatment of the relationship between 'agency' and 'structure' (as well as between 'practical knowledge' and 'official accounts'). Maurice Bloch, who clearly does not fit the 'functionalist' label, has made significant contributions to the kind of functional analysis of kinship proposed here. His distinctions between 'motives' and 'effects' (and between 'long-term' and 'short-term' effects) (Bloch 1973), as well as between 'moral meaning' and 'tactical use' (of kinship terms) (Bloch 1971), provide conceptual tools for grasping the dialectic between intentional social actions and their unintentional structural ramifications. We can conclude that although it is unproductive and misleading to quarrel about the primacy of 'meanings' versus 'uses' of kinship, it is nevertheless possible and necessary to analytically distinguish them; in doing so, the present volume focuses on the latter aspect.

Among the five perspectives discussed in the last section, not all have made functional issues part of their concern. While 'local meanings' and 'kinship "at home"'[15] have made little use of functional approaches, 'gender studies' have examined the role of kinship in creating/maintaining gender inequalities. Under the label of 'power and history' a fair share of functional issues have been raised, most of which relate to social inequalities. While several research projects conducted from the perspective of 'practice and personhood' have little to offer in this respect, Bourdieu's (few) contributions to kinship studies are probably the best examples of what we believe needs further attention. In addition to the contributions discussed above, the volume on *Interest and Emotion*, edited by Medick and Sabean (1984) addresses issues close to concerns highlighted in our volume.

The use of market metaphors (e.g. 'dividends') and the frequent treatment of the relationship between kinship and economy in the case studies of this volume warrant the question of whether the approach adopted here ought to convey the universality of market relations or to advocate economic reductionism. Neither form of 'economism' is intended. The usage of 'dividends' in the title of the volume can be seen as parallel to Bourdieu's usage of (cultural, social, symbolic, etc.) 'capital'. In both cases, the reference is to strategies and actions that are not limited to the pursuit of economic interests and go beyond the assumptions of rational choice theory. After all, the term 'dividend' is much older than its current application to stock market profits: according to the *Oxford English Dictionary*, the word is derived from the Latin *dividendum* ('that which is to be divided') and its first recorded English meanings are 'distribution' and 'share'. 'Dividends', then, refer to practices that are in no way bound to market institutions. Also, it is not intended to bolster the illusion that kinship can be explained by, or reduced to, economic rationale. While economic benefits are among the most visible 'dividends' of kinship, they are part of a much larger package that also includes emotion, mental health, group cohesion, etc.

Finally, a few comments on the relationship between the instrumentalist view adopted here and biologistic views of kinship. It could be argued that 'sociobiology' and related approaches are extreme cases of functionalism because they reduce kinship behaviour to the single issue of increasing 'inclusive fitness'. However, in contrast to our position, sociobiology provides an a priori answer to the question of what functions kinship can and does fulfil. Thus, in the same way that 'primordialist' views of ethnicity substitute an explanation of ethnicity through a reification of what needs to be explained, sociobiology turns a question into an answer. However, I believe that the issue of the relationship between kinship and biology still awaits a balanced answer. While the last twenty years were characterised by extreme positions – the complete decoupling of kinship and biology by culturalist and feminist approaches, on the one hand, and the reduction of everything to biology by sociobiology, on the other hand – none of these positions is entirely satisfying. After all, while it has become evident that biology alone is insufficient for a comprehensive understanding of what kinship *is* and *does*, it is equally hard to maintain that kinship has nothing to do with biology and procreation.[16]

## The chapters

While this introduction tries to chart some of the developments in kinship studies that have proven to be most relevant in the recent past, it by no means intends to provide prescriptions for the 'proper treatment' of the subject. Indeed, what I consider to be one of the best facets of this volume is that the authors do not write from a unified theoretical perspective, other than by addressing some of the broad issues outlined in the initial call for papers (see the Preface). While most chapters touch upon the various links between kinship and the 'economy' in one way or another, they do so from a multitude of perspectives and interests.

A notable characteristic of the chapters to come is that the word limits given to individual authors exceed the standard norm of comparable collections of essays. It seemed that the rich ethnographies on which all of the case studies are built deserved more room than the usual soundbites from the field. The authors were given ample space for contextualisation and elaboration of the cultural contexts in which people 'do kinship'. Thus, the theoretical framework of the volume becomes animated by ethnographies, which are more than mere illustrations of the perspective chosen. In addition to length, the ethnographic scope of the individual chapters is wide and provides coverage of a broad selection of different societies and social contexts. Each chapter can and does stand by itself. In the following brief synopsis I only highlight a few select issues; instead of being a concise summary, these paragraphs should encourage the reader to turn to the chapters themselves.

Mark Nuttall's contribution is of particular relevance to me because its subject matter – Inuit kinship – has been a reoccurring theoretical and practical challenge of my own field experiences in Alaska and the Russian Far East. His discussion of anthropological approaches to Inuit social organisation is an important contribution to a field that is struggling with the negative fall-out of concepts such as the 'Eskimo kinship system' and of notions such as 'anarchic' Inuit social organisation. Aptly entitled 'Choosing kin', Nuttall's case study from north-west Greenland explores how personal choice in the construction of kinship relations allows for the continued development of a mosaic of possible relatives. People can choose to become related to one another by avoiding their personal names and addressing one another with a kin term. Similarly, relationships regarded as unsatisfactory can be 'forgotten about' by using a personal name rather than a kin term as a form of address. However, the author warns that this flexibility should not be mistaken for 'formlessness'. Once kinship is acknowledged by both parties there are definite rules of conduct, moral obligations, rights and duties to fulfil. Furthermore, his case study demonstrates that neither the processes of acquiring personal names, nor the dynamic notions of personhood and identity, can be neglected in exploring Inuit kinship. Children are named for deceased people, and, as they grow older, they learn about and begin to negotiate a complex network of relationships that link them to an intricate pattern of genealogical and 'fictive' kin. In addition, Nuttall contrasts two modes of production – subsistence and commodity production – *vis-à-vis* kinship relations. The author demonstrates that subsistence, with its emphasis on sharing and non-exclusive ownership rights over non-human persons, is not determined by kinship but rather creates kinship. Commodity production, on the other hand, neither contributes to the re-creation of kinship bonds nor utilises the Inuit concept of social relatedness.

'Power and kinship in Shuar and Achuar society' by Elke Mader and Richard Gippelhauser questions the importance of kinship in a so-called egalitarian society. In particular, the relationship between leadership and kinship, or the potential that kinship and marriage ties hold for political power, is examined. The Dravidian kinship system found among the Shuar and Achuar is characterised by its high degree of flexibility. This flexibility manifests itself in the use of prefixes determining the degree of relatedness, which – to a certain degree – can be chosen according to individual preferences. It can also be seen in the affinalisation of remote kin and non-related persons, thus providing the possibility of establishing closer relations through marriage alliances. This offers multiple ways to manipulate kinship relations according to non-kinship categories. The chapter demonstrates how this flexibility relates to other essential features of Jivaroan society, such as their concepts of the person, the constructions of status and the dynamics of social and political groupings. A special place in Mader's and Gippelhauser's investigation is occupied by issues of spiritual power (vision quests, shamans, etc.). Here, kinship also provides an important building block for the forging of spiritual alliances, although the latter cannot be reduced to kinship. Kinship emerges as an integral part of a society in constant movement, characterised by a high degree of individualism and adaptability to change. The loose kinship rules and fluctuating political groupings do not represent a lack of social organisation but an organising principle. Thus, the dividends of kinship for social interaction in Jivaroan society are definitely limited but in no way negligible.

Gertraud Seiser's contribution strikes another familiar chord with the writer of these lines. The area and communities discussed in Chapter 4 are geographically close to my own home town, although I know little about the particular strategies of peasant livelihood described therein. 'On the importance of being the last one' puts an Austrian farming community into anthropological focus by addressing inheritance and marriage patterns, and, thus, highlights the benefits and burdens of kinship. Patterns of inheritance and alliance determine the social status of a person and his or her economic possibilities. In the community under consideration, the youngest son customarily inherits the peasant farm including all means of production, but he has to share his property with his wife. The other children have to marry out or live as subordinates to their younger brother and his wife. This situation causes structural conflicts within the so-called nuclear family and/or household. While the effects of primogeniture are reasonably well-described in the literature on European inheritance patterns, ulti-mogeniture has received comparatively little attention. In the case under consideration, one of its effects is that patrilineal succession is hard to maintain over several generations, which leads to a weak genealogical consciousness and a pronounced 'house ideology'. In this context, the institution of godparent-hood serves both to protect the interests of the children in the case of death or remarriage of one parent, and to strengthen the position of the farmwife (the godparents are ideally her sister and the latter's husband). It is noteworthy for anthropologists – who just recently discovered the analytical benefits of the 'house' – that European social historians have overemphasised the 'house' instead of relations of kinship and marriage between houses. In Seiser's case study, it is exactly these relations between households that guarantee the transmission of property and, thus, the social reproduction of inequality.

'Kinship, reciprocity and the world market' by Jenny B. White discusses the ways in which rural concepts of kinship are used within an urban and capitalist context. In working-class neighbourhoods of Istanbul, Turkey, kinship is metaphorically conferred on those people who do what kin do: that is, participate in relations of collective reciprocal assistance with no expectation of return. This 'fictive' kinship draws in resources, whether it be labour, goods, food, money or information, from unrelated outsiders, and is crucial for the economic survival of the urban poor. 'Fictive kinship' has also been harnessed to the world economy by providing a model for relations of production between pieceworkers and piecework distributors producing for export. By constructing their piecework labour as an expression of their social role, rather than as 'work for pay', women avoid the onus of working outside the home or taking over their husbands' role as provider. The male distributors also 'help' their neighbours by providing them with income opportunities. While the relationship is couched in the language of kinship, it is at base a capitalist relationship. Ironically, insistence that the women's production activities are simply socially contributed labour facilitates the exploitation of that labour, since the women do not keep track of the time spent working or feel free to demand a higher price per piece. Thus, through the alchemy of kinship, money and labour are converted to serve the reproduction of social solidarity.

In Chapter 6, Antónia Pedroso de Lima addresses the question 'Is blood thicker than economic interest in familial enterprises?', by discussing ethnographic material collected among the financial élite families of Lisbon. Pedroso de Lima thereby increases our small sample of ethnographies 'studying up' (Nader 1972). However, in contrast to the existing case studies, which were primarily conducted in US American contexts, the author illuminates the cultural notions of Portuguese business and kinship. Among the families of her sample – who have owned important enterprises for at least three generations – the relation between sentiments and economic interest assumes great centrality. Family members are business associates, but they share emotional feelings as well as economic interests and projects. These kinsmen who share the profits of the family business are also in competition for important managerial positions. At a later moment, they will have to fight among themselves for succession to leadership positions. Members who wish to proceed to these positions have to legitimate their position as guarantors of the common interests both in intra-familial and extra-familial contexts, thus combining distinct forms of leadership. Shared kinship relations and shared economic interests overlap continuously in social action. Thus, the crucial question is whether contemporary anthropology possesses the analytical categories to deal with the multidimensionally constructed cognitive patterns that rule these sentiments and economic interests.

Chapter 7 by Christoph Brumann is the only case study of this volume employing a cross-cultural perspective. In ' "Philoprogenitiveness" through the cracks', the author takes a comparative look at Utopian communes, i.e. groups whose members live and work together and share their property on idealistic grounds. The specific focus of his inquiry is whether the demands of 'community' conflict with those of 'family' and other kinship bonds. His major tool in assessing the issue is to correlate the longevity of particular communes with their strategies of regulating sexuality, marriage and nepotism. Previous theories have argued that family and kinship are inimical to communal survival, since they will create double loyalties by distracting members' attention from the wider group. Indeed, as the author demonstrates, many communes have tried to eliminate family and kinship bonds by introducing such practices as celibacy, group marriage or parent–child separation. A closer look at a sample of nineteenth- and twentieth-century North American, European and Japanese communes, however, reveals that no group-marriage commune has existed for longer than thirty-seven years. In contrast, all those communes that show the potential for healthy long-term survival are monogamous. Furthermore, the only three permanently successful cases (kibbutzim, Hutterite colonies and Bruderhof communities) are the ones that emphasise family and kinship most strongly. Family and kinship are controlled, however, by the fact that ultimate authority rests with the entire community and that members have to participate in sanctions against deviant members, even if they are their own spouses or children. In the end, Utopian communes are perfect illustrations of how difficult it is to get away from notions of family and kinship established by the wider culture in which its founding members grew up.

Finally, in my 'Concluding remarks' I attempt to reach a preliminary synthesis between the positions outlined in the Introduction and the presented case studies. First, the obvious variety of functions illustrated in the individual chapters is discussed. Instead of insisting on universal functions of kinship, or of using variation as a rationale for denying the usefulness of kinship as an analytical category, variation is viewed as resulting from a limited number of social constellations. Regarding the relationship between people and resources, or, in the words of Marilyn Strathern, the question of whether a society allows the substitution of people and things, 'kinship at large' seems to fulfil a variety of functions along a continuum, the extremes of which can be labelled 'inclusive' and 'exclusive' respectively. While 'inclusion' seems to prevail where access to labour or services is more important than to resources, 'exclusion' is a function of kinship relations in contexts where they regulate access to limited resources (such as arable land). Such a dichotomy of ideal-types juxtaposes 'flexible' kinship systems, in which relatives and allies are chosen, with societies in which kinship relations are binding and contain an element of competition. Finally, in trying to chart a fruitful course for future kinship studies, I call for the combination of two approaches that are often considered incompatible. On the one hand, we need more good and detailed ethnographies of what kinship is and does, especially in contexts where it is often assumed to be of little relevance, e.g. in so-called industrialised societies. On the other hand, these ethnographies need to be put into a comparative perspective, both regionally and topically, if we want to move beyond the celebration of cultural idiosyncrasies. I argue that such an approach will provide the best means to keep kinship studies vital and productive.

## Acknowledgements

I want to thank Janet Carsten, Andre Gingrich, Nelson Graburn, Stacie McIntosh, Antónia Pedroso de Lima and Michael Peletz for comments on an earlier draft of this chapter. Stacie McIntosh also provided valuable editorial assistance.

## Notes

1   One has to go back several decades to find a similar concentration of publications. For example, introductory texts and readers published in the early 1970s (e.g. Graburn 1971; Keesing 1975; Pasternak 1976; Schusky 1972, 1974) continued to be in use until the 1990s, because of the lack of more recent 'textbooks'. Graburn's *Readings in Kinship and Social Structure* (1971) is still unrivalled in its comprehensive treatment of approaches to kinship from the early days of anthropology to the 1960s.

2   Schneider's critique was more instrumental in highlighting the shortcomings of descent theory than in discrediting alliance theory. The latter approach was increasingly facing the empirical problem of marriage patterns – such as the 'close marriages' of the Near East – which did not fit easily into Lévi-Strauss's sweeping model.

3   Although other 'symbolic' anthropologists have applied similar approaches to other domains, the effects were quite different from Schneider's book. For example, Clifford Geertz's famous article 'Religion as a cultural system' (1973 [1966]) certainly did not mark the beginning of a crisis in the anthropological study of religions.

4   Ironically, one of the few other 'national traditions' I am familiar with, Soviet anthropology, was just about to explore innovative approaches that went beyond the dogmas of Morgan and Engels when kinship in the West was close to being pronounced 'dead'. For English language references to 'post-dogmatic' Soviet works on kinship see Butinov (1978), Chlenov (1978), Girenko (1978, 1984), Kryukov (1984), Levin (1974) and Popov (1978).

5   Not surprisingly, Fienup-Riordan's 1983 monograph is based on her Ph.D. dissertation, which she defended at the University of Chicago under the supervision of David Schneider.

6   For different but comparable accounts see, among others, Yanagisako and Collier (1987) and Peletz (1995). Yanagisako and Collier identify 'the cultural analysis of meaning', 'systemic models of inequality' and 'historical analysis' as facets of an analytical programme. Peletz lists 'kinship as symbols and structures', 'gender, power and difference', 'contradiction, paradox and ambivalence' and 'the repatriation of kinship studies and the new reproductive technologies' as major categories of advancement. While most of the other labels reoccur in my account in one way or another, I do not include Peletz's category of 'contradiction, paradox and ambivalence'. Although I definitely agree with Peletz's insight about the 'deeply Janus-faced condition of kinship' as a system with heavy moral entailments and burdensome obligations (Peletz 1996: 351), I view 'ambivalence' more as a future topic more fully to be explored (see Peletz forthcoming) than a field that has already contributed to the resurgence of kinship studies.

7   For a critical view of Collier's and Yanagisako's position see Scheffler (1991).

8   For applications of Bourdieu's writings on kinship to other case studies see Collier (1988) and Peletz (1996).

9   Sometimes, Arensberg's and Kimball's study on *Family and Community in Ireland* (1968 [1940]) is considered as one of the earliest prototypes of such an approach. However, despite its highly original treatment of family and kinship ties within a farming community, it cannot be considered 'anthropology at home'; to a certain degree, Ireland (together with the Mediterranean) filled the 'savage slot' of the early anthropology of Europe. Thus, Raymond Firth's *Two Studies of Kinship in London* (1956) – based on research conducted during the 1940s and 1950s – deserves credit as one of the first anthropological studies of that kind in the British context. The influential sociological study on *Family and Kinship in East London* (Young and Willmott 1957) followed on its heels.

10  Schneider's study was initially planned as a comparative study of urban kinship in Chicago and London (together with Firth). However, due to methodological problems, the planned joint monograph was never realised and the data from Chicago and London were analysed and published separately (personal communication with Nelson Graburn in early 1999, who was a founding fieldworker on Schneider's project).

11  Kelly's (1993: 521) definition that 'kinship relations are social relations predicated upon cultural conceptions that specify the processes by which an individual comes into being and develops into a complete (i.e., mature) social person' is highly relevant within the context of this book's perspectives.

12  Another facet of historical research – historical demography in kinship studies – can only be mentioned in passing. The works of Eugene Hammel, Peter Laslett, Kenneth Wachter and Richard Wall (e.g. Hammel and Laslett 1974; Laslett 1972, 1977; Wachter *et al.* 1978; Wall 1983) – which focus on the historical reconstruction of household composition and recruitment – are good examples of this approach.

13 The open-endedness of 'what kinship is', is also referenced in our usage of 'social relatedness' as a synonym for kinship.
14 This approach is best exemplified in the writings of Abner Cohen (e.g. 1969, 1974). An alternative label for this perspective is 'circumstantialist' (Glazer and Moynihan 1975: 19).
15 The accounts of historians of European kinship are a notable exception in this respect (see, for example, Duby 1994; Medick and Sabean 1984; Mitterauer and Sieder 1982; Sabean 1998).
16 Compare Laura Rival's (1998) critique of post-feminist and post-modern views that sexuality has nothing to do with the beginning and perpetuation of life.

# References

Arensberg, C.M. and Kimball, S.T. (1968 [1940]) *Family and Community in Ireland*, Cambridge, MA: Harvard University Press.
Barnard, A. and Good, A. (1984) *Research Practices in the Study of Kinship*, London: Academic Press.
Barnes, J.A. (1971) *Three Styles in the Study of Kinship*, Berkeley: University of California Press.
—— (1980) 'Kinship studies: Some impressions of the current state of play', *Man (N.S.)* 15: 293–303.
Barth, F. (1969) 'Introduction', in F. Barth (ed.) *Ethnic Groups and Boundaries: The Social Organization of Culture Difference*, Bergen: Universitetsforlaget.
Baumann, G. (1995) 'Managing a polyethnic milieu: Kinship and interaction in a London suburb', *The Journal of the Royal Anthropological Institute (N.S.)* 1: 725–41.
Bestard-Camps, J. (1991) *What's in a Relative? Household and Family in Formentera*, New York: Berg.
Bloch, M. (1971) 'The moral and tactical meaning of kinship', *Man (N.S.)* 6: 79–87.
—— (1973) 'The long term and the short term: The economic and political significance of the morality of kinship', in J. Goody (ed.) *The Character of Kinship*, Cambridge, UK: Cambridge University Press.
—— (1975) 'Property and the end of affinity', in M. Bloch (ed.) *Marxist Analyses and Social Anthropology*, New York: John Wiley.
—— (1978) 'Marriage amongst equals: An analysis of the marriage ceremony of the Merina of Madagascar', *Man (N.S.)* 13: 21–33.
Blu, K.I. (1977) 'Kinship and culture: Affinity and the role of the father in the Trobriands', in J.L. Dolgin, D.S. Kemnitzer and D.M. Schneider (eds) *Symbolic Anthropology: A Reader in the Study of Symbols and Meanings*, New York: Columbia University Press.
Boon, J.A. (1977) *The Anthropological Romance of Bali, 1597–1972: Dynamic Perspectives in Marriage and Caste, Politics and Religion*, Cambridge, UK: Cambridge University Press.

Borneman, J. (1992) *Belonging in the Two Berlins: Kin, State, Nation*, Cambridge, UK: Cambridge University Press.

Bouquet, M. (1993) *Reclaiming English Kinship: Portuguese Refractions of British Kinship Theory*, Manchester: Manchester University Press.

Bourdieu, P. (1977) *Outline of a Theory of Practice*, Cambridge, UK: Cambridge University Press.

—— (1990a) 'Land and matrimonial strategies', in *The Logic of Practice*, Stanford, CA: Stanford University Press.

—— (1990b) 'The social uses of kinship', in *The Logic of Practice*, Stanford, CA: Stanford University Press.

Butinov, N. (1978) 'Social organisation of horticulturalists (on the example of Oceania)', *Problems of the Contemporary World* 72: 117–26.

Carrithers, M., Collins, S. and Lukes, S. (eds) (1985) *The Category of the Person: Anthropology, Philosophy, History*, Cambridge, UK: Cambridge University Press.

Carsten, J. (1997) *The Heat of the Hearth: The Process of Kinship in a Malay Fishing Community*, Oxford: Oxford University Press.

Carsten, J. and Hugh-Jones, S. (eds) (1995) *About the House: Lévi-Strauss and Beyond*, Cambridge, UK: Cambridge University Press.

Chlenov, M. (1978) 'Geography of kinship systems of the peoples of Siberia and the Soviet Far East', *Problems of the Contemporary World* 72: 161–9.

Cohen, A. (1969) *Custom and Politics in Urban Africa: A Study of Hausa Migrants in Yoruba Towns*, Berkeley: University of California Press.

—— (1974) 'Introduction: The lesson of ethnicity', in A. Cohen (ed.) *Urban Ethnicity*, London: Tavistock Publications.

Cohen, A.P. (1994) *Self Consciousness: An Alternative Anthropology of Identity*, London: Routledge.

Collier, J.F. (1988) *Marriage and Inequality in Classless Societies*, Stanford, CA: Stanford University Press.

Collier, J.F. and Yanagisako, S.J. (1987) 'Introduction', in J.F. Collier and S.J. Yanagisako (eds) *Gender and Kinship: Essays Toward a Unified Analysis*, Stanford, CA: Stanford University Press.

Delaney, C. (1998) *Abraham on Trial: The Social Legacy of Biblical Myth*, Princeton, NJ: Princeton University Press.

Duby, G. (1994) *Love and Marriage in the Middle Ages*, Chicago: University of Chicago Press.

Engels, F. (1972 [1884]) *The Origin of the Family, Private Property and the State*. With an Introduction and Notes by Eleanor Burke Leacock, New York: International Publishers.

Farber, B. (1981) *Conceptions of Kinship*, New York: Elsevier.

Faubion, J.D. (1996) 'Kinship is dead. Long live kinship: A review article', *Comparative Studies in Society and History* 38: 67–91.

Fienup-Riordan, A. (1983) *The Nelson Island Eskimo: Social Structure and Ritual Distribution*, Anchorage: Alaska Pacific University Press.

Finch, J. (1997) 'Individuality and adaptability in English kinship', in M. Gullestad and M. Segalen (eds) *Family and Kinship in Europe*, London: Pinter.

Firth, R. (1956) *Two Studies of Kinship in London*, London: Athlone.

—— (1961 [1951]) *Elements of Social Organization*, Boston, MA: Beacon Press.

Firth, R., Hubert, J. and Forge, A. (1969) *Families and Their Relatives: Kinship in a Middle-Class Sector of London*, London: Routledge & Kegan Paul.

Fortes, M. (1949) *The Web of Kinship among the Tallensi: The Second Part of an Analysis of the Social Structure of a Trans-Volta Tribe*, London: Oxford University Press.

Fox, R. (1983) *Kinship and Marriage: An Anthropological Perspective*, Cambridge, UK: Cambridge University Press.

Franklin, S. (1997) *Embodied Progress: A Cultural Account of Assisted Conception*, London: Routledge.

Franklin, S. and Ragoné, H. (eds) (1998) *Reproducing Reproduction: Kinship, Power, and Technological Innovation*, Philadelphia: University of Pennsylvania Press.

Geertz, C. (1973 [1966]) 'Religion as a cultural system', in *The Interpretation of Cultures*, New York: Basic Books.

Geertz, H. and Geertz, C. (1975) *Kinship in Bali*, Chicago: University of Chicago Press.

Giddens, A. (1984) *The Constitution of Society: Outline of a Theory of Structuration*, Berkeley: University of California Press.

Gingrich, A. (1995) Review article: 'The prophet's smile and other puzzles. Studying Arab tribes and comparing close marriages', *Social Anthropology* 3: 147–70.

Ginsburg, F.D. (1989) *Contested Lives: The Abortion Debate in an American Community*, Berkeley: University of California Press.

Ginsburg, F. and Rapp, R. (eds) (1995) *Conceiving the New World Order: The Global Politics of Reproduction*, Berkeley: University of California Press.

Girenko, N. (1978) 'The classificatory principle and the division of the evolution of kinship systems into periods', *Problems of the Contemporary World* 72: 136–49.

—— (1984) 'Systems of kinship terms and systems of social categories', in T. Dragadze (ed.) *Kinship and Family in the Soviet Union: Field Studies*, London: Routledge & Kegan Paul.

Glazer, N. and Moynihan, D.P. (1975) 'Introduction', in N. Glazer and D.P. Moynihan (eds) *Ethnicity: Theory and Experience*, Cambridge, MA: Harvard University Press.

Godelier, M. (1975) 'Modes of production, kinship, and demographic structures', in M. Bloch (ed.) *Marxist Analyses and Social Anthropology*, New York: John Wiley.

Godelier, M., Trautmann, T.R. and Tjon Sie Fat, F.E. (eds) (1998) *Transformations of Kinship*, Washington, DC: Smithsonian Institution Press.

Goodenough, W.H. (1970) *Description and Comparison in Cultural Anthropology*, Chicago: Aldine Publishing Company.

Goody, J. (ed.) (1973) *The Character of Kinship*, Cambridge, UK: Cambridge University Press.

—— (1976) *Production and Reproduction: A Comparative Study of the Domestic Domain*, Cambridge, UK: Cambridge University Press.

—— (1983) *The Development of the Family and Marriage in Europe*, Cambridge, UK: Cambridge University Press.

—— (1990) *The Oriental, the Ancient and the Primitive: Systems of Marriage and the Family in the Pre-Industrial Societies of Eurasia*, Cambridge, UK: Cambridge University Press.

Graburn, N. (ed.) (1971) *Readings in Kinship and Social Structure*, New York: Harper & Row.

Gullestad, M. and Segalen, M. (eds) (1997) *Family and Kinship in Europe*, London: Pinter.

Hammel, E.A. and Laslett, P. (1974) 'Comparing household structure over time and between cultures', *Comparative Studies in Society and History* 16: 73–103.

Héritier, F. (1981) *L'Exercice de la parenté*, Paris: Éditions du Seuil.

—— (1994) *Les Deux Sœurs et leur mère: Anthropologie de l'inceste*, Paris: Odile Jacob.

Héritier-Augé, F. and Copet-Rougier, E. (eds) (1991–4) *Les Complexités de l'alliance*, Paris: Editions des Archives Contemporaines.

Holy, L. (1996) *Anthropological Perspectives on Kinship*, London: Pluto Press.

Homans, G.C. and Schneider, D.M. (1955) *Marriage, Authority, and Final Causes: A Study of Unilateral Cross-Cousin Marriage*. Glencoe, IL: The Free Press.

Howell, S. and Melhuus, M. (1993) 'The study of kinship; The study of person; a study of gender?', in T. de Valle (ed.) *Gendered Anthropology*, London: Routledge.

Hubert, J., Forge, A. and Firth, R. (1968) *Methods of Study of Middle-Class Kinship in London: A Working Paper on the History of an Anthropological Project, 1960–65*, London: Department of Anthropology, London School of Economics and Political Science.

Keesing, R.M. (1975) *Kin Groups and Social Structure*, Fort Worth, TX: Holt, Rinehart & Winston.

Kelly, R.C. (1993) *Constructing Inequality: The Fabrication of a Hierarchy of Virtue among the Etoro*, Ann Arbor: University of Michigan Press.

Kroeber, A.L. (1909) 'Classificatory systems of relationship', *The Journal of the Royal Anthropological Institute* 39: 77–84.

Kryukov, M.V. (1984) 'Towards a method of gathering field material on kinship systems', in T. Dragadze (ed.) *Family and Kinship in the Soviet Union: Field Studies*, London: Routledge & Kegan Paul.

Laslett, P. (ed.) (1972) *Household and Family in Past Time*, Cambridge, UK: Cambridge University Press.

—— (1977) *Family Life and Illicit Love in Earlier Generations: Essays in Historical Sociology*, Cambridge, UK: Cambridge University Press.

Leacock, E.B. (1981) *Myths of Male Dominance: Collected Articles on Women Cross-Culturally*, New York: Monthly Review Press.

Levin, Y. (1974) 'A description of systems of kinship terminology', in Y. Bromley (ed.) *Soviet Ethnology and Anthropology Today*, The Hague: Mouton.

Lévi-Strauss, C. (1949) *Les Structures élémentaires de la parenté*, Paris: Presses Universitaires de France.

—— (1969) *The Elementary Structures of Kinship*, Boston, MA: Beacon Press.

—— (1982) *The Way of the Masks*, Seattle: University of Washington Press.

—— (1985) *The View from Afar*, New York: Basic Books.

Lowie, R.H. (1917) *Culture and Ethnology*, New York: Holt, Rinehart & Winston.

Macdonald, C. (ed.) (1987) *De la hutte au palais: Sociétés 'à maisons' en Asie du Sud-Est insulaire*, Paris: Editions du CNRS.

McKinnon, S. (1995) 'American kinship/American incest: Asymmetries in a scientific discourse', in S. Yanagisako and C. Delaney (eds) *Naturalizing Power: Essays in Feminist Cultural Analysis*, New York: Routledge.

Maine, H.S. (1880 [1861]) *Ancient Law: Its Connections with the Early History of Society and its Relations to Modern Ideas*, London: John Murray.

Malinowski, B. (1930) 'Kinship', *Man* 30(2): 19–29.

—— (1944) *A Scientific Theory of Culture and Other Essays*, Chapel Hill: University of North Carolina Press.

Mauss, M. (1979 [1938]) 'A category of the human mind: The notion of person, the notion of "self"', in *Sociology and Psychology: Essays*, London: Routledge & Kegan Paul.

Maynes, M.J., Waltner, A., Soland, B. and Strasser, U. (eds) (1996) *Gender, Kinship, Power: A Comparative and Interdisciplinary History*, New York: Routledge.

Medick, H. and Sabean, D.W. (eds) (1984) *Interest and Emotion: Essays on the Study of Family and Kinship*, Cambridge, UK: Cambridge University Press.

Meillassoux, C. (1978) 'The social organisation of the peasantry: The economic basis of kinship', in D. Seddon (ed.) *Relations of Production: Marxist Approaches to Economic Anthropology*, London: Frank Cass.

—— (1981) *Maidens, Meal and Money: Capitalism and the Domestic Community*, Cambridge, UK: Cambridge University Press.

Mitterauer, M. and Sieder, R. (1982) *The European Family: Patriarchy to Partnership from the Middle Ages to the Present*, Chicago: University of Chicago Press.

Modell, J.S. (1994) *Kinship with Strangers: Adoption and Interpretations of Kinship in American Culture*, Berkeley: University of California Press.

Modjeska, N. (1982) 'Production and inequality: Perspectives from central New Guinea', in A. Strathern (ed.) *Inequality in New Guinea Highlands Societies*, Cambridge, UK: Cambridge University Press.

Murdock, G.P. (1949) *Social Structure*, New York: The Free Press.

Nader, L. (1972) 'Up the anthropologist – perspectives gained from studying up', in D. Hymes (ed.) *Reinventing Anthropology*, New York: Vintage Books.

Needham, R. (1962) *Structure and Sentiment: A Test Case in Social Anthropology*, Chicago: University of Chicago Press.

—— (1971) 'Remarks on the analysis of kinship and marriage', in R. Needham (ed.) *Rethinking Kinship and Marriage*, London: Tavistock Publications.

—— (1973) 'Prescription', *Oceania* 42: 166–81.

—— (1975) 'Polythetic classification: Convergence and consequences', *Man (N.S.)* 10: 349–69.

Nuttall, M. (1992) *Arctic Homeland: Kinship, Community and Development in Northwest Greenland*, Toronto: University of Toronto Press.

O'Laughlin, B. (1974) 'Mediation of contradiction: Why Mbum women do not eat chicken', in M.Z. Rosaldo and L. Lamphere (eds) *Woman, Culture, and Society*, Stanford, CA: Stanford University Press.

Ortner, S.B. (1984) 'Theory in anthropology since the sixties', *Comparative Studies in Society and History* 26: 126–66.

Ortner, S.B. and Whitehead, H. (eds) (1981) *Sexual Meanings: The Cultural Construction of Gender and Sexuality*, Cambridge, UK: Cambridge University Press.

Östör, Á., Fruzzetti, L. and Barnett, S. (eds) (1982) *Concepts of Person: Kinship, Caste, and Marriage in India*, Cambridge, MA: Harvard University Press.

Parkin, R. (1997) *Kinship: An Introduction to the Basic Concepts*, Oxford: Blackwell Publishers.

Pasternak, B. (1976) *Introduction to Kinship and Social Organization*, Englewood Cliffs, NJ: Prentice-Hall.

Peletz, M.G. (1995) 'Kinship studies in late twentieth-century anthropology', *Annual Review of Anthropology* 24: 343–72.

—— (1996) *Reason and Passion: Representations of Gender in a Malay Society*, Berkeley: University of California Press.

—— (forthcoming) 'Ambivalence in kinship since the forties', in S. Franklin and S. McKinnon (eds) *Relative Values: New Directions in Kinship Study*, Berkeley: University of California Press.

Pina-Cabral, J. de (1989) 'L'Héritage de Maine: Repenser les catégories descriptives dans l'étude de la famille en Europe', *Ethnologie française* 19: 329–40.

Pine, F. (1996) 'Naming the house and naming the land: Kinship and social groups in Highland Poland', *The Journal of the Royal Anthropological Institute (N.S.)* 2: 443–59.

Popov, V. (1978) 'Bifurcate-merging system of kinship terms as a source of ethnosociological information (on the example of the Akan peoples)', *Problems of the Contemporary World* 72: 150–60.

Radcliffe-Brown, A.R. (1950) 'Introduction', in A.R. Radcliffe-Brown and D. Forde (eds) *African Systems of Kinship and Marriage*, London: Oxford University Press.

Rival, L. (1998) 'Androgynous parents and guest children: The Huaorani couvade', *The Journal of the Royal Anthropological Institute (N.S.)* 4: 619–42.

Robin, J. (1980) *Elmdon: Continuity and Change in a North-west Essex Village, 1861–1964*, Cambridge, UK: Cambridge University Press.

Roschelle, A.R. (1997) *No More Kin: Exploring Race, Class, and Gender in Family Networks*, Thousand Oaks, CA: Sage Publications.

Rubin, G. (1975) 'The traffic in women: Notes on the "political economy" of sex', in R.R. Reiter (ed.) *Toward an Anthropology of Women*, New York: Monthly Review Press.

Sabean, D.W. (1998) *Kinship in Neckarhausen, 1700–1870*, Cambridge, UK: Cambridge University Press.

Sacks, K. (1974) 'Engels revisited: Women, the organization of production, and private property', in M.Z. Rosaldo and L. Lamphere (eds) *Woman, Culture, and Society*, Stanford, CA: Stanford University Press.

—— (1982) *Sisters and Wives: The Past and Future of Sexual Equality*, Urbana: University of Illinois Press.

Scheffler, H.W. (1978) *Australian Kin Classification*, Cambridge, UK: Cambridge University Press.

—— (1991) 'Sexism and naturalism in the study of kinship', in M. di Leonardo (ed.) *Gender at the Crossroads of Knowledge: Feminist Anthropology in the Postmodern Era*, Berkeley: University of California Press.

Scheffler, H.W. and Lounsbury, F.G. (1971) *A Study in Structural Semantics: The Sirionó Kinship System*, Englewood Cliffs, NJ: Prentice-Hall.

Schneider, D.M. (1965a) 'Some muddles in the models: Or, how the system really works', in *The Relevance of Models for Social Anthropology*, London: Tavistock Publications.

—— (1965b) 'Kinship and biology', in H.J. Coale (ed.) *Aspects of the Analysis of Family Structure*, Princeton, NJ: Princeton University Press.

—— (1968) *American Kinship: A Cultural Account*, Englewood Cliffs, NJ: Prentice-Hall.

—— (1972) 'What is kinship all about?', in P. Reining (ed.) *Kinship Studies in the Morgan Centennial Year*, Washington, DC: The Anthropological Society of Washington.

—— (1980) *American Kinship: A Cultural Account*, second edition, Chicago: University of Chicago Press.

—— (1984) *A Critique of the Study of Kinship*, Ann Arbor: University of Michigan Press.

Schneider, D.M. and Smith, R.T. (1973) *Class Differences and Sex Roles in American Kinship and Family Structure*, Englewood Cliffs, NJ: Prentice-Hall.

Schusky, E.L. (1972) *Manual for Kinship Analysis*, New York: Holt, Rinehart & Winston.

—— (1974) *Variation in Kinship*, New York: Holt, Rinehart & Winston.

Segalen, M. (1983) *Love and Power in the Peasant Family: Rural France in the Nineteenth Century*, Chicago: University of Chicago Press.

—— (1986) *Historical Anthropology of the Family*, Cambridge, UK: Cambridge University Press.

Spiro, M.E. (1977) *Kinship and Marriage in Burma: A Cultural and Psychodynamic Analysis*, Berkeley: University of California Press.

Steinberg, N. (1993) *Kinship and Marriage in Genesis: A Household Economics Perspective*, Minneapolis, MN: Fortress Press.

Stone, L. (1997) *Kinship and Gender: An Introduction*, Boulder, CO: Westview Press.

Strathern, M. (1981) *Kinship at the Core: An Anthropology of Elmdon a Village in North-west Essex in the Nineteen-sixties*, Cambridge, UK: Cambridge University Press.

—— (1984) 'Marriage exchanges: A Melanesian comment', *Annual Review of Anthropology* 13: 41–73.

—— (1985) 'Kinship and economy: Constitutive orders of a provisional kind', *American Ethnologist* 12: 191–209.

—— (1987) 'Producing difference: Connections and disconnections in two New Guinea Highland kinship systems', in J.F. Collier and S.J. Yanagisako (eds) *Gender and Kinship: Essays Toward a Unified Analysis*, Stanford, CA: Stanford University Press.

—— (1988) *The Gender of the Gift: Problems with Women and Problems with Society in Melanesia*, Berkeley: University of California Press.

—— (1992a) *After Nature: English Kinship in the Late Twentieth Century*, Cambridge, UK: Cambridge University Press.

—— (1992b) *Reproducing the Future: Anthropology, Kinship and the New Reproductive Technologies*, London: Routledge.

—— (1997) 'Marilyn Strathern on kinship', *EASA Newsletter* 19: 6–9.

Terray, E. (1972) *Marxism and 'Primitive' Societies: Two Studies*, New York: Monthly Review Press.

Trautmann, T.R. (1987) *Lewis Henry Morgan and the Invention of Kinship*, Berkeley: University of California Press.

Wachter, K.W., Hammel, E.A. and Laslett, P. (1978) *Statistical Studies of Historical Social Structure*, New York: Academic Press.

Wall, R. (ed.) (1983) *Family Forms in Historic Europe*, Cambridge, UK: Cambridge University Press.

Weston, K. (1997) *Families We Choose: Lesbians, Gays, Kinship*, New York: Columbia University Press.

—— (1998) *Long Slow Burn: Sexuality and Social Science*, New York: Routledge.

Witherspoon, G. (1975) *Navajo Kinship and Marriage*, Chicago: University of Chicago Press.

Wolfram, S. (1987) *In-Laws and Outlaws: Kinship and Marriage in England*, New York: St Martin's Press.

Yanagisako, S.J. (1978) 'Variance in American kinship: Implications for cultural analysis', *American Ethnologist* 5: 15–29.

—— (1985) *Transforming the Past: Tradition and Kinship among Japanese Americans*, Stanford, CA: Stanford University Press.

—— (1987) 'Mixed metaphors: Native and anthropological models of gender and kinship domains', in J.F. Collier and S.J. Yanagisako (eds) *Gender and Kinship: Essays Toward a Unified Analysis*, Stanford, CA: Stanford University Press.

Yanagisako, S.J. and Collier, J.F. (1987) 'Toward a unified analysis of gender and kinship', in J.F. Collier and S.J. Yanagisako (eds) *Gender and Kinship: Essays Toward a Unified Analysis*, Stanford, CA: Stanford University Press.

Yanagisako, S. and Delaney, C. (eds) (1995) *Naturalizing Power: Essays in Feminist Cultural Analysis*, New York: Routledge.

Young, M. and Willmott, P. (1957) *Family and Kinship in East London*, London: Routledge & Kegan Paul.

# Chapter 2

# Choosing kin

## Sharing and subsistence in a Greenlandic hunting community

*Mark Nuttall*

The anthropological study of Inuit kinship has not been without controversy. While anthropologists have generally agreed that kinship is the very foundation of Inuit social organisation, most have produced conflicting accounts that have provided a rich source for academic debate and argument. Some suggest that Inuit social organisation is either rigidly structured, or formless and flexible. Others emphasise that kinship is biologically prescribed and the primary means of regulating interpersonal relations, while some take an opposing view and, rejecting the idea that kinship is the underlying framework for Inuit social life, stress instead the importance of locality and negotiation, and argue that kinship is merely a rhetorical language for social relations. Such debates have done little to dispel the general feeling amongst anthropologists who do not specialise in the cultures of the Arctic, that Inuit studies have contributed little to general anthropological theory precisely because Inuit social life and social organisation is hard to categorise. If anything, Inuit social organisation is hard to categorise because there is no homogeneous Inuit culture – although 'Eskimo' and 'Inuit' have been used as terms in both academic and popular literature as if they were descriptive of a single cultural group. However, if there is unity in diversity in Inuit societies across the Arctic it is to be found in the importance of kinship for constituting and framing social interaction, rather than the existence of an 'Inuit type' kinship system.

In this chapter I argue that kinship is both the foundation for social relatedness and social organisation, and the key organising principle for subsistence activities in Kangersuatsiaq, a village in north-west Greenland. However, I reject the notion that in Kangersuatsiaq kinship is biologically prescribed. This is immediately apparent to anyone who tries to collect genealogies, work out an individual's kin reckoning or simply listen to the way people use kinship terms in situations of both reference and address. The boundaries of kindred- and descent-based groups, as people in Kangersuatsiaq define them, are shifting constantly, as are the interpersonal relationships that are defined in terms of kinship. Kinship in Kangersuatsiaq may appear to have distinct biological roots, but in practice it is flexible and integrates non-biological social relationships that are considered to be as 'real' as any biological relationship. Kinship relationships are not always permanent states, and although it may be possible to talk of a kinship *system* in Kangersuatsiaq, it is a system that is inherently flexible and allows extensive improvisation in that people can choose their kin. Kinship in Kangersuatsiaq is more accurately described as a complex network and intricate pattern of relationships that includes both the living and the dead. When people die their names and their kinship relations carry on in new-born children, so that people retain their social presence despite their physical absence. As I have argued elsewhere, people continually define and bring into existence 'real' relationships that are not based on biology (Nuttall 1992). Kinship is a cultural reservoir from which individuals draw items they can use to define and construct everyday social interaction. To understand kinship in this part of Greenland it is important to focus on the meanings that individuals attribute to kinship terms and kinship terminologies, rather than accepting at face value that terminologies refer to strict genealogical relationships.

Yet, while I suggest that kinship is flexible, I argue that it is not formless. Nor are particular roles without obligation. Kinship in Kangersuatsiaq is all pervasive: because kinship ties are reaffirmed or created through the naming of children after the deceased, or simply by applying a kin term to someone who may not be a biological relative, almost everyone can trace or establish some kind of kinship relationship with everyone else in the village. If a relationship does not exist, then one can be created. At the same time, people can deactivate kinship relationships if they regard them as unsatisfactory. People are therefore not constrained by a rigid consanguineal kinship system, but can choose much of their universe of kin. Thus, daily life in Kangersuatsiaq is inextricably bound up with kinship and people carry out and talk about most social and economic activities – hunting, fishing, other kinds of work, visiting, gossiping, or whatever – with reference to kin relationships. But however they construct their own relationships, they are bound to behave in prescribed ways.

After summarising some of the key issues in the anthropological study of kinship, I discuss how kinship works in Kangersuatsiaq. I then place particular emphasis on how kinship structures and defines the social organisation of subsistence, but describe how kinship as the key organising principle for seal hunting, whaling, fishing, sharing and exchange is beginning to look precarious as Greenland moves increasingly towards a market-based economy. While kinship remains important in Kangersuatsiaq, changes in wider Greenlandic society mean that people no longer live and work only within a spatially defined community of common interest expressed through kinship relations. Some people are involved more and more in occupational networks that are dispersed and based on contractual relations. For those involved in the harvesting of marine mammals and in small-scale fishing, it is not always easy to reconcile the need to meet the obligations of kinship relationships, with the need to be competitive and survive in a rapidly modernising circumpolar country. As the Greenland Home Rule government places more emphasis on the commercial trade of seal meat, whale meat and other products of what, for most people, remains subsistence hunting, there is a clash between two cultures: one small-scale, emphasising kinship, reciprocity and cultural identity, the other market-orientated within a context of nation-building.

## Anthropological models of Inuit kinship

Early ethnographic accounts of Inuit kinship (e.g. Birket-Smith 1924; Boas 1964 [1888]; Holm 1914; Rasmussen 1931) focused almost exclusively on terminology and did little to contribute to an understanding of Inuit social organisation. Rather, eskimologists were inspired and constrained somewhat by Morgan's (1870) description of kinship terminologies from Greenland and the Canadian Arctic, and Spier's (1925) definition of an 'Eskimo' type kinship system. Morgan worked from the extremely limited sources available at the time and assumed there was a great deal of cultural uniformity right across the North American Arctic. Based on material gathered by Diamond Jenness (1922), Spier's 'Eskimo' type system grouped cross and parallel cousins together by virtue of having one term to identify each, two terms for grandparents, four terms for parents' siblings, one term for grandchildren and simple nepotic terms. Spier also argued that siblings are distinguished by age and he saw this system as characteristic of the entire Inuit area.

Following Spier's lead, a great deal of anthropological research on Inuit kinship networks tended to look for underlying structures and logic that had cross-cultural validity (e.g. Murdock 1949). Murdock's 'Eskimo' type system placed the nuclear family at the centre of Inuit social organisation. He went beyond Spier by emphasising descent and the terminological separation of cousins and siblings. But Murdock's contribution to kinship studies was the way in which he argued that the term 'Eskimo' type could be applied cross-culturally beyond the Arctic, and could best describe Western European social organisation. Instead of merely describing a system of kinship reckoning in remote corners of the Arctic, the 'Eskimo' type system came to be used to designate a form of social structure. Although the 'Eskimo' type kinship system was later critiqued for the way it sought to exemplify the social structure of Inuit societies (e.g. Giddings 1952), and although anthropologists were baffled when they discovered deviations from the 'Eskimo' type system (and Spier himself had noted that there were some striking differences), the very diversity of Inuit culture was ignored and misunderstood as anthropologists focused on descent systems, cousin terminologies or clan organisation and attempted to build models of pan-Inuit social structure (e.g. Sperry 1952; Fainberg 1967). The anthropological study of Inuit kinship has been charac-terised by its attempts to look for underlying structure and logic, and has produced an academic language rich in terminologies, descriptive models and concepts. This has been the intellectual straitjacket from which many students of Inuit culture have found themselves unable to escape.

It fell to Damas (1963, 1964, 1968) and Guemple (1965, 1972a, 1972b) to break with tradition and argue, respectively, that the social context of kinship terminology, rather than the terms themselves, was the all important factor in determining and organising Inuit social rela-tionships, and that non-kinship-based alliances were more important than kinship in structuring social relations. Working on material gath-ered among the Iglulingmiut of the central Canadian Arctic, Damas described in intricate detail how kinship was the foundation for the formation of Inuit social groups. In particular, Damas argued how Inuit notions of *ungayuq* ('affection' and 'closeness') and *naalaqtuq* ('respect' and 'obedience') went some considerable way in structuring kinship relations. The extremely detailed work produced by Damas has been influential and other anthropologists have also described the importance of *ungayuq* and *naalaqtuq*. For example, for the people of Clyde River on Baffin Island, Wenzel (1981) has suggested that these notions not only determine how kin relate and behave towards one another, but structure Inuit ecological relations as well.

However, while Damas argued that kinship was centrally important in organising and regulating social life and interpersonal behaviour,

Guemple's work amongst the Qiqiqtamiut of the Belcher Islands emphasised that 'kinship' is essentially based on negotiation and may be better seen as a metaphor for non-genealogically defined and mutually beneficial alliances, such as spouse exchange, adoption, naming and ritual sponsorship. For Guemple (1979: 93) 'social relatedness begins in the local group, not in the kinship tie', and is inherently socio-cultural rather than biological. Thus, kinship ties are only recognised and validated through proximity – people are recognised as kin if they live in the same community, not because they have any genealogical connection. For the Qiqiqtamiut, Guemple argues, anyone living in a settlement, hunting camp or regional hunting group can become a relative. But for this relationship to exist, people must not only reside together, they must co-operate with one another according to traditional rules (such as generalised reciprocity) and maintain regular contact. If they fail to do so, they cease to be relatives. But the range of potential relatives is vast – virtually all Inuit can become relatives if they come into contact with one another. Similarly, in Graburn's (1964) analysis of Inuit groups on the Ungava coast, he argues that social relatedness begins with residence and co-operation, i.e. that kinship only becomes meaningful and assumes significance if people are members of the same household or co-operate together in hunting and fishing activities. Furthermore, in Guemple's analysis Inuit social organisation is egalitarian rather than hierarchical, and through the creation of alliances the dividends of kinship are economic as well as social. For Guemple, the language of kinship is a rhetorical one that causes anthropologists to ignore the negotiated character of all social relationships.

Guemple has his critics, most notably Burch (1975) who firmly argues against the idea of kinship as negotiation and being anything other than biologically determined. Rather than being formless, flexible and fluid, Burch argues that his material on Inupiaq kinship in northern Alaska shows precisely that kinship is vitally important in structuring specific kin relations and prescribing how people must act and relate to one another. Others have criticised Guemple by pointing out that there are no situations similar to the Belcher Islands anywhere else in the Arctic, or have argued that Inuit societies that have hierarchies, or are at least ranked, such as in north-west Alaska, show that kinship is not the great leveller Guemple claims it to be.

While I still find his work readable and refreshing, I would criticise Guemple myself for seeing Inuit kinship as unimportant and for focusing instead on locality and negotiation. My own experience of

Inuit kinship comes not only from Kangersuatsiaq, but also from field-work carried out in villages in north, south and east Greenland, where kinship is central to social and economic life. Whatever the particulari-ties of kinship in these villages, it nonetheless shapes, informs, influences and determines how people relate to one another and is central to the way people conceptualise and define their social worlds. In Greenland social relatedness does not always begin in the local group – for example, as we shall see later, children are often named after deceased people who lived in different villages. Once named, they become the kin of the surviving relatives of the deceased. Yet, while I do not follow Guemple all the way, I also disagree with Burch that (based on my own understanding of how things work in Greenland, at least) kinship is biologically determined and support Guemple's posi-tion that kinship is metaphorical and flexible. In addition, Schweitzer (1994) has recently argued for the Bering Strait Inupiaq that 'becoming a relative' is not limited to biological means and that prag-matic and strategic choices are part of the process. Kinship is a rhetoric of social relatedness, as Guemple argues (Guemple 1972a), but I cannot agree with him that it is not the underlying skeleton of the social system and is unimportant. In Kangersuatsiaq, kinship – whether based on biology or affinity – is real as long as people see it as such.

Although Fienup-Riordan (1983) broke the mould with her emphasis on complementary oppositions underpinning Yup'ik social organisation in south-west Alaska, the anthropological study of Inuit kinship has not yet shaken off the intellectual legacy of the biology versus locality or structure versus formlessness debates. This is partly to do with a changing research agenda. The tremendous social and economic changes in the Arctic over the last few decades, the politici-sation of Inuit culture and the increasingly influential role that Inuit communities play in deciding what type of research should be carried out, all mean that anthropologists have interests other than kinship systems, such as self-determination movements, indigenous knowledge and environmental management, sustainable development and subsis-tence economies. The work of the likes of Damas, Guemple and Burch remains highly influential because few studies of contemporary Inuit social organisation that have emerged over the last decade or so have entered the anthropological consciousness in quite the same way.

I have previously suggested that we must move away from restrictions imposed by earlier anthropological models of Inuit kinship (Nuttall 1992), and have argued that kinship relationships should not be defined as fictive if they are not biologically determined. Rather, in

Greenlandic villages kin categories vary in meaning and their significance lies in the way they permit individuals freedom to employ them
in any way they choose. It is in this sense that kinship is symbolic and it
is through kinship that people find expression in their social worlds
(Nuttall 1992: 93). However, there is another compelling reason why
we should dispense with looking for a distinctively Inuit type of kinship
system. The sheer number of studies of Inuit kinship based on research
with Inuit groups in Siberia, Alaska, Canada and Greenland shows that
the very diversity of Inuit society defies generalisation. There is no
homogeneous form of Inuit social organisation and the search for a
pan-Inuit type kinship system is a fruitless one. Kinship, however, *is*
important for Inuit peoples, but the forms it takes differ from area to
area.

With this premise, and against the background of this brief summary of anthropological models of Inuit kinship, in the rest of this
chapter I discuss how kinship remains at the very core of social and
economic life for the people of Kangersuatsiaq, a village in north-west
Greenland. While advocating a move away from being restricted by
existing models of Inuit kinship, I am nonetheless all too self-conscious
that I am stumbling around the 'kinship as inherently socio-cultural'
camp led by Guemple. However, I do not seek to show how Greenland Inuit kinship lends credence to a particular anthropologist's
observations about how kinship operates in Alaska or Canada, or dispel
anyone else's arguments about flexibility or structure, or so on,
although my material may address many of these issues and theoretical
perspectives. Rather, I wish to show that kinship is the key organising
principle for social life, subsistence hunting and fishing, and sharing in
one particular village. But instead of kinship relationships being biologically determined and structured, or negotiated on the basis of locality
and geographical closeness (i.e. Guemple's notion that relatedness
begins in the local group), or forms of alliance functioning to support
inadequate or weak kinship ties, I suggest that what is significant about
kinship in this part of Greenland is that it is based largely on choice, or
at least people can choose their kinship relationships. Yet, while kinship
in Kangersuatsiaq may point to the argument that many students of
Inuit kinship advance in favour of recognising the inherent flexibility of
kinship, I argue that once people choose their kin there are definite
prescriptions about how they should relate to one another. In other
words, you can choose your kin, but you cannot choose how to behave
towards and with them.

## The setting

Kangersuatsiaq is a small hunting community of about 200 people in the southern part of the district of Upernavik in north-west Greenland. Upernavik district comprises ten villages served by the administrative centre of Upernavik town. Geographically, Upernavik district is a pattern of islands with several large peninsulas jutting out from Greenland's inland ice. In common with other Greenlandic communities, identity and a sense of place is expressed with the suffix -*miut*, meaning 'people of'. The people of Kangersuatsiaq refer to themselves, and are referred to by others, as Kangersuatsiarmiut ('people of Kangersuatsiaq'), but more often prefer to call themselves Kangersuatsiarmiit (-*miut* becomes -*miit* in the Kangersuatsiaq dialect). In this way the Kangersuatsiarmiit express their attachment to their locality and distinguish themselves from the inhabitants of other nearby villages, such as the people of Søndre Upernavik (Søndre Upernavimmiut) and Kullorsuaq (Kullorsuarmiut).

The villages in Upernavik district are spatially organised to allow easy access to their respective resource areas (Haller 1986). Kangersuatsiaq is also known throughout Greenland as Prøven, meaning 'tried'. Throughout the 1770s attempts were made by the Danes to establish the netting of beluga whales at the site of the present-day village, and the history of Kangersuatsiaq is said to start from this date (Greenland was a Danish colony from 1721–1953 and achieved Home Rule from Denmark in 1979). While beluga whaling remained vitally important to the local economy during the nineteenth century, the Kangersuatsiarmiit subsisted mainly by the harvesting of seals. Although a small-scale inshore commercial fishery has developed throughout Upernavik district over the last decade, seal hunting not only forms part of a larger cultural system, it continues to provide the foundation for both a secure kin-based network and a sense of community in Kangersuatsiaq (Nuttall 1992). Hunters rely on catching ringed seals during winter and spring, and to a lesser extent in summer. Harp seals are more important in late summer and autumn. In addition, beluga, minke and fin whales, narwhals, walrus and certain species of seabirds, such as guillemots, eider ducks, little auks, barnacle geese and kitti-wakes are also harvested.

Hunting entails an ideological and ritual responsibility to both animals and the environment. Hunters must ensure that a reciprocal relationship between the hunter and the natural world is maintained. Human beings must follow a code of correct ways of acting in relation to the environment and ensure that animals and animal spirits are propitiated. Hunters are held to account: they are responsible for ensuring the stability and continuity of a multiplicity of spiritual relationships between humans and animals (which are seen as non-human persons). Following Ellen (1982: 175), I suggest an encompassing definition of subsistence is 'all the uses to which a species may be put'. In Kangersuatsiaq, like many other Greenlandic hunting communities, dependence on marine mammals for food and survival is reflected in community hunting regulations and the attitude of hunters towards the animals they hunt. For example, the hunting household uses the meat, fat and skin of the seal, and complex local rules determine how the products of the catch are shared and distributed. While the Kangersuatsiarmiit hunt and fish primarily to acquire food for themselves, and although hunting has not acquired a purely commercial incentive, some products of the hunt (e.g. sealskins, whale meat) and the fishery are sold to Royal Greenland (a Greenland Home Rule government-owned company responsible for Greenland's fishing, production and export business). Until recently the sale of sealskins was the only source of income for many people. However, most families in Kangersuatsiaq now derive little income from hunting. The market value of sealskin prices has dropped considerably over the last few years, partly as a result of the activities of animal rights groups, which were influential in forcing European trade bans on importing seal products. Although originally directed towards the harvesting of harp and hooded seal pups off Atlantic Canada, the anti-sealing campaigns (directed by several environmental organisations such as Greenpeace) were extended in the late 1970s to include aboriginal seal hunting in the Arctic. Environmental organisations, and more specifically animal rights groups, argued that by adopting modern Western technology such as rifles and speedboats, the Inuit had effectively removed themselves from any traditional context. While the skins of adult seals hunted in Greenland are exempt from the European ban, the trade in sealskins is only made possible because it is subsidised by the Greenland Home Rule government. Despite this subsidy, the effects of the ban have still been felt in Greenland and have intensified the marginal role of seal hunting in the country. Many hunters now find it increasingly difficult to continue their customary way of life.

Like many other villages in Greenland, Kangersuatsiaq is characterised by its mixed economy, combining the informal sector of customary and traditional subsistence activities (which provide the primary source of food for many households), with the formal sector of wage-earning possibilities. The informal sector is not easy to measure or analyse, combining as it does hunting and fishing based on long-term, consistent patterns of use and seasonal variation, non-accumulation of capital, sharing of wild foods, the generational transmission of knowledge and non-monetary exchange based on kinship groups and other networks of close social association. While some people hunt or fish, others work in paid employment. Casual labour in the village fish-processing plant or for the municipal authorities, or working on fishing vessels based at larger ports in Greenland are often seen as activities necessary for supplementing the subsistence economy. In more than two-thirds of families dependent on subsistence hunting and fishing, at least one partner is a wage-earner. But it is also the case that in other parts of Greenland, where commercial fishing is dominant and greater opportunities exist for wage-earning, the hunting of seals and other sea mammals is important either as a full-time occupation or as a supplement to wage labour.

## Choosing kin

Social relationships in Kangersuatsiaq are defined in terms of being either kin or non-kin based. Kinship is multifaceted, embracing genealogy, consanguinity, affinity, friendship, name-sharing, birthday partners, age-sets, the living and the dead. Kinship is bilateral and the term for personal kindred or close extended family is *ilaqutariit*. The root of this word, *ila-*, means 'a part', or 'a companion', and a member of the *ilaqutariit* is called an *ilaqutaq*, 'someone who belongs'. Individual households are suffixed with *-kkut* (e.g. Josepikkut – Josepi's household) and there are usually several *-kkut* in an *ilaqutariit*. The Kangersuatsiarmiit distinguish between an *ilaqutaq* and an *eqqarleq*, someone who is a genealogical or affinal relative belonging to another *ilaqutariit*. *Eqqarleq* derives from *eqqaq*, meaning 'the immediate vicinity/area', or 'close to'. As a form of address and reference *eqqarleq* is not necessarily always applied to distant kin, but its use depends on how a person defines his or her relationship with another person. One vitally important feature of kinship in Kangersuatsiaq is that kin relationships can be created if individuals choose to regard a non-kin relationship as something similar to a genealogical or affinal link. Just as people work out and define social relationships in terms of being kin or non-kin based, they can also decide how closely related they feel to someone. While it may be rare to hear that somebody regards a sibling as an *eqqarleq*, an *eqqarleq* such as a second cousin's spouse may be regarded as a sibling by somebody and referred to as an *ilaqutaq*, even if those people have no consanguineal or affinal relationship.

Like many other Inuit communities, Greenlanders generally use kin terms in preference to personal names to refer to and address people irrespective of any genealogical or affinal connection. The Kangersuatsiarmiit are no exception to this rule. To establish and continue a kinship relationship is easy enough – kin terms are simply used for both reference and address, and personal names are avoided in most situations of daily interaction. As forms of address, kin terms are used usually in the possessive: for example, *ataataga* (my father), *paniga* (my daughter). So, a man or a woman who regards their second cousin's (*illuusaq*) wife as a sister will use the appropriate kinship term (a man will call the woman either *aleqa* for older sister, or *najak* for younger sister; a woman will call her *angaju* for older sister, or *nukaq* for younger sister). The woman who is now regarded as a sister will reciprocate by using the appropriate kinship term for brother or sister (*ani* for older brother, or *aqqaluk* for younger brother; *angaju* or *nukaq* for older or younger sister respectively). Such use of kin terms illustrates Schneider's (1968) argument that the recording and listing of kinship terms does not mean that their designation will follow accordingly. The central thesis of my earlier work on Greenland Inuit kinship (Nuttall 1992) is that kin terms are symbols that allow for the imputation of idiosyncratic meaning and form part of a much larger set of symbols and implicit meanings that people use actively and consciously to construct the idea of community.

While relationships can be created if people regard others as particular categories of kin, genealogical relationships can also be 'forgotten about' if a person regards that relationship as unsatisfactory, uncomfortable or strained (Guemple 1979; Nuttall 1992: 82–3). Guemple (1972c) has argued that this is made possible because of the negotiated nature of the Inuit kinship system. In this way, genealogical relationships can be rendered obsolete or subordinated to other social relationships. In Kangersuatsiaq it is common to hear people talking about a member of their *ilaqutariit* as if they were actually an *eqqarleq* and vice versa. Other people may deny any kin connection whatsoever. In some cases, this may be because two members of an *ilaqutariit* have fallen out. To deny a kinship connection is a way for people to disown one another.

There may be pragmatic reasons to deny a kin tie, especially when first cousins are involved in a sexual relationship. People are heard to say things like 'She used to be my relative but she's now my woman', or 'She used to be my cousin' (Nuttall 1992: 83). By choosing to ignore or deny a relationship, that relationship ceases to exist. Rosaldo (1980: 183) also makes a similar point when she says that kin ties can be 'discovered', or people can choose to forget or cease to know a kin tie. But there are usually limits to what relationship can be denied, such as parents, grandparents and siblings. Heinrich (1963) distinguished between optative and non-optative categories of kinship. Optative kin can include anyone with whom an individual wants to consider kin, while non-optative kin includes grandparents, parents and siblings. People can fall in and out of the former category, but, as I have already pointed out, it is not really acceptable to deny the existence of one's parents, siblings, grandparents and possibly aunts and uncles. Optative kinship networks are flexible to the point where incompatible relations between individuals can be remedied by substituting them for more effective and meaningful ones (Guemple 1979). In this way, unlike the situation described by Burch (1975) in northwest Alaska, biology does not structure kinship relationships and determine how people who are biologically related should behave towards one another. In Kangersuatsiaq, alternatively, kinship is not ascribed but a matter of choice. Unlike Guemple's observation that, for the Qiqiqtamiut, people become relatives if they reside in the same locality, maintain regular contact and share game according to well-defined rules, the Kangersuatsiarmiit do not forget kin if someone moves away from the village, or does not share seal meat. Unless an individual decides otherwise, people remain kin despite physical absence and also if they choose not to share meat or fish (however, while people are not obligated to maintain the same kinship relations if they do not wish, they do have an obligation to share).

Although kinship in Kangersuatsiaq may be flexible, I do not subscribe to a view taken by some anthropologists who see anarchy, rather than structure, in the 'formless' Inuit social world. I agree with Burch (1975) that flexibility is not about formlessness but about allowing individuals the opportunity to move around a complex network of relationships: to reposition themselves and others how they see fit simply by regarding social relationships in terms of kinship or non-kinship. The reasons for doing so are various, complex, often intensely personal and sometimes pragmatic. There may be sexual reasons (as discussed above, where cousins are involved in a sexual relationship), or, as discussed below, two people who have an especially strong friendship may commemorate it by turning it into a kinship relationship. More practical reasons for choosing one's kin may relate to subsistence activities, where a man may have no brothers but may need to depend on close male kin for participating in hunting and fishing activities. In this way, friends who help out may be regarded as kin and the relationship established with a kinship term. While the flexibility of the kinship system allows individuals to choose who they want to have as their relative (or who they do not wish to have as a relative), it does not give them licence to decide how they should behave with that person; however, if two women who are cousins decide to discontinue that kinship connection by dropping the kin term, 'forgetting' about the biological relationship and using one another's personal name as a form of address, then the obligation to behave in a prescribed way will cease. If two unrelated persons wish to regard themselves as being like cousins, then they can establish that relationship by addressing one another with the kin term for cousin (*illoq*). But by doing so they must recognise that they are expected to behave as if they were cousins and must treat one another with respect and as equals, regardless of any age difference. If the two are men and are both hunters, then there may be certain obligations to share hunting equipment or to give catch-shares from large sea mammals, such as walrus or bearded seals, to each other's households.

Such institutionalised prescriptions may, by association, also extend to some of the genealogical and affinal kin of the individuals concerned. For example, two men who could trace no genealogical or affinal connection considered their friendship to be like the relationship between close brothers. The older man, Peter, called the younger man, Jens, by the kin term for younger brother (*nukaq*), while Jens addressed Peter as *angaju*. Jens called Peter's older sister *aleqa* and she reciprocated by calling Jens *aqqaluk*. Jens, who was unmarried, paid his 'older sister' to prepare the skins of the seals he caught, and she occasionally cooked for him and washed and repaired his clothes. Her husband called Jens *sakiatsiaq* (wife's brother) and their children called him *angak* (mother's brother). In return, Jens called his *aleqa*'s husband *sakiatsiaq* (a term also used for sister's husband) and their children (two boys) each by the term *ujoroq*. Jens also called Peter's parents by the terms for mother (*anaana*) and father (*ataata*), and Peter did the same to Jens's parents. Jens, through his kinship relationship with his *angaju* Peter, acquired an older sister, a brother-in-law, two nephews and another set of parents in addition to his biological parents. Jens would regularly give all of these people gifts of seal meat or fish (*pajugat*). A notable exclusion from Jens's kinship network, however, was Peter's younger sister with whom Jens once had a sexual relationship. Jens simply addressed her by her first name and she remained, for Jens, non-kin. Yet, Peter called a woman in the village with whom he could otherwise trace no genealogical or affinal tie 'younger sister' (*najak*) because he considered her to be exactly that. That woman called Peter *ani* (older brother) and, because Peter and Jens considered themselves brothers, she applied the same term to Jens.

It is easy to see how an individual's universe of kin can expand to include anyone they wish to consider a relative. These people are not fictive kin: they are 'real' in the same sense as biological kin. Ultimately, the Kangersuatsiarmiit can, if they so wish, distinguish between biological or fictive kinship. The use of the suffix -*piaq*, meaning 'one's own', 'personal' or 'real' can be used to distinguish biological kin from fictive kin, who can be identified by the suffix -*siaq*, meaning 'borrowed', 'bought' or 'found'. However, in Kangersuatsiaq I have only heard such distinctions used as terms of reference rather than address, and then only in conversations I had with people about genealogies. The use of a kin term is not usually suffixed as a means of discriminating between categories of biological or fictive kin. Again, I argue that fictive kin are considered to be as 'real' as biological kin and the use of -*piaq* or -*siaq* would be making a distinction between categories of kin that the Kangersuatsiarmiit do not necessarily worry about. An adopted son, for example, will be addressed as *erneq*, rather than *ernersiaq*. The use of such terminology suggests that the relationship between parents and son is regarded as if the child was really the parents' biological offspring.

The thing that underlies kinship in Kangersuatsiaq is the continual redistribution or recycling of names and name-souls, and this re-establishes existing relationships, establishes new ones and reconstitutes social life in the village. When a person dies, their name and name-soul live on in a new-born child. Kinship relationships are then able to continue. They are reaffirmed, re-expressed and modified. People, through their names, are located within a complex web of social relationships that encompass both the living and the dead. It is to the importance of naming that I now turn.

## Names, personhood and identity

During the long, dark polar winter, brilliant displays of aurora borealis, the northern lights, can often be seen on clear nights. Scientific explanation for auroral displays, that the northern lights are electrical discharges in the ionosphere of the earth, is at odds with indigenous accounts in Kangersuatsiaq. For the Kangersuatsiarmiit the northern lights both follow the end of human life and at the same time precede the birth of children. The Kangersuatsiarmiit call the northern lights *arsarnerit*, saying that they are the souls of dead people playing football with a walrus skull, or with an inflated seal bladder. By way of explanation it is necessary to consider Kangersuatsiarmiit ideas of the person.

The Kangersuatsiarmiit see the person (*inuk*) as consisting of body (*timi*), soul (*tarneq*) and name/name-soul (*ateq*). The body (*timi*) is subject to disease and decay, while the soul (*tarneq*) is a person's life force and is affected by the state of health that the body is in. The name is regarded as both a social and spiritual component of the person. When a person dies, his/her name-soul leaves the body and is said to be 'homeless' until it is recalled to reside in the body of a newborn child. It is during this period following life that a person's soul becomes an *arsartoq*, a ball player, and the soul of an unborn child. By playing ball in the night sky, the souls of the deceased remind the living that they are never too far away and are waiting to return home.

A person who is named after a dead person is called an *atsiaq* (pl. *atsiat*), but the first same-sex child to be born after the death of another person is called that person's *ateqqaataa*. The dead person, who can have more than one *atsiaq*, is known as the *atsiaq*'s *aqqa*. *Aqqa* is another word for name. Throughout many parts of the Inuit area the name is not tied to either sex, and a child can receive the name of a deceased male or female. But in Greenland all personal names are gender specific (because they are Danish names) and generally a child can only be named after a person of the same sex. This can cause problems if, say, a man whose name is Jens has died and three girls are then born. Are people to wait until a baby boy is born? There will be concern that Jens's name will be cold, lonely and homeless for too long. People can get around this potentially disturbing situation by calling one of the girls Jensine (usually the first to be born, if she has not yet received a name). However, a similar improvisation of naming does not occur if a woman dies and a baby boy is born shortly after.

The *atsiaq* does not necessarily have to be born into the deceased's community. It is quite common to find *atsiat* in other villages named after people from Kangersuatsiaq. Often, people discuss that the *aqqa* has decided where her or his *atsiaq* will be born. As one woman told me, after hearing that the *atsiaq* of a 63-year-old man named Johannsi

had been born in the village of Upernavik Kujalleq (south of Kangersuatsiaq) one week after his death:

> 'Three days after Johannsi died, I had a dream that he came to
> visit. He walked in the kitchen and took off his cap and coat.
> He sat down, drank some coffee and talked about seal hunting.
> Suddenly, he got up and put his cap and coat back on. He said he
> had to go home and I followed him to the door. He started to
> walk away and I called after him and said that he was going in the
> wrong direction, that his house was the other way. He replied that
> he was going home and started to walk in the direction of
> Upernavik Kujalleq.'

Johannsi's *ateqqaataa* linked two previously unrelated families in
Kangersuatsiaq and Upernavik Kujalleq. Again, this goes against
Guemple's argument that kinship begins in the local group and that
people only become relatives if they maintain regular contact.
Johannsi's family and the family of his *ateqqaataa* do not have
frequent contact, but gifts of salmon, narwhal meat and beluga whale
meat pass between them at appropriate seasons. Despite the birth of an
*ateqqaataa* in another village, the first same-sex child born in
Kangersuatsiaq after a death will receive the name of the deceased
person. The *ateqqaataa* who lives in another village remains important
to the family of the deceased, but having an *atsiaq* living in
Kangersuatsiaq acquires deep significance. In the case of Johannsi, a
baby boy was born in Kangersuatsiaq some weeks after the birth of
Johannsi's *ateqqaataa*. Although the boy was named after Johannsi
and became his *atsiaq*, the relationship between the two families in
Kangersuatsiaq and Upernavik Kujalleq based on the birth of the first
child was not forgotten about, even though Johannsi's family developed stronger relationships with the second boy's family.

As an *atsiaq* a child enters into a multiplicity of relationships with
the surviving relatives of its *aqqa*, who will all address the child by the
kin term they would have applied to their dead relative. The child
grows up to use corresponding terms of address, which means that the
actual use of kinship terminology diverges considerably from the use of
terms that denote genealogical and affinal relationship. For example, a
dead woman's *atsiaq* will be called 'mother' (*anaana*) by that woman's
children, and 'wife' (*nuliaq*) by her husband. In addition to her *aqqa*'s
father calling her 'daughter' (*panik*), she will be called 'daughter' by her
genitor. Furthermore, it may be that an *atsiaq* belongs genealogically

to his/her *aqqa*'s family, which complicates the use of terminology further. For example, an *atsiaq* who is named after his maternal grandfather will address his mother as 'daughter', his father as 'daughter's husband' (*ningaaq*), and his grandmother as 'wife' (*nuliaq*).

Children are constantly asked questions about these relationships by their parents, older siblings and the various kin of the *aqqa*. They are not only asked about their genealogical relationships: they are also asked about the people they are named after and they learn about their relationships with their *aqqa*'s family. Children learn to identify their own positions in the kinship networks of their parents and where they fit into other patterns as *atsiat*. Children learn to navigate their way across the convoluted terrain of the social landscape by knowing the answers to such constant questions as 'Who is your father's *atsiaq*?', 'Why do you call your cousin grandfather?', 'What are the names of your two mothers?' (i.e. the names of biological mother and the mother of the child's *aqqa*), 'Whose name does your sister have?' In this way children learn the identities of those they are named after and acquire a knowledge of the various and often extensive relationships that link them, their parents and other members of their *ilaqutariit* to a substantial number of people in Kangersuatsiaq and beyond.

As children are named after people who had previously occupied positions as kin, to some extent roles and interaction between *atsiat* and the family of the *aqqa* are prescribed. Names are also something to be shared with other people: children, as *atsiat*, not only enter into a complexity of relationships with their genealogical families and those kin of the *aqqa*, they also continue their close social association with name-sharers (*atiik*; name-sharer). Again, personal names are avoided as terms of address and the reciprocal form of address is '*atiitsara*', 'my name-sharer'. A child called David, for example, will be the name-sharer of all those who have the same name and the relationship will already have been established between his *aqqa* and all other men called David. There are endless possibilities for entering into other relationships established through name-sharing. But here it all boils down to choice. People can choose how far they wish to develop a relationship based on the kin terms applied to a name-sharer's close kin. For some people, the relationship may be nothing more than a way of addressing one another, while for others it may be emotionally charged. There are several cases in Kangersuatsiaq where name-sharers do not in fact share a name. These people are close friends, or have a close association as hunting and fishing partners. They choose to become name-sharers and so address one another as *atiitsara* usually on the basis of a shared experience, such as surviving a difficult time on the sea ice during a winter hunting trip. Sharing a name, then, is not necessarily a prerequisite for establishing a name-sharing relationship. To call someone *atiitsara* is a way of commemorating that experience.

The naming of a child means that the social and spiritual essence of the deceased person is reincarnated in the newborn, and to some extent receiving the name of a deceased person predetermines an individual's kinship reckoning. People choose to believe or deny that personal characteristics are also reincarnated, but on the whole there is a general belief that names confer personality. For some people, children simply receive the name of a deceased relative and do not assume any of a person's qualities or behaviour. Others, however, believe that personal characteristics are also reborn and relatives often look for signs of these when a child is growing up. Elsewhere (Nuttall 1992, 1994a) I have described how people in Kangersuatsiaq, through their names, do not disappear from the social map at death. They remain part of the community and continue to extend their network of social alignments. Naming illustrates and conveys one of the most outstanding aspects of Inuit culture: the emphasis on continuity, rather than finality, of both person and community. The link between person and name is inseparable: it is not an arbitrary association that is severed at death but a bond that integrates each and every person in Kangersuatsiaq, both living and dead, present and absent, in a complex network of interpersonal relationships.

So far, I have talked about how kinship is the foundation of social relations in Kangersuatsiaq and shown how the Kangersuatsiarmiit can choose their kin, and also how they continue their relationships with deceased relatives through *atsiat*. Relationships can be created or forgotten about, and people are also related to one another through an elaborate network of name relationships. But how constraining is kinship, and what limits does it place on the individual? As we have seen, the individual can transcend the network of genealogical kin into which he or she is born. But in creating new relationships there are still prescribed ways of relating and behaving towards the people one wishes to have as one's relatives. Furthermore, as all Kangersuatsiarmiit are *atsiat* they are part of several other networks of relatives that they may or may not have chosen. Although it can happen (Nuttall 1992), it is not easy for a person to disengage themselves from relationships established by virtue of their status as an *atsiaq*. Like one's biological parents and siblings, it is rare for the parents and siblings of an *atsiaq*'s *aqqa* to be regarded as optative kin – other relatives are a different matter, though.

## Kinship and the social organisation of subsistence

Given that kinship provides the foundation for social relationships in Kangersuatsiaq, and that the Kangersuatsiarmiit depend on hunting and fishing for their livelihoods, does kinship also influence the organisation of ecological and economic relations, and structure economic activity and the relationships between those engaged in commodity production? Certainly, the way in which social organisation provides the framework for how Inuit organise environmental relations, or vice versa, has been of some interest (e.g. Wenzel 1981). However, in this final section, I am concerned less with questions of whether the environment shapes Inuit social organisation, and more with how relationships between people engaged in commodity production are cultural constructs. Kinship may underlie the social organisation of subsistence, but decisions relating to hunting and subsistence activities (i.e. who hunts with whom, who shares with whom, etc.), while largely made with reference to kinship, are not always driven by it. Kinship does not determine the relationships of those involved in commodity production, although kin relationships are expressed and reconstituted, or even brought into being, through hunting, fishing and sharing. You do not always have to hunt or fish with your kin, but an unrelated hunting partner may end up as your kin, nonetheless.

*Ilaqutariit* form quite distinct groups, reflected in mutual assistance, distribution and sharing of meat and fish, and each household can usually rely on co-operation in economic activities from others in the same *ilaqutariit*. Yet, hunting partnerships and the social organisation of fishing crews tend not to be based solely on relationships within an individual's *ilaqutariit*. It is indeed common to find fathers and sons, brothers and other consanguineal kin such as cousins, working together when seal hunting, or whaling, or fishing. But the intricate sociological configurations of the kinship network also provide a framework for how people work out the social organisation of subsistence hunting and fishing, so that two name-sharers, or people connected through *atsiaq* relations, may work together in preference to working with consanguineal kin. So, although some hunting partnerships and the social organisation of some fishing crews may remain within the *ilaqutariit*, people do not have to be genealogical kin to hunt or fish together. In short, because the success of hunters and fishers is defined largely in terms of their competence (Nuttall 1998a), no one is going to want to hunt or fish with their kin (whether father, brother or cousin) if they are incompetent at hunting and fishing.

In most cases, seal hunting, some long-line fishing and the harvesting of seabirds is carried out by a hunter working on his own. Whale hunts, on the other hand, are collective. But if a hunter does wish to go on seal-hunting expeditions, or go halibut fishing with someone, then they are not restricted to having to work with their immediate genealogical kin. This is quite important, especially if a hunter's brother is a lazy or incompetent hunter, or if his father is too old to hunt, or his cousin is away from the village working on a fishing boat. Most hunters are usually in a position to choose good, reliable hunting and fishing partners from a wide range of relatives who are not consanguineal kin. In this way, it is possible that one hunter may be part of several hunting partnerships, working with relatives of his *aqqa*, for example. It is also rare for a man to hunt or fish with someone to whom he does not apply a kinship term or have a name-sharing relationship with. By virtue of being hunting partners, and given the extremes of the environment in which they hunt, two men may have had experiences together on the sea ice, or have lifelong friendships, which they have chosen to commemorate with a kin term. They may be unrelated genealogically, but they can become each other's kin nonetheless. Kinship thus underlies the social organisation of subsistence and commodity production, but it is a very wide and flexible kinship network that individual hunters and fishers can usually draw on. They can choose the relatives they want to hunt with beyond the network of kin they are related to through biological and consanguineal ties.

While kinship is important for commodity production, gaining access to resources is not usually dependent on kinship. No one owns animals, for instance, nor do individual *ilaqutariit* or households own and control territory and place restrictions on who can and cannot hunt in a particular place. There are some notable exceptions, however. The use of summer camps, where many *ilaqutariit* spend several weeks a year, is based on the allocation of rights to use by the community to individual families. These rights recognise criteria of 'ownership' of summer campsites as being based on regular occupation, maintenance of the sites and storage of equipment. Individual hunters also have rights to set nets for salmon, seals and beluga whales at particular places near the mainland, or around small islands. These netting sites cannot be used by others. Sons usually inherit the right to use such sites from their fathers. At other points in the landscape, hunters maintain storage sites used for equipment or as meat caches. Hunting equipment may be kept close to netting sites, seal meat is stored for use as dog food when hunters are away for several days, and extra supplies of benzine are taken out to places near the main summer fishing camps. Such sites have recognised conditions of use. Hunters and their families have exclusive rights to tenure only as long as they continue to use and maintain those sites. If a hunter fails to maintain or use his netting sites, storage sites or campsites, then, after a 'reasonable length of time' has elapsed (there are long and heated discussions in Kangersuatsiaq about what constitutes a reasonable length of time), others can move in and use those sites.

While gaining access to resources and organising hunting and fishing crews is not necessarily dependent on having specific kinship relations, kin relationships are certainly very useful if a hunter wishes to use someone else's boat, or has a problem with his outboard engine and needs to borrow another for a day. If this need arises, or if it is Sunday and the store is closed and it is not possible to buy bullets or benzine, or if one needs hooks for one's fishing lines, then these things can be obtained from one's relatives – be they one's father, brother, name-sharer, the father of one's wife's *atsiaq* and so on. Kinship is thus advantageous and people are obliged to share with anyone they count as kin. The person who has loaned the hunter his boat, or has given him bullets can also rely on that action to be reciprocated – if not immediately, then at some future point. The return may come in the form of a similar loan, or a meat-gift, or whatever the person has to give that may be needed or appreciated. Such reciprocity points to the importance of sharing and distribution in Kangersuatsiaq.

As I have explored at length elsewhere (Nuttall 1992), the Kangersuatsiarmiit have extensive, detailed, intimate and complex knowledge of their local environment and the resources on which they depend. Seal hunting and other subsistence activities do not only provide the nutritional means for survival; hunting and fishing are important for cultural identity and embody notions of a specific relationship between humans and animals that continues to define and shape local culture and livelihoods. Hunting encapsulates relations that are posed in ideological, natural and cultural terms, and central to subsistence hunting in Greenland is the sharing and distribution of meat. Much of the meat from sea mammals is shared out to members of the hunter's *ilaqutariit*, to other relatives, and to people who are linked through *atsiaq* and name-sharing relationships. However, while kin are the principal recipients of catch shares, kinship alone is not the principle that governs sharing practices and patterns. It may be that sharing reinforces and helps to sustain kinship relations, but it is the relationship people have with animals and the environment, in addition to the relations they have with other persons, which goes some way to determine patterns of sharing and distribution.

For example, when hunters return to the village with several seals or with a large sea mammal such as a walrus, bearded seal or beluga whale, people will quickly make their way to the beach carrying plastic buckets or polythene bags and will watch as the animals are cut up, thus expressing a request for a share of the catch. The Kangersuatsiarmiit believe that animals give themselves up to hunters. In turn, the hunter gives the animal to other people. When hunters have meat to give and share they do so freely and willingly, although it is the hunter's wife who often decides on what shares will be given to whom. Quite often, there are particular parts of the catch that are given to particular people based on their kinship relations with the hunter, although optative kin may not always receive a share.

Other shares are handed out to people who are recognised as being unable to hunt for themselves, such as old people and even the incompetent and lazy. Gifts of meat are also taken to people's homes even if they have not requested the meat. The giving of meat parallels the giving of the seal to the hunter, in that what comes freely is given away freely (Nuttall 1992). In order to survive and to be able to provide for his family, a hunter requires skill, prowess and knowledge. Yet there are people in Kangersuatsiaq who do not have the means (whether physical, intellectual, skilful, economic or so on) to hunt for themselves and their families. Networks of kinship and sharing ensure that such inability to hunt does not result in the marginalisation and starvation of the less competent (Nuttall 1998a).

Free distribution of meat from seals and other marine mammals is an acknowledgement of the debt owed to the animal in coming to the hunter and a denial that any one person has exclusive claims to ownership of the animals that are caught. As well as reaffirming fundamental values towards animals and the environment, the sharing and distribution of meat both expresses and sustains social relationships. Through sharing and giving meat, what was an individual success in hunting by one person becomes a distinctive statement of the importance of kinship relations and community. But it is also a statement of the complex social relations between humans, animals and the environment. This is illustrated perhaps most vividly by *ningeq*, the distribution of catch shares from large sea mammals such as beluga whales, walrus and bearded seals. When a hunter has caught one of these creatures, others are entitled to a share of the meat simply by arriving on the scene as the hunter is preparing to land his catch. Other hunters make a claim to a share by touching the animal with the toe of a boot, with the tip of a harpoon or ice chisel, or by helping to haul the animal on to the ice edge or to bring it to shore for flensing. It is customary among the Kangersuatsiarmiit for the first hunter to arrive on the scene of the kill to direct the cutting up of the catch into meat packages, with the hunter who actually made the kill assisting. The shares are divided according to the order of arrival, or the first to touch the animal. Thus, while the hunters present may be kin, kinship does not play a part in influencing who gets what. It is possible, although in practice often unlikely, for an entire walrus or beluga to be shared out among people who are not kin. Whatever form the distribution may take, the hunter who made the kill always ends up with more than enough meat for his own needs.

Sharing and exchange in Kangersuatsiaq need to be understood with reference to the sense of social relatedness the Kangersuatsiarmiit feel they have with each other, with animals and with the environment, which is perceived as a 'giving environment' in the way that Bird-David (1990) has argued that most hunter-gatherers conceptualise the natural world. Bird-David argues that hunter-gatherers are distinguished from other peoples by their particular views of the environment, and of themselves, and by a particular type of economy that she calls a 'cosmic economy of sharing'. Like many other hunting societies, the Kangersuatsiarmiit do not only regard the environment as 'giving': sharing the products of the hunt is a social event that demonstrates relatedness, affection and concern. Cultural identity is founded upon and derives meaning from a culturally embedded system of shared relations. As with many other Inuit communities that depend on hunting (see, for example, Wenzel 1991), when meat is shared and exchanged in Kangersuatsiaq it is done so on the understanding that hunters have an obligation to distribute much of what they catch. This obligation to share underlies the customary ideology of subsistence in Kangersuatsiaq and contributes to the reproduction of kinship ties and other close social relationships. While this obligation to share remains strong, as I discuss below, there is an increasing commoditisation of hunting and some hunters prefer to try to sell meat from narwhal and beluga hunting (and, increasingly, from seal hunting), rather than distributing the meat freely to people other than their immediate family.

The sale of whale meat and other Greenlandic foods, such as seal and fish, is being encouraged by the Greenlandic Home Rule government, although on a larger scale than the local-level economy. Although the Home Rule government aspires to greater political, financial and economic independence from Denmark (Nuttall 1994b), Greenland remains in an economically vulnerable position because it relies to a large extent on imports. Greenland has only twice had a positive balance of external trade since 1980 (in 1989 and 1990) and this almost permanent deficit is only made possible to withstand because the Greenlandic economy is supported by block grants from Denmark.

As well as other goods, Greenland relies to a great extent on imported foodstuffs, mainly from Denmark. To ease this reliance, hunters in small settlements such as Kangersuatsiaq are being encouraged to sell part or most of what they catch to Royal Greenland, the country's meat and fish processing and marketing company, rather than share or sell the meat within the village. Royal Greenland owns the majority of Greenland's land-based production facilities, and also has sixteen large, and more than forty smaller, processing plants. It also employs almost 3,000 people worldwide, as a consequence of its global processing and operating offices. The Home Rule government considers the production, distribution and exchange of food products from hunting and fishing as vital to the development of local, small-scale sustainable community development (Greenland Home Rule Government 1995; Marquadt and Caulfield 1996).

There is already a market for Greenlandic foods within Greenland, mainly in the large west-coast towns where many people do not have the time, means or ability to hunt, yet value and rely on Greenlandic meat and fish products as the basis of their diet, or look upon Greenlandic foods as delicacies. Royal Greenland is concerned with the expansion of this market and the corresponding increase in production necessary to meet demand. This increase in the production, distribution and exchange of hunting and fishing products is also a central aspect of the Home Rule government's policy for creating sustainable conditions in the settlements, and in the process easing the subsidies that make it possible for many villages to survive. In many parts of Greenland, however, there is local opposition, or reluctance, to sell seal and whale meat to the Royal Greenland processing plants that are to be found in many villages.

For example, the Home Rule government has recently invested 12.6 million Dkr in a new processing plant in Kuummiut, a village in east Greenland. It was hoped that hunters and fishers from other settlements in the district would sell their catch to the plant. There is a lot of active hunting of sea mammals in east Greenland, but hunters have been failing to sell meat from narwhal and seal hunting, as well as the meat from successful polar-bear hunts. Hunters in east Greenland, like hunters in many other parts of the country, sell only about half of what they catch, mainly at the *kalaaliaraq*, a market found at the harbour in larger towns. They keep the rest for themselves and their families. Royal Greenland has failed to recognise the essence of sharing as a fundamental part of the hunting culture, as well as understanding the immediate gains for a hunter who sells meat privately rather than to the Royal Greenland processing plant (Nuttall 1998b). Any meat that is sold is surplus and the money earned is essential for the economic viability of the hunter's household. Although some hunters do see the incentive to earn money as overriding other concerns such as sharing, for the most part when hunting is done to satisfy a market demand beyond the local community or regional economy, then the customary ideology of subsistence and notions of sharing and giving are disrupted and threatened.

The reality for small villages such as Kangersuatsiaq is that, in modern Greenland, people rely increasingly on occupational associations in addition to, or in place of, kinship relations. As is already the case in many North Atlantic fishing societies, in occupational terms, spatially defined communities of common interest expressed through close kinship relations have been replaced by dispersed networks based on occupational associations and formalised contractual relations (Nuttall and Burnett 1998). In an increasingly technical and modernising Greenland, hunting is becoming more 'commercialised', while fishing has become more technologically complex. Fishermen, for example, are investing in bigger and increasingly sophisticated boats to fish the waters in different parts of Greenland. While, in some cases, male kinsmen such as brothers are investing in these vessels together, crew members are not always kin, but well-qualified non-kin who receive wages rather than shares in the profits of the catch.

While I have argued that kinship does not determine or control the social organisation of commodity production, the ideology of subsistence and sharing sustains, renews and brings into being kinship relations. Kinship has certain dividends and entails moral obligation, and people choose, and wish to sustain, the relationships they see as rich and meaningful to them. Now that the incentive for economic production in modern Greenland is increasingly market-driven, rather than framed by kinship, economic gain makes for social loss.

## References

Bird-David, N. (1990) 'The giving environment: Another perspective on the economic system of hunter-gatherers', *Current Anthropology* 31(2): 189–96.

Birket-Smith, K. (1924) 'Ethnography of the Egedesminde district, with aspects of the general culture of West Greenland', *Meddelelser om Grønland* 66.

Boas, F. (1964 [1888]) *The Central Eskimo*, Lincoln: University of Nebraska Press.

Burch, E.S., Jr (1975) *Eskimo Kinsmen: Changing Family Relationships in Northwest Alaska*, St Paul, MN: West Publishing.

Damas, D. (1963) *Iglulingmiut Kinship and Local Groupings: A Structural Approach*, Ottawa: National Museum of Canada.

—— (1964) 'The patterning of the Iglulingmiut kinship system', *Ethnology* 3: 377–88.

—— (1968) 'Iglulingmiut kinship terminology and behaviour, consanguines', in V.F. Valentine and F.G. Vallee (eds) *Eskimo of the Canadian Arctic*, Toronto: McClelland and Stewart.

Diamond Jenness (1922) 'The life of the Copper Eskimos', *Report of the Canadian Arctic Expedition vol. 12*.

Ellen, R. (1982) *Environment, Subsistence and System*, Cambridge, UK: Cambridge University Press.

Fainberg, L. (1967) 'On the question of the Eskimo kinship system', *Arctic Anthropology* 4: 244–56.

Fienup-Riordan, A. (1983) *The Nelson Island Eskimo: Social Structure and Ritual Distribution*, Anchorage: Alaska Pacific University Press.

Giddings, J.L. (1952) 'Observations on the "Eskimo Type" of kinship and social structure', *Anthropological Papers of the University of Alaska* 9(1): 5–10.

Graburn, N. (1964) *Taqamiut Eskimo Kinship Terminology*, Ottawa: Northern Coordination and Research Centre.

Greenland Home Rule Government (1995) *Greenland 1995–96 Statistical Yearbook*, Nuuk: Statistics Greenland.

Guemple, L. (1965) 'Saunik: Name sharing as a factor governing Eskimo kinship terms', *Ethnology* 4: 323–35.

—— (1972a) 'Eskimo band organization and the "D.P. Camp" hypothesis', *Arctic Anthropology* 9: 80–112.

—— (1972b) 'Introduction', in L. Guemple (ed.) *Alliance in Eskimo Society*, Seattle: University of Washington Press.

—— (1972c) 'Kinship and alliance in Belcher Island Eskimo society', in L. Guemple (ed.) *Alliance in Eskimo Society*, Seattle: University of Washington Press.

—— (1979) *Inuit Adoption*, Ottawa: National Museum of Man.

Haller, A. (1986) *The Spatial Organization of the Marine Mammal Hunting Culture in the Upernavik District, Greenland*, Bamberg: Universität Bamberg.

Heinrich, A. (1963) 'Personal names, social structure, and functional integration', *Anthropology and Sociology Papers of the Department of Sociology, Anthropology and Social Welfare, Montana State University, Missoula, Montana* 27: 1–12.

Holm, G.F. (1914) 'Ethnological sketch of the Angmagsalik Eskimo', *Meddelelser om Grønland* 39.

Marquadt, O. and Caulfield, R. (1996) 'Development of West Greenlandic markets for country foods since the 18th century', *Arctic* 49(2): 107–19.

Morgan, L.H. (1870) *Systems of Consanguinity and Affinity of the Human Family*, Washington, DC: Smithsonian Institution.

Murdock, G.P. (1949) *Social Structure*, New York: Macmillan.

Nuttall, M. (1992) *Arctic Homeland: Kinship, Community and Development in Northwest Greenland*, Toronto: University of Toronto Press.

—— (1994a) 'The name never dies: Greenland Inuit ideas of the person', in A. Mills and R. Slobodin (eds) *Amerindian Rebirth: Reincarnation Belief among North American Indians and Inuit*, Toronto: University of Toronto Press.

—— (1994b) 'Greenland: Emergence of an Inuit homeland', in Minority Rights Group (ed.) *Polar Peoples: Self-Determination and Development*, London: Minority Rights Publications.

—— (1998a) 'States and categories: Indigenous models of personhood in northwest Greenland', in R. Jenkins (ed.) *Questions of Competence: Culture, Classification and Intellectual Incompetence*, Cambridge, UK: Cambridge University Press.

—— (1998b) *Protecting the Arctic: Indigenous Peoples and Cultural Survival*, Chur, Switzerland: Harwood Academic Publishers.

Nuttall, M. and Burnett, K. (1998) 'The negotiation and management of crisis in the Scottish fishing industry', in D. Symes (ed.) *Northern Waters: Management Issues and Practice*, Oxford: Blackwell Science.

Rasmussen, K. (1931) 'The Netsilik Eskimos. Social life and spiritual culture', *Report of the Fifth Thule Expedition 1921–24*, 8: 1–2.

Rosaldo, M. (1980) *Knowledge and Passion*, Cambridge, UK: Cambridge University Press.

Schneider, D. (1968) *American Kinship: A Cultural Account*, Englewood Cliffs, NJ: Prentice Hall.

Schweitzer, P. (1994) 'How to become a relative: Kinship and social interaction in the Bering Strait region', paper presented at the 3rd Biannual EASA Conference, June 1994, Oslo.

Sperry, John D. (1952) 'Eskimo kinship', MA thesis, Department of Anthropology, Columbia University.

Spier, L. (1925) 'The distribution of kinship systems in North America', *University of Washington Papers in Anthropology* 1(2): 69–88.

Wenzel, G. (1981) *Clyde Inuit Adaptation and Ecology: The Organisation of Subsistence*, Ottawa: National Museum of Man.

—— (1991) *Animal Rights, Human Rights: Ideology, Ecology and Economy in the Canadian Arctic*, Toronto: Toronto University Press.

# Chapter 3

# Power and kinship in Shuar and Achuar society

*Elke Mader and Richard Gippelhauser*

The issue of power has been a long-standing topic in the anthropology of Lowland South America. The discussions about leadership in Amerindian societies have been characterised by questions about the modes of power or powerlessness attributed to 'chiefs'. Since the publication of Lowie's article on the 'Political Organisation among the American Aborigenes' (Lowie 1948) a set of problems concerning the construction and enactment of power in Amazonian societies has been addressed. One line of investigation has focused on the nature of power and leadership, and its relationships to the principles of social organisation in Lowland South America. The notion of the powerless chief and the specific social conditions that determine his existence have been approached from various points of view, with some authors emphasising the importance of balanced social relations. For example, Lévi-Strauss's study of chieftainship among the Nambikuara describes various forms of reciprocity that characterise the relationship between chief and commoners (Lévi-Strauss 1967). In continuation of this line of thought, Clastres argued that special social mechanisms create an egalitarian *société contre l'état*, which is immune to the institutionalisation of centralised political power and the emergence of a state (Clastres 1976 [1974]). An important feature in this context is the separation of religious and secular power-positions.

Questions concerning the relationship between religious and political power have lately been addressed in novel ways. Lowie's and Clastres's argument – that a concentration of secular and religious offices in one person or institution will lead to centralised and coercive power – has been contested by Santos Granero. He demonstrates that in the case of the Amuesha of Peru such a combination does not lead to stratification and the formation of state-like structures. 'Mystical means' play an important part in the construction of power and

authority in the Amazon region, but they do not constitute a base for
the development of stable socio-political formations (Santos Granero
1993). The notion of the powerless chief has also been contested.
Descola suggests dismissing this concept and studying these social
systems and their forms of leadership under the heading of 'societies
without chiefs'. He also suggests a more thorough investigation into
the different concepts of power that prevail in Lowland South America
(Descola 1988).

To understand the issue of power in Lowland South America it is
necessary to look at the complexity of interactive social and ideological
processes that constitute the construction of power. In the following
we will present a case study that investigates some of these processes
among the Shuar and Achuar, focusing on the relationship between
power and kinship. We will look at the role of kinship in the construction and enactment of power in three contexts: the acquisition of
spiritual power during the vision quest; the establishment of political
power and leadership in the dynamic network of social and political
groups; and the construction of shamanic power.[1]

The Shuar and Achuar are part of the Jivaroan language family,
which consists of five ethno-linguisitic groups and approximately
110,000 people, living on both sides of the border between Ecuador
and Peru. Their livelihood depends on tropical forest agriculture with
varying degrees of interaction with the national economy. This ethnic
and cultural ensemble shares a set of common features but also encom-
passes regional varieties. On the one hand, there are some differences
concerning various aspects of social organisation, cosmology, myth and
ritual. On the other hand, there is great variation in regard to the
impact of the interaction with the respective national societies. In the
following we will refer to the Shuar and the southern Achuar,[2] and
concentrate on their traditional social organisation, as witnessed during
various periods of fieldwork among the Achuar of the Peruvian
Changkuap River (Rio Huasaga) between 1975 and 1991. Other data
are based on our fieldwork among the Shuar of the Upano valley
between 1990 and 1994.

In Jivaroan society every individual is part of a local group that
forms the core of social relations and the matrix for social events. Such
local communities consist of approximately fifteen to fifty people who
share a house or live in several buildings that form a cluster of houses.[3]
Usually a local group consists of one or several monogamous or polygynous families. Gender relations are in some contexts balanced, e.g. in
the economic and ritual spheres, where men and women perform

complementary and interactive tasks. Other fields of action, e.g. politics and shamanism, are clearly dominated by men.

The members of a local community share the same space and its natural resources, and are united by close kin ties, binding economic and social obligations, and strong emotional bonds. The mutual claims and obligations between them are part of the ideal of 'living well' (*penker pujustín*) that forms a framework for individual action. Everybody is expected to be as efficient as possible in their respective tasks and are supposed to put their capacities or products at the disposal of other members of the local group. The specific obligations between individuals are defined by age, kinship and gender. Husbands and wives, for instance, have mutual claims on the work capacity of their spouses; mothers on that of their unmarried children. Among men there is a strong tendency towards close economic co-operation between affines, whereas cognates only work together on limited occasions. This tendency is not restricted to co-operation within the local community, a fact that is evident in the composition of work parties that include individuals from different local groups (see Gippelhauser and Mader 1990: 36–54).[4] The relationship of a young married man to his father-in-law is characterised by especially strong obligations. Brideservice implies that a son-in-law has to support his father-in-law in all activities, at least for a period of several years.[5] During that time a son-in-law has to assume many of his bride-father's activities in addition to his own tasks. Refusal to fulfil brideservice obligations would jeopardise a marriage.

However, the local communities are not bounded entities. Social ties and economic, political and emotional relations between individuals connect members of different local groups on various levels. Social life evolves around individual actions and their assessment, which incorporates and affects different sets of persons.[6] The space of individual action is public and private at the same time, for the house serves simultaneously as a scene of domestic and political events. Interaction is also influenced to a large extent by the permanent presence of conflict, which can escalate from domestic problems to feuding and blood revenge. Until approximately 1950, armed conflicts (*mesét*) often went hand-in-hand with headhunting, which meant the acquisition of head-trophies of enemies during an attack. The head-trophies would be transformed into shrunken heads (*tsantsa*) in the course of various rituals. The *tsantsa* ceremonies were part of the spiritual dimension of warfare, aimed at undermining the enemy's strength and transferring that strength to one's own group.

The framework for individual action and social relationships includes various dimensions. In the centre of interaction is the densely inter-woven local community, but, in addition, every individual is part of a network of relations that incorporates persons from several local groups. This results in a continuum of close and loose relationships, which undergo changes in the course of concrete events. These rela-tionships are shaped by structural preconditions as well as by properties and actions of individuals, and constitute an arena for the construction of power. In the following we want to look at various dimensions of this interactive system, especially the significance of kinship.

## The flexibility of kinship

A common feature among all Jivaroan peoples is the Dravidian kinship system, based on bilateral cross-cousin marriage throughout the gener-ations. It does not feature special terms for affinal relatives, which are included in that kin-class to which they would belong if continuous cross-cousin marriage had taken place. This creates a rule with mathe-matical logic, through which the exact relationship to even very distant kinfolk can be defined if only one connecting link is known. Thus, in ego's own and the first ascending and descending generations there are only two terms for each sex – one for 'cognates', one for 'affines' – and both are used in the sense of Dumont (1953).

Kinship terminology determines whom one can marry, not only who is excluded from one's marriage pool. This positive marriage rule says that spouses have to be taken from the kin-class *wajér* (cross-cousin or in-law of the other sex and the same generation). The ideal partner is a *nekás wajér*, a 'real' bilateral cross-cousin. This way one marries children of one's father's *saír* (cross-cousin, brother-in-law), one's children marry the children of one's own *saír* and so on. Thus, the affinal relationship is passed down through the generations.

In ego's own generation the terminological system shows a certain peculiarity, generally known as 'Jivaroan sibling terminology', but in fact comprising all kin of this generation. Male and female speakers use common terms for relatives of different sex and different terms for relatives of the same sex. This is due to the fact that among cross-sex relatives the essential distinguishing criterion is marriageability, which is of similar importance for both sexes, whereas towards relatives of the same sex, males and females have different sets of rights and obliga-tions.

The concept of descent is of very little importance to the Jivaroan peoples. Most individuals do not know the names of their ancestors of the third ascending generation; quite a few are not even aware of the names of their grandparents. This creates genealogies of little depth, but permits almost unlimited collateral extension. The filiation is bilateral and there are no descent groups. The only recognisable kin group is the kindred, an ego-oriented bilateral network of kin that includes affines, has shifting boundaries and does not function as a corporate group. There is no name for the kindred in the Jivaroan languages, but it is possible to identify two ideal-types of kindred, one 'minimal' and one 'maximal', which can be more or less clearly defined.[7] The maximal kindred includes all individuals to whom any kind of kin-relationship can be traced. Therefore, it consists of most people with whom one has regular contact: for instance, the majority of the inhabitants of one's own river system; quite a few people from other rivers; and sometimes even members from other ethnic groups. The minimal kindred includes only one's closest kin, cognates and affines alike, and all preferential marriage partners. Although there seems to be an endogamous tendency, most spouses are taken from outside the minimal kindred.[8]

The rule of post-nuptial residence is quite clear-cut. After his wedding a young man has to move to the local group of his father-in-law, and he stays there for several years or until the latter dies. Then he can become leader of his own local group or join any other of his choice. It can be shown statistically that a significant majority (about 70 per cent) follows this rule.[9] Thus, women stay with their original local group, in which they form its stable core, and are related to other group members primarily through consanguineal ties. The young men have to leave their parental local community to join their father-in-law, the *saír* (cross-cousin, brother-in-law) of their father. Only their sons could marry back into the group of their grandfather. Without the double bias of a masculinist point of view and a descent-orientated perspective, this system has to be called 'exchange of young men'. Thereby, leaders of local groups belonging to the affinal kin-class *saír* exchange sons, according to the residence rules. Between local groups whose leaders belong to cognatic categories (*yatsúr*), an exchange of young men is not possible. Rather than being a direct reciprocal system, the exchange of young men links a large number of dispersed local communities into a network of marriage alliances and reaches a certain balance only through the generations.

An important feature of the Jivaroan kinship system is the flexibility with which it allows a person to shape an individual set of kin-relations within certain boundaries. Through the use of the prefixes *nekás* (true) and *kaná* (separated, distant) in connection with kinship terms, one can determine the collateral extension of one's personal kindred and thus manipulate the social distance between individuals. The possibilities of this manipulation increase with growing genealogical distance, which here also refers to affines. Undeniably *nekás* (true) are all members of the minimal kindred. It is not possible to deny your father or mother, brother or sister, father-in-law or mother-in-law by referring to them as *kaná*, as distant or separated persons, or to evade the clear set of obligations connected to such relationships, e.g. economic co-operation or blood revenge. This would lead to open conflicts and a loss of prestige. With these exceptions, an individual can choose his or her own 'true' kin group out of the numerous members of the maximal kindred by declaring certain persons as *nekás* and others as *kaná*. In this context it is possible to state the closeness of social, economic or political relationships without negative consequences.

On the outskirts of the maximal kindred, where relationships are very remote, there exists a further possibility to manipulate social distance. Collateral relatives of the cognatic category of great genealogical distance can be affinalised by addressing them with affinal terms corresponding to their generational position. Thus, they are incorporated into a kin-class by which marriage alliances can be established, creating a much closer social relationship. Furthermore, close social ties that equal those of the minimal kindred can be established between persons that do not have any kind of kin-relationship or even do not belong to the same ethnic groups. This is made possible through the '*amíku*-system'.[10] *Amíkri* are persons linked by a formalised partnership that implies a certain set of economic and social ties. In regard to their mutual social obligations, *amíku*-partners are considered as part of the minimal kindred, and are as closely related as *nekás yatsúr* or *nekás saír* (real brother or cross-cousin).

Kinship is characterised, on the one hand, by binding relationships as manifest in the minimal kindred, and, on the other hand, by negotiable relationships, which allow a personal choice of close or distant relatedness with certain individuals within the maximal kindred. Kinship sets up a framework within which an individual can make personal choices. Social relations that exceed the local communities and the minimal kindred are prestructured, but not determined, by kinship. The absence of descent groups, the Dravidian system with its wide collateral extension, and the possibility to manipulate the closeness of kin ties to a certain extent all lead to a highly flexible system.

This flexibility of kinship forms a framework for the construction of power that is based on a set of ideas about the person, his or her capacities, and specific forms of spiritual power that have to be acquired during a vision quest.

## Visions and powerful persons

[In my vision][11] I walked around and came to a big tree. The tree turned into a man with a lance in his hand, he had long hair, he was my grandfather Pedro Tsenkush. He talked to me: 'My grandson, what are you doing here?' Everything had changed, I was on a path in the middle of the forest.

I asked: 'Are you my grandfather?' He carried a lance that was full of blood.

Suddenly he gave me the lance and said: 'Take it, I give it to you, with this [lance] nothing can destroy you, you will be strong in warfare, you will feel neither compassion nor fear, you will do the right things.' He put the lance into my hand and said: 'Take it, it is yours!' I was frightened, everything was full of blood, but he urged me forward: 'Come on, let us go, let us go!' He took me to a place where a jaguar was devouring people. There he touched me with his powerful breath,[12] then he disappeared.

Now I was alone with the jaguar. The jaguar devoured the people, then he turned around and came towards me. I had the lance in my hand and just when I wanted to attack the jaguar he turned into a man and talked to me. He said: 'I am jaguar, I am a jaguar-man, my name is jaguar, but I am a man. I am everywhere, I wander across the entire land. You will have the power to do so as well, but your lance will not touch me.' Then he disappeared and I was alone in a strong storm with heavy rain.

(Interview with Alejandro Yurank Tsakimp, Sucúa 1991)

The human being (*shuar*) is conceived of as a fluctuating conglomerate of physical and spiritual components with flowing transitions to other entities of the world.[13] Thus, humans, plants and animals share a common spiritual element, *wakán*, which enables them to communicate with each other. This kind of 'soul', associated with vitality, physical appearance, reflexivity and emotions, is given to everybody by birth equally. It represents the stable core of the person in the sense that it does not undergo changes during the lifetime of an individual. But the Shuar notion of the person does not refer to a stable and bounded entity: rather, it is associated with a process of transformations. Various spiritual elements are acquired and incorporated into an individual or get lost again in the course of certain events. Though these components of the person are accessible to everybody, they are not equally distributed among individuals and groups. Elders generally control a higher quantity and greater variety of these spiritual elements than younger people. The acquisition of specific elements is also regarded as a precondition for certain activities, and thus reflects gender roles and the social division of tasks. The social person in the sense of Fortes (1973: 283–8) is thus created and constantly recreated during the lifetime of an individual.

The concept of the person in this society is closely related to the notion of power. Power (*kakárma*) is regarded as an attribute of the person, and is connected with certain spiritual components of the human being. The most important component is *arútam*, which is acquired by men and women during various vision quests.[14] Visions are induced by fasting and psychoactive substances (*Datura arborea*, *Banisteriopsis caapi* or tobacco), and ideally include two distinct sequences of visionary encounters. During the first part of the vision, *arútam* usually appears in a metaphoric shape, often as an animal. The second part is related to the actual acquisition of *arútam* through a transfer of power from a deceased person to the vision-seeker. A person who has thus acquired *arútam* is called *wáimiaku* – 'one who has seen'. The incorporation of *arútam* by that person becomes manifest as individual qualities and abilities that are a precondition for success in various fields of action. Furthermore, visionary images are regarded as an omen: a person's fate is, to a large extent, determined by the vision's content.

Let us now take a closer look at the first part of the vision, especially at its powerful imagery. The images that can appear during this stage consist of approximately forty different figures and represent a complex set of symbols that are related to certain capabilities, qualities or events. The imagery of the vision refers to various spheres of life. *Arútam*-power, which is represented by such figures, can bring about economic, social or political success, strength in warfare and in other conflicts, as well as a long and healthy life. Any specific image is interpreted according to its context and often covers a wide range of significations. Carlos Utitiaj, a Shuar teacher from Sucúa, told us about various possibilities in regard to the signification of a visionary encounter with a comet (*payár*):

A good warrior, who saw a comet [in his vision], can make use of its velocity. He can surprise his enemies with a swift attack. This is very important in warfare, a good warrior has to be strong and fast.

The comet can also signify that a warrior will never be killed in a fight. Here again a person makes use of the comet's velocity. Sometimes a warrior has to escape his enemies. In that case he is like a comet who crosses the sky within seconds and disappears. Nobody can catch up with him, if he is pursued by his enemies they cannot follow him. Such is a warrior who has encountered this *arútam*, who has received the power of the comet. ...

Another aspect [of the comet's power] is related to work; persons who have encountered a comet will be more brilliant than all other members of their family because they never get tired of working. They work with pleasure, they always participate [at somebody's invitation to work]. Such persons outdo others because they work with pleasure.

The power of the comet can also take effect in regard to social relations. A comet is bigger than other stars, he sparkles more, he distinguishes himself from others. In the same way people who have seen a comet [in their vision] are superior to others. They are easy-going, cheerful, they like to joke. Such qualities make them likeable, nobody gets angry at them, even if they commit some error. Their cheerfulness is transmitted to everybody and everybody forgets their faults. That is how a comet-vision affects social life.

If today somebody sees a comet in a vision, we do not talk of war anymore. We say: This person is fast and efficient in his activities. In his business, on his farm he is swift as a comet. Or somebody has a fast mind, he or she grasps everything quickly and thinks fast. Today we have stopped to be warriors in the old way, but in the intellectual sphere a warrior's qualities are just as important. Today you have to think fast, at least you have to think well before you act.

Who would not like to be such a comet? I would love to be a comet in the spiritual and intellectual world!

(Interview with Carlos Utitiaj, Sucúa, 1994)

The concept of *arútam* is thus related to certain personal qualities. They are expressed in various spheres of action and distinguish one individual from another. In their interpretation of visions, the Shuar emphasise certain features of personality and behaviour that they regard as especially desirable. Among these features one can distinguish three clusters of qualities that are closely related to each other and are of major importance for social relations. The first cluster refers to superiority and strength; the second to unassailability and invulnerability (in the concrete, as well as the figurative, meaning of the term); and the third to charismatic attraction and popularity. These personal qualities are essential for the construction of status and therefore represent an important component of social interaction.

Let us now look at the second part of the vision. Here the person on a vision quest encounters an anthropomorphic figure. This appearance is also referred to as *arútam* and the figure is regarded as the bearer or owner of special capabilities. In the course of this visionary sequence, a transfer of power from one person to another – strictly speaking, from a dead to a living person – takes place.

> After the death of a *wáimiaku* [a person who disposes of *arútam*] something like this can happen. During the night my mother's aunt died, a bad storm came up. A gale was blowing, there was heavy rain, it was like a hurricane, the rivers were in flood.[15]
>
> Let us assume somebody would have been so lucky to have spent this very night in the forest. If he would have taken just a little bit of tobacco, the deceased person would have appeared to him in a dream [vision] for sure. She would have talked to him and shown him everything she had achieved in her life [and thus transferred her power to him].
>
> (Interview with Carlos Utitiaj, Sucúa, 1994)

The relationship between the anthropomorphic figure of *arútam* and the vision-seeker is determined to a certain degree by kinship, which is expressed in various parts of the visionary experience. In this context one has to take a closer look at the relationship between the different facets of *arútam*, especially in regard to its human and non-human components. Let us start with an *ánent*, a ritual chant sung by men during a vision quest:

> My fathers
> You, who have made yourself jaguar
> turn yourself into words
> become only words
> Come to me

From face to face
step in front of me

My grandfathers
What are you?
What have you become?
Into what did you transform yourself?
If you are anaconda
If you are jaguar
If you are comet
Turn yourself into words
Step in front of me
from face to face

My old men
What have you become?
Are you perhaps anaconda?
Become words
Step in front of me
Appear to me.[16]

In this ritual song that helps to persuade *arútam* to appear in a vision, the possible *arútam*-apparitions are addressed directly several times. These spiritual beings are called fathers (*aparu*), grandfathers (*apáchuru*) and Great Old Men (*úunt*). On the one hand, the terms of address postulate kin-relations between the *arútam*-figures and the vision-seeker, while on the other hand they emphasise age and status. Calling the apparitions grandfathers or Great Old Men reflects a respectful attitude towards elder people with power and knowledge. The various forms of address are used as synonyms in the course of the chant and reflect the wide range of possible degrees of relatedness between the *arútam*-apparitions and the vision-seeker.

Generally, *arútam*-apparitions are addressed as elder relatives, most frequently as grandfather (*apáchur*) or grandmother (*nukúchur*), and in some cases also as father (*apar*) or mother (*nukur*). The terms *apáchur* and *nukúchur* refer to all bilateral relatives (cognates as well as affines) of the grandparent generation (as terms of reference). Therefore, paternal and maternal grandparents along with their siblings, parallel cousins, cross-cousins and all other relatives of the same sex and generation are referred to by the same terms. According to the Dravidian system, there is no distinction between cognates and affines in this generation. Thus, the kinship terms most frequently applied to *arútam*-apparitions refer to a large, fairly unspecific group of relatives of the grandparents' generation and includes cognates as well as affines.[17] The form of address corresponds to the variety of anthropomorphic apparitions in individual visions.[18] The apparitions can take the form of deceased relatives of the grandparent or parent generation, of individuals who may or may not be known to the vision-seeker. The *arútam*-figures are usually of the same sex as the vision-seeker, but exceptions are possible.

Let us return for a moment to the above-mentioned ritual song. The chant demonstrates the concept of *arútam* as a multidimensional entity that is comprised of various components. *Arútam* is addressed as a person and simultaneously refers to an impersonal power with specific qualities expressed by its metaphoric shape, e.g. as a jaguar or an anaconda. In the song these apparitions are referred to as beings into which the grandfathers have transformed themselves. The singer also pleads with the 'grandfathers' to appear to him, to turn themselves into words[19] and, thus, to transfer their power unto him or her. The words of the *arútam* apparitions are regarded as a form of condensed power that can be transferred from one being to another.

The apparitions during an *arútam*-vision thus contain several components that affect the vision-seeker and the process of power-transmission in different ways. Kin-relations between the person on a vision quest and the human dimension of *arútam* (the figure of the power-bearer) are meant to motivate the '*arútam*-grandfathers' to feel compassion for the vision-seeker and, thus, to transfer their abilities to their younger relative. The non-human aspects of the apparitions determine the specific orientation of that power. The narratives of visions show that some individuals emphasise a specific kin-relationship to the anthropomorphic apparition, while others are not very explicit about it.[20] Furthermore, the different visions a person experiences during his or her lifetime usually include encounters with a variety of *arútam*-persons. Sometimes these are relatives; at other times they are strangers or supernatural beings, such as mythological figures.

Images and persons that provide power in the course of a vision are also subject to culture change. They can be regarded as icons of power that reflect the relations of power in the social world of the Shuar and Achuar at a given time. The visionary apparitions in 'modern times' often exceed the traditional contexts of power and knowledge. Social and economic change demands new abilities and new forms of know-ledge to cope with life: qualities that cannot be transferred to the vision-seeker from a Shuar grandfather. Instead, they derive from representatives of other cultures, who are regarded as masters of the correspondent activities. The increasing replacement of Shuar grandfathers or grandmothers as power-givers by non-Shuar priests, teachers, doctors and *colonos* (mestizo settlers and farmers) reflects changes regarding the assessment of personal qualities and the distribution of power in the social environment of the Shuar people:

> A friend of mine took *maikiúa* (datura) when he was a child; he was very young and his parents accompanied him [when he went on the vision quest]. When he was under the influence of *maikiúa*, he stood up and picked up two wooden sticks – his parents observed it. He walked around, clapped the sticks to a rhythm and said: 'I am Chinese, I am Chinese and a great karate-fighter!' He jumped around and shouted like a Chinese karate-fighter. He shouted: 'I jump, I fly, I am a great master!'
>
> After his vision had passed, my friend told his parents that he had received the words [power] to become a master of karate from a Chinese. Later in his life, this man won the national competitions in karate in Ecuador and he was placed second in the South American competitions. He participated in a lot of international fights and he also took part in a movie. He is Shuar, a brother of my wife, but today he lives in the United States. He is a master and runs a karate-school in California.
>
> (Interview with Carlos Utitiaj, Sucúa, 1994)

The vision quest aims at an integration of different forms of power and capacities into one person. The relationship between vision-seekers and the visionary power-givers forms part of the process of the acquisition of *arútam*, so kinship plays an important role in structuring access to spiritual power. The *arútam*-apparitions neither appear automatically in a vision, nor is every vision quest successful. Various forms of ritual action, as well as the correct interaction with the various appearances during the vision, are necessary to make the *arútam*-figures appear and concede their power to the person on the quest.[21] Generosity in this context can be expected from close kin rather than from strangers. Nevertheless, one tries to gain access to every possible power source, whether from within the set of relatives of the vision-seeker or from other people.

These notions of person and power go hand-in-hand with the high value the Shuar and Achuar place on the individual and his or her specific qualities. Such properties determine a person's reputation and social status, which depends on age as well as on personal achievements. Status is not inherited or determined by belonging to some clearly defined group, but has to be achieved by individual action and its social assessment. Especially high value is thereby put on strength, as expressed in 'powerful speech' (*kakáram chicham*), and on superiority in various fields of action. Everybody aims at being respected or being famous (*náatin*) in his or her social network for some special achievements – for raising large quantities of pigs and poultry, brewing excellent beer, having extensive knowledge of magical songs or being a superior warrior or shaman. Another highly appreciated quality is charismatic power, which is conceived of as the power of a person to attract others, be it to lure game into the reach of a hunter, to bring spiritual entities into the sphere of influence of a shaman or to induce followers into a political alliance. The notions of person and power, as well as the construction of status, emphasise the importance of the individual and his or her abilities and reputation. This is not only expressed in the concept of the person: it also affects the formation of kin-groups and socio-political groups.

## Kin, conflict and the construction of power

The construction of power and leadership is closely related to the formation of socio-political groups. In order to take a closer look at theses processes let us return to the fields of interaction between local communities. The local groups are interconnected by different forms of alliances, which can be defined in the widest sense of the term as 'alliances that imply an obligation for mutual support' (Oppitz 1988: 9–10). In Shuar and Achuar society, such obligations are either stable and attached to close kin ties or they are negotiable and have to be acquired and maintained repeatedly. The alliances are also orientated towards specific persons with their individual properties and capabilities. A person becomes an attractive alliance-partner if he or she displays the required qualifications: the most desirable allies in an armed conflict are outstanding warriors; on occasions of organising a ceremony, they are women and men who are renowned masters of chants; in cases of illness, an alliance with a powerful shaman is demanded.

What are these different forms of alliances and in what contexts do they take effect? Let us look first at the marriage alliance, which connects different local communities and establishes close social ties, especially between male affines. In this society, a spouse can be chosen from among a large number of persons belonging to the marriageable kin-class. Cross-cousins are the preferred marriage partners, but decisions are also influenced by non-kinship criteria. Besides an emotional attachment between the future husband and wife, the reputation of the individuals involved, their abilities in their respective areas of action and the social status of the bride's father are of main importance in the decision-making process. The potential father-in-law and son-in-law are connected through mutual interests: the prestige of the former depends to a great extent on the abilities of his sons-in-law, who are his closest followers, while the son-in-law can raise his social status when that of his father-in-law rises. Dominated by elder men, the politics of marriage aims at the individual accumulation of binding social and economic obligations with persons of high capabilities. The group of people connected through marriage alliances – usually identical to the local community – can also be the core for the temporary formation of larger socio-political groups.

Another type of alliance represents the so-called *amíku*-system. Certain individuals create close social bonds over large geographical distances through a formalised exchange of trade goods or of shamanic knowledge and power. These relationships last a lifetime and establish binding mutual social obligations that equal those of closest kin (see Harner 1972: 125–32). Larger socio-political alliances, connecting several local groups and specific individuals over a greater distance, are loose and fluctuating followerships centred around Great Old Men (*uúnt*). Such followerships form a network of alliances that are realised only in the context of certain events, such as economic and ritual co-operation or armed conflicts.

An individual household has a high degree of autonomy in economic and political matters. Such a constellation of individuals can provide for the subsistence of their members and can hardly be coerced into an action of which it does not approve. Nevertheless, a lot of tasks can be managed more easily and efficiently if a larger group of people co-operates. This applies especially to male activities (e.g. clearing gardens, construction of houses) that are only required periodically and can be optimised by short-term co-operation.[22] On such occasions the man who is in charge of a certain task invites people to support him in this effort. An 'invitation to work' (*takát iniámpramu*) is directed at men of all local communities in the neighbourhood.[23] They are at liberty to either accept the invitation, or to excuse themselves because of urgent work in their own household or because of bad dreams.[24] The organisation of ceremonies (*namper*) follows the same pattern. A father, for instance, organises an initiation ceremony (*nua tsankram*) for his daughter, and invites other people to participate. Such an invitation always implies a request to contribute to the feast with food and drink, as well as with ritual knowledge. Ritual specialists, for instance men and women who are regarded as masters of songs (*anéntin*), are invited specifically to fulfil certain tasks. The same organising principle applies to 'invitations to kill' (*ipiámamu*) during armed conflicts. If a person wants to attack somebody in the course of a blood revenge or to defend his local community against enemies, he has to call on people who will support him in his venture.

The different forms of alliances and the concrete events during which they become manifest are a central feature of the construction and demonstration of power in this society. These events involve groups of people that have to be invited ('invitation' – *ipíamu* or *untsúmma*) by the interested individual. The composition of such groups varies according to the social relations and the prestige of the participants. The core is made up of persons who are connected to the interested party by binding social ties – his closest kin and his *amíku*, who are obliged to follow his call. Whereas any adult man can motivate a few close relatives to co-operate with him on certain occasions, the number of participants rises with the increasing prestige of the organiser. The more prestige and power a person has, the more people are interested in establishing close social relations with him. Even remote collateral relatives want to become his *nekás*, his true or close kin, and demonstrate their closeness by participating in his projects.

Invitations to build a house or to celebrate a ritual are thus complex social events that exceed their specific purpose. An invitation to work represents a temporary accumulation of work capacity and skills, and also serves to demonstrate and stage social relations. The same principle applies to ceremonies, which always include ritual, social and political elements. All of these events create a public that assesses individual action. On such occasions a person can demonstrate his or her abilities in certain fields of action and can prove to be a reliable ally. Furthermore, co-operation in the economic and ritual sphere expresses the distribution of power in a social network at a certain time. It shows the status and influence of specific individuals, confirms established alliances and creates new ones.

The political dimension of such alliances is most evident in the context of feuding and warfare (*mesét*).[25] Any kind of armed conflict is called *mesét*, no matter if the opponents belong to the same ethnic group or to different ones. The only distinction that is made depends on the number of people involved. If there are more than two local communities participating in a conflict, it is called *uún mesét* (great war). This term is applied to any kind of war, from the skirmishes between two alliances of moderate size to the Second World War.

Women and shamans are always mentioned in the same breath as the main causes of conflicts that are usually connected with accusations of adultery or witchcraft. Such conflicts cover a wide range of discourse and action: from misunderstandings between husband and wife; to strained relations between local groups (due to accusations of sorcery); and to armed conflicts among groups of allies. This can lead to long-lasting cycles of blood revenge which create a climate of permanent tension and potential armed conflict between hostile individuals or groups. Such a situation is expressed in the following narrative by an Achuar from the Changkuap River:

> I was still a child when it happened. My brother-in-law, Alejo, went down to the river, he wanted to take a bath. ... So he went to the river and was approaching the enemies [who lay in an ambush]. He had just taken off his clothes and was on his way into the water when the shots hit him. Dead, he fell into the water. His brother ran back to the house screaming. We were in the house, my mother was making beer, my grandmother and the other women also, they were laughing and joking. He rushed in and yelled: 'The enemies have shot Alejo!' Everybody then began to scream and to run back and forth in confusion. I first did not know what had happened. Everybody then ran outside and all of a sudden we heard some shots, but it was not the enemies, one of our men had shot [at the enemies].
>
> My mother and my grandmother ran towards the river. I wanted to follow them, but they sent me back to the house and shouted to me: 'Son, you must stay here, it is too dangerous, they will kill you, you are a boy. Therefore stay in the house, we will go [to the river] and bring him back.'
>
> In those days I was a child and did not know what death is, and how one dies, I had never seen a corpse before. Then they came back and carried the body of my brother-in-law. I looked at him for a long time, I saw the wounds in his body. That is how the war began. ... In those days, when they killed my brother-in-law, I was still too young, but I would have liked to participate [in the feuding], I wanted to fight. Today we meet our enemies quite often, and I think sometimes: This matter, this war, has been over

for a long time and those who killed my brother-in-law then [about twenty years ago] have also died, they are dead. If one considers that, one can almost forget the *mesét* (feud). Lately these people who were our enemies began to participate in our *comunidad* (village), and I think sometimes: Isn't it strange, why do these people come? They are our enemies after all. If I was not responsible for this village, I would be the first to attack them. That's how I feel until today, and I don't want to see my enemies here. But what can one do today? This community was formed and why should one think too much about such things.

But [about two years ago] somebody sent people to kill my father,[26] and I always say to my father: 'If they kill you, I will take revenge for you in any case.' Am I not a grown man? I have got enough experience as a warrior, for when I was young they were leading many wars and I took part in them with great enjoyment.

(Interview with Petsain Kukush, Puerto Rubina, 1991)

Because of such incidents, the members of various communities are divided into fluctuating groups of friends and foes, and into uneasy alliances. This phenomenon is not limited to the more traditional Jivaroan groups: it can also be observed among the Shuar who have experienced major social and political changes during the past decades. Conflicts remain an important feature of the construction of power and the formation of social groups, even if they are seldom decided by weapons these days (see Rubenstein 1995: 38–63).

Let us take a closer look at feuding. The composition of war alliances follows the same principles as described above in the context of economic co-operation. It is based on kin relations and influenced by the social status of the man who invites others to support him in organising and preparing the raid. Furthermore, friendships and hostilities that date back to old conflicts once again gain importance. Before each action the alliances are negotiated anew, because the strategy in each case depends on the composition of the war party and the strength of the followerships participating. Success in an armed conflict is only possible when the man leading the venture can convince a sufficiently large group of people to join his side.

An attack is usually the result of a death that has not been revenged. A close relative of the deceased, usually a male member of the minimal kindred, takes the initiative and fulfils his obligation for blood revenge. If such a person is not a very powerful man, meaning if he does not have a large enough followership, he cannot take revenge on his own.

When somebody wants to start a war, he cannot do it on his own, he has to go to a Great Old Man, to somebody like myself. This man spreads the word, he announces the war. This old man is not obliged to take part in the attack, he can stay in his house as well. Only his people have to set out [for the raid].

(Interview with Kukush, Puerto Rubina, 1991)

The man interested in organising a raid applies to the Great Old Man closest to him in his social network. The latter then decides if he will make the respective case his own (see Warren 1988). Even if somebody makes the decision to act on his own, he has to receive the consent of the *uúnt* of his alliance group. Thus, the Great Old Men control the politics of conflict in their sphere of influence. While young men who want to gain prestige through the participation in an armed venture are usually in favour of a raid, the *uúnt* are often interested in avoiding the escalation of a conflict that could destabilise the current distribution of power. Whether a Great Old Man decides on war depends largely on his own relationships with the people involved. Old hostilities are often responsible for his decision to organise an attack. In such a case, he becomes the *meséta uúntri* ('lord of the war').[27] As such he calls the *ayámrin* (persons who help to carry out a revenge) and pronounces an 'invitation to kill'. While he can depend with certainty on a number of warriors from his own household or his minimal kindred, other men of his followership are not necessarily obliged to take part in his war.

When a man invites to kill (*ipiámamu*) he says: 'Come to my aid, my enemies want to extinguish me, they are fighting against me.' So he talks and he sends messages to his *amikri* [friends, trade-partners], for example, from here to Kukush or to Purabacocha. He sends messages to attract all men, who are very powerful and have good luck, who are extraordinarily brave. Those who are strong and brave come. One tries to get up to twenty persons [for a raid].

When the message has spread, they all assemble to attack the enemies together. The *amikri* and *saír* (cross-cousin, brother-in-law) come to help. They say: 'I also will carry your beer,' which means that I will support you, 'I also am a man!' They stand with their guns raised high and speak with power: 'Take me with you to this battle, show me where the warriors of the enemy live, take me with you, I will help you. I also am a man, I also will kill, I also had a good vision, I want to kill because I dreamt it [in the vision].'

So they talk. Then the host answers: 'Well, well, well, I will take you with me.'

(Interview with Súkut, Changkuap River, 1991)

The men who follow the call gather in the house of the warlord. The participants affirm their mutual alliance in the form of ritualised speeches, and they discuss organisation, strategy and the distribution of tasks.[28] The tactics of an attack are usually based on an interaction of *anánkartin* (spies or persons who outwit the enemy) and *maátin* (killers). Killers are often called from distant communities; they are in most cases *amíku* or relatives that live far away but are connected to the interested party by close kin ties. The persons who prepare a raid (*anánkartin*) are usually asked to pretend peaceful interactions with the enemy to make an attack easier. Persons who have close relations with the hostile group are ideal for this task:

> In order to catch your enemies easily, you first send a person who knows them very well. Well, you send somebody who goes there to pay a visit, but he really is a spy (*anánkartin*). You send him to catch them easily. After his first visit he has to come back without any problems. On his second visit you kill your enemies. Then the enemies also rise and continue the war, and that way the war spreads.
>
> (Interview with Kukush, Puerto Rubina, 1991)

An attack is thus made easy by persons whose position in the conflict is misjudged by the enemy.[29] Such persons can be members of the minimal kindred or of the local group of the adversary. Their role can be understood better if we take a look at the shifting boundaries of kin groups. Individual personal kindreds (minimal as well as maximal) overlap, with no segmentation, as in the case of unilineal kin groups. Every individual is thus a member of several overlapping kindreds at the same time. This can lead to uncertain loyalties in certain cases of conflict, as an individual can be equally related to both parties (Gippelhauser 1985: 233–5). The decision of such individuals to join one side can be decisive for the success of a raid. In this context, the manipulation of relationships by means of the notions of *nekás* (true) and *kaná* (separated, distant) is of vital importance.

Alliances in the context of warfare are based on kin ties and established social relations. Nevertheless, their composition in a given case of conflict is not quite predictable. The affiliation of individuals with one party or another is often negotiable, and the decision to finally join one side can be made for different reasons. On the one hand, such decisions are influenced by earlier hostilities between the persons involved in a conflict; on the other, they depend on the power and charismatic attraction of the respective warlords (*meséta uúntri*).

The followership of a Great Old Man (*uúnt*) is neither very stable nor a bounded group. Even in the core of the followership, personal changes can take place. After several years of brideservice, a man might leave a father-in-law who has little influence by marrying a second wife and thus joining a more powerful bride-giver. Such a move might lead to some gossip, but might, as well, represent a decisive step in the social career of a man. The ability to manipulate alliances without losing prestige is an important talent that requires great social and political skills. An alliance group lives and dies with the person in its centre – the respective Great Old Man (*uúnt*) – and his power and charismatic attraction. Furthermore, a man who builds up a followership has no guarantee that he can uphold it over a long period of time. Even if he succeeds in keeping a large alliance group together for most of his lifetime, his influence will decrease when he becomes old and infirm, and his followership will form new alliances around other powerful men. In this way, a Great Old Man (*uúnt*) slowly turns into a 'Little Old Man' (*uúntach*), who is respected and enjoys the fame of an old warrior, but who is no longer the focus of social and political events.

Socio-political groups and the powerful persons who lead them are created in the course of concrete conflicts. These political constellations usually do not last beyond the immediate conflict, as they tend to dissolve due to internal tensions and have to be renegotiated and reconstructed for any new instance of conflict. In some cases, a fusion of normally hostile alliances can take place. Several groups may join together to fight against a common enemy, and postpone their smaller internal conflicts for the time being (see Uriarte 1989: 160).[30]

Such processes usually imply a transformation of the composition of alliance groups. Whereas some people will stay with their old alliance partners, others may join another faction. Thus, influential men are constantly trying to attract experienced warriors to their own followership and to negotiate alliances with other men of influence. This tug-of-war game is based on the non-existence of permanently bounded groups with an obligatory membership. Overlapping boundaries between different personal kindreds enable an individual to deliberately choose a faction that best suits his interests. The ability to change sides often makes it unclear to which alliance group one belongs. Such loose attachments lead to permanent insecurity about loyalties and form the basis of political manoeuvrings and power games.

## Shamanic power

Shamans (*uwishín*) are a special kind of powerful person. They have spiritual power entities and magical objects at their disposal that allow them to exercise influence upon other persons' bodies, thoughts and emotions. Thereby, they can cause and heal disease and misfortune.[31] Shamans are mostly men, but the few women shamans are said to have special powers.[32] The Jivaroans distinguish between two types of shamanic activity according to their intentions: healing (*tsuákratin*) and bewitching (*wawékratin*). Whether a shaman is regarded as a healer or sorcerer depends mainly on his social relations with the people involved in his actions. The members of his local community and his alliance group usually respect him as a healer and as an expert on spiritual knowledge, while people from other communities may see the same person as a sorcerer who causes disease, misfortune and death.

All shamanic activities are based on control over a large quantity of spiritual power elements. These are mainly conceptualised as magical darts (*tsentsak*) – little arrows of light in various shapes and colours – or as spirit helpers (*pasuk*) in the form of animals and mythical figures. In everyday life, the magical darts rest in the body of the shaman, embedded in a sticky substance called *chunta*.

If a shaman wants to apply his powers for healing or bewitching he has to activate them. To do so, he will drink *natem* (*Banisteriopsis caapi*), a psychoactive substance. This enables him to call his spirit helpers, who rest in the forest and rivers around his house. While his spirit helpers (e.g. a jaguar, an anaconda or Tsunki, the mythical lord of shamanic power) stand guard around him, he can start to move his power darts. They move from his stomach to his mouth and can be moved further by breath or with the aid of spirit helpers. During a healing ceremony, the darts float around him, covering him with a bright, multicoloured layer of light. This coat of light and his spirit helpers protect him from the attacks of enemy shamans. They also make him attractive to the hostile darts located in the body of the patient. The darts of his enemy, who inflicted the illness, are supposed to fall in love with him so that he can suck them out easily and heal the patient. If this does not work, they must be removed by force.

A healing ceremony represents a power fight between enemy shamans over the control of their darts and spirit helpers. To attract and manipulate hostile darts and spirit helpers, the healer must have the same type of powerful entities at his disposal. The greatest danger for the healer is the powers of his adversary, especially if the healer is not equipped with the same type of power and, thus, cannot control the powers of the adversary.

In the course of a diagnosis and healing, the shaman who removes the disease-producing elements can determine their origin and the identity of the sorcerer:

> If a woman is very sick her husband or her brother might bring her to see me, so that I can cure her. It can happen that he says: 'Cure her, and when she is cured, send the darts against him [the sorcerer].' They [the patients] ask me for that, they want me to bewitch the other shaman with the very same powers that caused their illness. They want him to suffer the same misfortune. They say: 'Let us see how he will feel, when he has to suffer the same illness.' If I have the respective knowledge, I can do it, I can punish the sorcerer. That is why a sorcerer always has to be cautious. He has to drink *natem* [*Banisteriopsis caapi*] and he has to call his darts and spirit helpers to protect him.
>
> (Interview with a shaman, Sucúa, 1991)

Should the disease be a fatal one and attributed to a particular shaman, the instance becomes a case of blood revenge. This can be carried out, on the material level, by killing the respective shaman or, on the spiritual level, by commissioning a friendly shaman to send the fatal darts back towards the sorcerer and thereby execute vengeance. The context of shamanic activities is therefore characterised by conflict. Besides the spiritual conflicts among adversaries, social conflicts related to witchcraft accusations are a major feature in every shaman's life. Even if he is famous for his power and knowledge, and – for that reason – enjoys a very high social status, the assessment of his activities is always ambivalent. Some people regard him as an important ally who defends them against disease and misfortune, while others regard him as an aggressive enemy who causes illness and death.

Because of their abilities to accuse others of witchcraft, shamans play a decisive role in the construction and manipulation of conflicts (see also Descola and Lory 1982). This gives them a special political power, but it also implies a dangerous life. Time and again shamans are at the centre of violent altercations in which they frequently become the victim. Powerful shamans are often Great Old Men (*uúnt*) with their own group of followers. Furthermore, they have special alliances with other influential leaders and warriors, in order to defend themselves efficiently when problems arise.

Let us now look at the role of kinship in the construction of shamanic power. On the one hand, kinship exercises an influence on the acquisition of power. On the other, it influences the political power play of practising shamans. The strength and effectiveness of a shaman is based on the accumulation of power elements (the darts and spirit helpers), a process closely related to his training. To become a shaman one first has to obtain a vision that indicates a calling and then become an apprentice to a master shaman. After a period of training, the novice is given a certain set of darts, spirit helpers and other spiritual entities or magical objects that form the foundation of his power. During this process, master and novice enter into a spiritual and social alliance, which implies that both partners have to defend each other against hostile shamans and other adversaries (see Harner 1972).

This primary transmission of shamanic power usually takes place within the minimal kindred, in most cases from father to son. Shamans want their power 'to stay in the family', and sometimes endow a little boy or even a newborn baby with a magical dart that protects him and marks him as a potential shaman. Growing up with a shaman as a father also gives a child a perfect opportunity to observe and learn. The actual training usually starts after the apprentice has completed puberty, lasts for several years and often leads to joint shamanic practice. The training and transmission of power establishes an extraordinarily strong bond between father and son, which also becomes manifest through co-residence in the same household during adulthood.

But the acquisition of power and knowledge does not represent a single event in a shaman's life. It is rather the first step in a continuous quest for power that lasts a lifetime. During his professional career a shaman enters into various *amiku* relationships with practitioners from other local communities, other ethnic groups and other shamanic traditions. By training with and acquiring power from five to fifteen different masters,[33] he establishes a network of alliances that reach beyond kin relations and ethnic boundaries. This combination of close ties within the minimal kindred (in this case among male cognates) and additional alliances, with a variety of powerful persons of different groups, reproduces the same principles of interaction of closeness and distance as described in other contexts. In regard to a shaman's position as an important political actor, kinship pre-structures his possibilities of action in the same way as outlined above for other actors in the political process. These are marked by close social ties, within the minimal kindred and the local group, which also form the basis for political alliances through which a shaman can become a member of the followership of a Great Old Man or stand at the centre of his own. Shamans are tied into social networks with two different sets of strings that follow a similar pattern. They control a network of spiritual alliances in addition to their normal participation in social groups as members of a local community, a kindred, a marriage alliance and a larger political alliance.

## Conclusions

The construction of power in this society consists of various ideological, religious, social and political processes. Secular and religious power cannot be divided into antagonistic or dichotomous categories. On the one hand, everybody's personal power is based on spiritual elements; on the other, shamanic power is, to a large extent, interwoven with political power. Power among the Jivaroans thus constitutes an interactive continuum of socio-political and spiritual elements that can lead to different positions of leadership. The non-state type of political organisation of this society is not based on a balance between secular and religious power positions, but rather on a 'culture of conflict' that turns both forms of power into contested and elusive personal assets. Furthermore, all forms of power are related to kinship but are not determined by it.

In the context of the vision quest, the acquisition of spiritual power (*arútam*) can be regarded as an example of the variety of 'mystical means' that are of great significance for the construction of power in Amazonian societies (Santos Granero 1993). This type of power is conceptualised as an attribute that can be accumulated and/or lost during a person's lifetime. *Arútam* is not limited to a certain group of specialists, but, rather, is regarded as a precondition for success in various fields of action. Thus, it constitutes an important spiritual element in the construction of political power. Kinship is of significance in regard to access to *arútam*, as it is preferable to have close kin relations to the spirits of the deceased who are supposed to appear in the vision and transfer their abilities and power to the vision-seeker.

Shamans have additional forms of power at their disposal, which they use primarily for healing and/or causing illness and misfortune. Shamans form an active part in the politics of conflict. The acquisition of shamanic power is, on the one hand, linked to close kin ties, as power and knowledge are initially transferred mostly from father to son. On the other hand, all shamans are part of extensive networks that link practitioners of different regions and local traditions into a system of exchange of knowledge and power that reaches far beyond kin-group boundaries.

In the socio-political context, relations of power represent a fluctuating hierarchical continuum of individuals who exert influence upon others. Political power derives from personal abilities and reputation in combination with the skill to manipulate relatedness to other individuals in different contexts, allowing individuals to actively shape their social networks. This dimension of the construction of power is based on the flexibility of kinship, where social closeness or distance are subject to fluctuations and can be manipulated within certain boundaries.

The relationship between power and kinship among the Shuar and Achuar generally contains three dimensions. First, kin relations do represent a meaningful aggregate of social relations: they provide close social ties within the minimal kindred and the local group, and they form the base for the construction of larger socio-political entities. These close kin ties also provide a foundation for access to power in political, spiritual and religious contexts. Second, the flexibility of the kinship system enables a person to manipulate relatedness in various contexts. In regard to the formation of larger socio-political groups, kin relations are negotiable to a certain degree, and represent an integral part of a social system in constant flux. Nevertheless, kinship predefines interpersonal relations and provides a network of possibilities for agency: along its lines an individual can exert his influence and make choices according to personal preferences and political opportunity. Third, some aspects of power transcend kin groups and ethnic boundaries. In the context of the vision quest, the power-givers are sometimes completely unrelated to the vision-seeker. In the context of alliances, shamanic and non-shamanic *amiku*-partnerships construct close social and/or spiritual ties to otherwise unrelated people. These relationships represent important assets to all powerful persons.

The dividends of kinship for the construction and enactment of power in this society are limited, but cannot be neglected. They represent one of various organising principles of society and may be understood better by looking at their relationship with other aspects of agency and their ideological framework.

## Acknowledgements

We are grateful to Adam Kuper for his comments on a draft of this article, and to Tracie Cogdill for her editorial assistance.

## Notes

1    Two of those contexts – political leadership and shamanic power – are strongly dominated by men, which gives this study a certain 'male bias'. This does not mean, however, that women are powerless in this society, but rather that it is impossible to discuss all the different contexts of power within this chapter. For various aspects of female power in Shuar and Achuar society, see Mader (1997, 1999).

2    For an analysis of the social organisation of the northern Achuar, see Taylor (1984) and Descola (1993b).

3    Settlement patterns in Jivaroan societies vary to a certain degree. This is due to: differences in habitat; differences in population densities as a result of historic events (e.g. the depopulation of certain areas during the rubber boom); and culture change (e.g. the establishment of '*centros*' in the territory of the Shuar Federation in Ecuador). The data presented here refer to the Peruvian Changkuap River (Rio Huasaga) and might very well differ from other areas.

4    A recent study from Kurintsa, a Shiwiar community in Ecuador, shows similar results (Sugiyama 1997, personal communication). Co-operation among different persons and local groups will be discussed later in connection with the formation of socio-political groups.

5    The length of brideservice varies between different regions within the Jivaroan ensemble.

6    A similar type of social interaction is described by Thomas (1982) for the Pemon.

7    Based on Murdock's (1964) suggestion, but adapted to Dravidian systems by including affines (Gippelhauser 1985: 231–7).

8    'Endogamous nexi', as described by Taylor (1984) and Descola (1993a) for the Ecuadorian Achuar, could not be found in the Changkuap region of Peru.

9    These data were collected in the Changkuap region between 1975 and 1979; see Gippelhauser (1985: 251–306).

10   The term *amíku* derives from the Spanish word *amigo* (friend). According to Harner, the system appears among the Jivaroan peoples around 1910 and is related to the increasing circulation of industrial goods (Harner 1963: 74–84; see also Mader and Gippelhauser 1989: 42–3).

11   Square brackets [ ] indicate additions by the authors for a better understanding of the text; parentheses ( ) indicate translations of indigenous terms.

12 Powerful breath (*umpúm*) can transfer spiritual power from one person to another; it is also used by shamans to affect a person's health or dreams.

13 On the concept of the person among the Shuar and Achuar, see Mader (1999) and Taylor (1993).

14 Other spiritual components are limited to shamans and are mainly acquired from other shamans during various periods of apprenticeship.

15 Stormy weather is generally regarded as a sign of a possible *arútam*-apparition.

16 Exerpts from a chant by Uwijínt, quoted from Pellizzaro (1978, vol. 1: 123–5).

17 This applies, to a certain extent, to G+1. Due to bifurcate merging, the term *apar* includes several male relatives of G+1: F, FB, MZH, as well as more distant male relatives of the same generation of the cognatic category according to the collateral extension (see Gippelhauser and Mader 1990: 55–61).

18 These remarks are based on the analysis of thirty-five narratives of visionary experiences by Shuar and Achuar (see Mader 1999).

19 *Chichamtínui ajásame* means 'turn yourself into words'.

20 The narrative presented at the beginning of this section shows both possibilities in the course of one vision. The first anthropomorphic apparition is clearly identified and addressed as the seeker's grandfather, the second apparition – the 'jaguar-man' – is not referred to in terms of kinship.

21 For the ritual context of the vision quest, see Mader 1999.

22 Women's economic activities are mostly carried out continuously by adult women with the help of their husbands or unmarried daughters (see Mader 1985: 382–434).

23 This refers to Achuar settlement patterns on the Peruvian Changkuap River, where a lot of local groups live fairly close to each other along the river. In other areas (e.g. among the Ecuadorian Shiwiar of the Pastaza Province), local communities are more dispersed and co-operation on these occasions is usually limited to the members of the respective communities.

24 Certain dreams are bad omens for specific activities, so to avoid any mishap a person has to spend the day resting in the house.

25 On Achuar warfare and feuding, see also Descola (1993b: 293–325) and Uriarte (1989).

26 The attackers fled after being discovered.

27 The term *meséta uúntri* is usually translated into Spanish as '*dueño de la guerra*' – lord or owner of the war.

28 For the social and ritual preparation of an attack, see Karsten (1935: 279–92) and Descola (1993a: 293–325, 417–32).

29 This strategy was successfully applied several times on the Changkuap River. For its significance in Shuar warfare, see also Hendricks (1993: 155–67).

30 This strategy proved to be very efficient in fending off the Inca and Spanish intrusions. A good example is the 'Jivaro Revolt' of 1599, a simultaneous attack on several Spanish townships in the Upano and Santiago area. The strategy was based on the short-term mobilisation of large groups of Jivaro warriors, which dissolved and dispersed after successful attacks. This method ensured that counter-attacks would fail. The significance of fluctuating

alliances in regard to the resistance against outside aggression is also described by Uriarte (1989: 156–77).

31  Due to their extensive ritual knowledge they often also held the position of a *wea*, a leader of ceremonies. These rituals (initiation ceremonies, collective vision quests, etc.) were common among the Shuar until approximately 1960, subsequently disappearing because of the influence of missionaries (see Mader 1999). Shuar shamans thus traditionally combined elements of both horizontal and vertical shamanism (Hugh-Jones 1994).

32  On female shamans among the Shuar, see Perruchon (1997).

33  These additional training periods can last from a few days to a few months. Long-distance relations of Shuar shamans have been documented for some time. The most common inter-ethnic relations are those between Shuar and Canelos Quichua. The latter were highly regarded for their knowledge of 'white man's magic'. Harner has pointed out that Canelo shamans were ranked higher than Shuar shamans, and even today every Shuar *uwishín* tries to obtain knowledge and power from at least one Canelo Quichua (Harner 1972). But some contacts went to even more distant areas: for example, Disselhoff mentions relations between Shuar shamans and the famous *brujos* of Santo Domingo de los Colorados (in the Ecuadorian coastal region) in the 1930s (Disselhoff 1939). During past decades intercultural contacts have intensified as settlers from different parts of Ecuador populate large parts of traditional Shuar territory. Furthermore, new infrastructures, like roads and buses, facilitate journeys to foreign masters in the search for new knowledge and power.

## References

Clastres, P. (1976 [1974]) *Staatsfeinde. Studien zur politischen Anthropologie*, Frankfurt am Main: Suhrkamp.

Descola, P. (1988) 'La Chefferie amérindienne dans l'anthropologie politique', *Revue Française de Sciences Politique* 38 (5): 818–27.

—— (1993a) 'Les Affinités sélectives. Alliance, guerre et prédation dans l'ensemble jivaro', *L'Homme* 33(2–4): 171–90.

—— (1993b) *Les Lances du crépuscule. Relation Jivaros, Haute Amazonie*, Paris: Plon.

Descola, P. and Lory, J.-L. (1982) 'Les Guerriers de l'invisible. Sociologie comparative de l'ágression chamanique en Popouaisie Nouvelle-Guinée (Baruya) et en Haute-Amazonie (Achuar)', *L' Ethnographie* 87–8: 85–109.

Disselhoff, H. (1939) '"Brujos" im Hochland von Ekuador', *Zeitschrift für Ethnologie* 71: 300–5.

Dumont, L. (1953) 'The Dravidian kinship terminology as an expression of marriage', *Man* 53: 34–9.

Fortes, M. (1973) 'On the concept of the person among the Tallensi', in G. Dieterlen (ed.) *La Notion de la Personne en Afrique Noir*, Paris: Editions du Centre de la Recherche Scientifique.

Gippelhauser, R. (1985) 'Verwandtschafts- und Sozialorganisation der Achuara des peruanischen Amazonas', unpublished Ph.D. thesis, University of Vienna.

Gippelhauser, R. and Mader, E. (1990) *Die Achuara-Jivaro. Wirtschaftliche und soziale Organisationsformen am peruanischen Amazonas*, Vienna: Verlag der österreichischen Akademie der Wissenschaften.

Harner, M. (1963) 'Machetes, shotguns and society: An inquiry into the social impact of technological change among the Jivaro Indians', unpublished Ph.D. thesis, University of California, Berkeley.

—— (1972) *The Jivaro: People of the Sacred Waterfalls*, London: Robert Hale & Company.

Hendricks, J.W. (1993) *To Drink of Death: The Narrative of a Shuar Warrior*, Tucson: University of Arizona Press.

Hugh-Jones, S. (1994) 'Shamans, prophets, priests, and pastors', in N. Thomas and C. Humphrey (eds) *Shamanism, History, and the State*, Ann Arbor: University of Michigan Press.

Karsten, R. (1935) *Headhunters of Western Amazonas. The Life and Culture of the Jibaro Indians of Eastern Ecuador and Peru*, Helsingfors: Societas Scietiorum Finnica.

Lévi-Strauss, C. (1967) 'The social and psychological aspects of chieftainship in a primitive tribe: The Nambikuara of northwestern Mato Grosso', in R. Cohen and J. Middleton (eds) *Comparative Political Systems: Studies in the Politics of Pre-Industrial Societies*, Garden City: Natural History Press.

Lowie, R.H. (1948) 'Some aspects of political organisation among the American aborigenes', *The Journal of the Royal Anthropological Institute* 78: 11–24.

Mader, E. (1985) 'Subsistenz und Arbeitsorganisation der Achuara des peruanischen Amazonas', unpublished Ph.D. thesis, University of Vienna.

—— (1997) 'Waimiaku: Las visiones y relaciones de género en la cultura shuar', in M. Perrin and M. Perruchon (eds) *Complementariedad entre homber y mujer. Relaciones de género desde la perspectiva amerindia*, Quito: Abya Yala.

—— (1999) *Metamorfosis del poder. Persona, mito y visión en la sociedad de Shuar y Achuar*, Quito: Abya Yala.

Mader, E. and Gippelhauser, R. (1989) 'Kinfolk or tradepartners? Cultural adaptation to economic change on the Peruvian Amazon', in A. Gingrich, S. and S. Haas, and G. Paleczek (eds) *Kinship, Social Change and Evolution. Proceedings of a Symposium held on the Occasion of W. Dostal's 60th Birthday*, Horn, Austria: Verlag Ferdinand Berger.

Murdock, G.P. (1964) 'The kindred', *American Anthropologist* 66: 129–32.

Oppitz, M. (1988) *Frau für Fron. Die Dreierallianz bei den Magar West-Nepals*, Frankfurt am Main: Suhrkamp.

Pellizzaro, S. (1978) *Mitologia Shuar* (12 vols) (Mundo Shuar, Serie F), Quito: Abya Yala.

Perruchon, M. (1997) 'Llegar a ser una Mujer-Hombre. Chamanismo y relaciones de género entre los shuar', in M. Perrin and M. Perruchon (eds) *Complementariedad entre homber y mujer. Relaciones de genéro desde la perspectiva amerindia*, Quito: Abya Yala.

Rubenstein, S. (1995) 'Death in a distant place or the politics of shamanism', unpublished Ph.D. thesis, Columbia University.

Santos Granero, F. (1993) 'From prisoner of the group to darling of the gods: An approach to the issue of power in Lowland South America', *L'Homme* 33 (2–4): 213–30.

Seymour-Smith, C. (1991) 'Women have no affines and men no kin: The politics of the Jivaroan gender relation', *Man (N.S.)* 26(4): 629–49.

Taylor, A.-C. (1984) 'La allianza matrimonial y sus variaciones estructurales en las sociedades Jibaro (Shuar, Achuar, Aguaruna y Huambisa)', in M. Brown (ed.) *Relaciones Interetnicas y Adapción Cultural entre Shuar, Achuar, Aguaruna y Canelos Quichua*, Quito: Abya Yala.

—— (1993) 'Remembering to forget: Identity, mourning and memory among the Jivaro', *Man (N.S.)* 28: 653–78.

Thomas, D.J. (1982) *Order without Government. The Society of the Pemon Indians of Venezuela*, Urbana: University of Illinois Press.

Uriarte, L. (1989) 'Native blowguns and national guns: The Achuar Jivaroans and the dialectics of power in the Peruvian Amazon', unpublished Ph.D. thesis, University of Illinois at Urbana-Champaign.

Warren, P. (1988) 'Rappresentazioni Cognitive e Gestione Sociale delle Malattie tra gli Jívaro-Achuar', *L'Uomo* 1: 99–133.

# Chapter 4

# On the importance of being the last one

## Inheritance and marriage in an Austrian peasant community

### Gertraud Seiser

> Land holding cannot be created, regardless how diligent one may
> be; it may only be obtained through inheritance or marriage.
>
> (Ilien and Jeggle 1978: 88)

For the people of Unterweissenbach (Mühlviertel, Upper Austria),[1]
the connection between emotion and material interests, and between
economy and kinship, has been a matter of permanent concern.
Whenever I questioned my interview partners on kinship and marriage,
they always wanted to talk about property, houses, land ownership and
money. At the same time, any conversation about family affairs revealed
diverging interests within the so-called nuclear family, the household or
the kin group. Rosenbaum (1982: 116–7) called this conflict 'structural', given the central meaning attributed to a person's ownership
over arable land. In this chapter I will discuss the reasons for these
diverging interests, such as inheritance practices, marriage patterns and
kin relations, as found within a relatively marginal, rural area of Austria.
In the past, high social status came with the ownership of a farmhouse,
and only a son or a daughter could assume land ownership, social
status and decision-making power from their parents. It will be illustrated below how social inequality and stratification were reproduced
at the crossroads between kinship and economic interests.

There is ample literature on European inheritance patterns that
routinely juxtaposes partible and impartible inheritance norms.[2] My
contribution is intended to be more descriptive than theoretical and
acknowledges the fact that – among the impartible forms of transmission of patrimony to the next generation – primogeniture (i.e.
succession by the first-born) is described particularly frequently. If
mentioned at all, the transmission of property and rights to the
youngest child (ultimogeniture) is simply seen as a variation of primo-

geniture (e.g. Sieder 1987: 44). Below I will present the results of my fieldwork conducted in an area characterised by ultimogeniture. I will contrast my findings with the insights produced by social anthropology and social history in studying primogeniture, the predominant impartible inheritance pattern. I will argue that the consequences of these two inheritance practices are quite different. Following a brief description of economic practices in the area studied, I will characterise the respective inheritance and marriage patterns that existed between 1920 and 1960. Regarding the methods chosen, I have primarily used the narrative interview format. It would therefore be incorrect to claim further historical depth. Moreover, the fundamental changes in economic and social structures that took place since 1960 will only be briefly mentioned in this chapter.

The study area of my research is called Mühlviertel. This region is part of Upper Austria and is situated between the Danube River and the Czech Republic. It is forested hillside country, which was characterised by extreme poverty and underdevelopment as late as the 1960s. Unfavourable economic and climatic conditions, the limited availability of usable land, the underdeveloped infrastructure and (between 1948 and 1989) its proximity to the Iron Curtain contributed to this situation. Between 1920 and 1960, the economic activity most characteristic for the area in question may be described as 'peasant family farming'. The peasant family farm constituted the basic, multi-dimensional unit of social organisation (Shanin 1987: 3–4; Hettlage 1989: 11–12). It was primarily composed of members of the family who performed the work necessary for the maintenance of the farm as an economic entity. A farm satisfied the major part of a family's consumption needs and secured payment of taxes and other dues. The family farm was the most important element of everyday life, linking property, production, consumption, welfare, social reproduction, identity and prestige. Husbandry and stock-farming constituted the major sources of income within the mixed economy, and functioned at a low level of specialisation. Fertile, arable land was available only to a limited degree; as a result, land ownership assumed particular importance. As in most parts of Western Europe, family ownership or individual ownership of the means of production, i.e. of buildings, machinery, land and livestock, predominated in the area studied. Descent and alliance were defined in terms of land ownership, as well as by the way in which land was passed on, with specific reference to the 'house' (see Segalen 1986: 62).

In addition, there were big differences between the individual farmhouses or land holdings in terms of size, land quality and economic resources. The rural lower class settled around villages and larger townships, working as day labourers and/or local craftsmen. They always owned or leased a small piece of land that they worked for subsistence purposes. These small- and medium-sized farming units had to rely on non-agricultural sources of income, mostly small trades, depending on agriculture or income from seasonal paid labour elsewhere. Only about one-third of the farms in the community studied were able to provide adequate means for a family of five to six persons.

Until the 1960s, all of the 'large' farmers displayed a distinct self-perception as 'rich' farmers with a sense of social differentiation – an attitude that served to set them apart from those who had to rely on additional sources of income. The constantly rising earnings in the industrial sector (as compared to those in agriculture), the expansion of the transport infrastructure and the alternative opportunity of commuting to the urban area of Linz led – at the beginning of the 1960s – to a development that saw the small farmers and the residual heirs of the farms soon possess more liquid capital than the former 'rich' farmers. The reversal of the existing patterns was succeeded by the devaluation of the status of the 'rich farmers' in the village hierarchy. After the 1970s, the farm needed the heir much more than the heir needed the farm (see also Planck 1978: 205).

## Family structure

Initially, I will make some general observations regarding the characteristics of peasant family structure and labour organisation during the pre-industrial period as identified in German-language publications by social and economic historians, as well as by folklore studies of Central Europe. Viewing the peasant family as a residential unit, one will find, on average, two to three generations living together in one household, possibly including non-married brothers and/or sisters of the (male or female) farmer (Sieder 1987: 17). In the area studied there are usually three to four adults living on the farm – including the retired farmers. The individual members are in a close working relationship with each other. It is this working relationship – between at least the majority of the family members living in one household – that Mitterauer (1990: 140) considers to constitute the essential difference of family farming from non-agricultural family forms. Family farming is characterised by a unity of production, consumption and family life, which includes non-salaried working 'members of the family' and farm-hands who are integrated into the household (Ortmayr 1986: 336–8), as well as by the overall control that the 'head of the house' (*majordomus*)[3] holds over everyone living in the household (Rosenbaum 1982: 116; Sieder 1987: 17–8; Weber-Kellermann 1974: 15). Referring to one of the founders of German ethnology, Wilhelm Heinrich Riehl (1855), Otto Brunner (1978) suggested the term 'whole house' (*das ganze Haus*)[4] for this type of social organisation. Chayanov (Tschajanow 1923; Chayanov 1986 [1966]) was the first to analyse the ability of these peasant family farms to retreat, in times of economic crisis, from the caprices of the market (partly and temporarily), and to retain the farm as the basis of living for the future by increasing labour while reducing the level of consumption. This phenomenon has since been repeatedly described (see, for example, Medick 1978; Brunner 1978: 85). Sufficient evidence can be found in the study area for this type of economic strategy, which was used by the farming population at least until the end of the 1950s.

The descriptions and analyses of the social structure of the peasant population of Austria focus on the investigation of household units and of social strata (Ortmayr 1989: 115).[5] Studies based on the methods and analytical instruments provided by social anthropology, however, have uncovered a vast net of relationships and co-operation among individual households. There is plenty of literature on the different forms of mutual relationships between the social class of peasants and the rural lower class (for example Ortmayr 1984, 1986; Mitterauer 1986). In regard to the relationship between individual farming units of approximately equal social standing, however, I did not come across anything noteworthy in German-language literature,[6] apart from scattered evidence that neighbours would occasionally co-operate. Zonabend (1987) states that French regional ethnography tended to neglect the importance of alliance and descent patterns in favour of the residential unit;[7] I am of the opinion that this applies, even more so, to Austrian studies of family structure and the organisation of labour in rural societies.

The persons I interviewed reported a wide variety of activities (co-operation, festivities and mutual assistance commitments in the event of catastrophes) involving persons from other farms. The composition of such groups was repeatedly justified by kinship relations, and/or neighbourly ties and relationships established by marriage were routinely counted as kinship. The term used to describe these relatives was 'relatives coming with the marriage'. For example, the decision of who would be invited to a funeral or to help in the construction of a family home was never left to pure chance or to individual discretion:

instead, it was embedded in a system of rights and duties. I will now focus on some of the phenomena that are frequently associated with activities shared among individual households. These are: social stratification; the transfer of patrimonial rights to the succeeding generation; marriage; the importance of the concept of 'the house'; kinship and neighbourhood. All of these phenomena mentioned are closely interwoven. I will try to identify mutual dependencies wherever possible.

## Social stratification and social categories

The peasant society in the area studied was stratified,[8] and the resources of the farming enterprises differed widely. What was termed 'a house' by the resident population began at a size of about 1,000 square meters of land and extended to about 100 hectares of land for farming purposes. As a consequence, enormous differences existed between these 'houses', both in terms of their ability to provide a sufficient economic basis for the respective members of the household, as well as in terms of social prestige.

The literature on this issue differentiates between 'full-scale farmers' and the 'rural lower class' (or 'sub-peasant population').[9] As stated by Mitterauer (1992: 34), there is no all-encompassing indigenous term for these groups. In the area studied, the following categories are used: *grossi Baun* ('big farmers'), *mittlari Baun* ('medium-size farmers'), *kloani Eachta* ('small farms'), *Kuahaisl* (literally, a 'cow shack'), *Goasshaisl* (literally, a 'goat shack'), *I-Haisl* ('small cottages') and *Deastleit* ('farm-hands').[10] The boundary between the 'full-size farmers' and the rural lower class is not only blurred, it is also shifting. Over the past seventy years, this boundary has constantly been moving – depending on the overall social context and on the size of the household that had to be cared for. All groups of people living with the peasant couple and their children in one farmhouse or one farming unit, including the farm labourers, farm co-habitants (*Inwohner*), retired farming couples with a right to life annuity (*Altbauern im Ausgedinge*) and the vagrant non-working residents (*Einleger*),[11] constitute another problem of classification. Depending on whether they are classified according to age, degree of kinship, relative social status, or whether one uses a longitudinal or a cross-section in time, the results of such classifications may differ widely from each other. In the above-mentioned study, Michael Mitterauer (1992) points out these problems. One reason for the difficulty in classifying these groups – in particular farmers and farm labourers – lies in the relationship between farm size and family structure, which I will address in greater detail below.

The predominance of the nuclear family was a special characteristic of rural family structures in countries of Northern, Central and Western Europe, in addition to – and caused by – advanced marriage age. This resulted in a change in the relationship between consumer and producer within a family cycle, while the area of the arable land remained the same. There was a considerable need for non-family labour, if a farming couple had just married and their children were not yet fit for farm work, and if the retired parent farmers had to be cared for. Fifteen years later, the situation would have changed considerably. In most cases, the retired parent farmers would have died, while all of the children would be able to work, but not yet ready to get married. A peasant household with many children was able, or forced, to send their children to other houses as farm-hands (see Planck 1978; Ortmayr 1984; Burguière and Lebrun 1997). 'Thus, the central function of the farmhands was to supplement the lack of child labour' (Rosenbaum 1982: 66).[12]

## Marriage and transfer of property

How did this predominant nuclear family reproduce its structure again and again? On the level of descent and succession, the central event is the transmission of patrimony to the next generation.[13] In the area studied, impartible inheritance norms with ultimogeniture largely prevailed; in regard to property rights, a form known as 'shared farm ownership' (*Ehegattenhof*) was widespread. This meant that each of the spouses owned one-half of the entire property. This inheritance pattern had a direct bearing on the social structure of the peasant society; in fact, it was – by and large – the decisive local factor in producing and reproducing this kind of social structure. The options available to the individual members of a sibling group were thus distributed unequally by two factors: on the one hand, by inheritance practices and, on the other, by matrimonial strategies. Isogamy[14] is a marital practice that reproduces social inequalities: those children from a sibling group who were not able to marry into an equally large farm were destined for a lower social class. Of course, this is seen from the perspective of the farm owners – not from the viewpoint of those groups of persons who find themselves already at lower social levels.

Under the rules of ultimogeniture, the final social status of farm children was unclear prior to marriage and before the farm was handed over. Given the actual marriage age, the decision as to whether one would eventually become farmer or farm-hand was not made until age thirty or so. I would like to illustrate these generalisations using the following examples.

In 1920, a generational transfer of the farming unit took place on the Meier farm.[15] Two daughters were born in 1921 and 1922, then three boys (in 1924, 1927 and 1929). The son (who was born in 1927 and who took over the farm in 1961) after having married a daughter from a neighbouring farm, recounted: 'Until 1937, one male and one female servant worked at the farm. Thereafter, it was up to us children to do the work. First the girls, until 1952, then it was me until 1961.' The eldest daughter married a widowed baker with seven children under the age of twelve in a village thirty kilometres away; the second wedded a farmer in the area studied. The eldest son married the heiress of a farm close by; the youngest – who, according to the rules of ulti-mogeniture was the logical heir of the farm – was considered too weak and sickly to take over the farm. He took up an apprenticeship in Linz and married the daughter of a poor 'goat shack' farmer.

A similar situation was found at the Gruber farm. At the time Lini was born in 1934, one female servant was still employed on the farm. By and by, her older sisters took over this function. When Lini finished school at age fourteen in 1948, two farmers from nearby came to ask whether she would like to work as a 'female servant' with them. Her father finally sent her to the farm where he thought she would be needed most. She left home on Candlemas Day (February 2), the day of general rotation of servant and farm-hand personnel in western and eastern Austria (Piegler 1959). However, her time as stable maid on a foreign farm did not last very long. When her sister got married in March, she had to assume her sister's duties at home. Her eldest brother was killed in the Second World War; the second son returned from the war after a short period of internment, worked for a few years as a farm-hand on the farm and later took up a blue-collar job in Linz. On the occasion of his marriage, his father bought him a piece of land to build a family home. The eldest sister married the heir of a nearby farm, while the second daughter worked for almost fifteen years on the farm of her parents. Then, she successfully insisted on a love match with a non-inheriting farmer's son who, at that time, worked as a stableman. She, too, received a piece of land when she got married to build a cow shack (*Kuahaisl*). Lini wedded the heir of a neighbouring farm, and the youngest son took over his parents' farm after he had married the daughter of another neighbouring farmer.

Thus, of the ten children of two different farms described here, all of whom had married between 1952 and 1961, two men inherited the farm of their parents; both wedded daughters of neighbouring farms. Four of the children married into farms one to five kilometres away, one daughter married into a small trade business, and three children established blue-collar households, which partly gave them the opportunity for small-scale farming with no more than one or two cows, one or two pigs and some goats.

When describing the changes in social status these people experienced, one has to take into account the enormous changes in terms of economy and prestige that occurred during the past forty years between farmers and workers in the Mühlviertel. When the three persons who established blue-collar households got married (between 1952 and 1956), it was seen as an enormous social decline, and their relative social standing changed fundamentally in the course of the subsequent twenty years.

Until the 1950s, poorer families were forced to send some of their offspring to wealthier farms where these children, often only between seven and nine years old, had to tend small flocks of animals (sheep, goats or geese). The children of the farmers remained on the farm of their parents for a longer time. They were not sent off to work until the next child in age would take over their duties. The number of children on a farm had a decisive impact on the social position of the individual sons and daughters. Within the area studied, even the larger farms could not afford to keep more than three to four teenage or grown-up children at home. Asked whether children from larger farms, too, had to work on other farms, the farmer's wife from a medium-sized farm noted: 'If there were a lot, even the farmers' children were sent off. At the Nagel farm there were eight children, and, of course, they could not keep all of them at home.'

Although the social differences between owners of 'large' and 'medium-sized' farms were felt to be rather substantial, the number of children within a group of siblings was of great importance for the social starting position of each child. For example, if there were a large number of children being raised on a large farm, this was likely to reduce their opportunities for inheritance and, above all, the dowry of these children, who because of this were considered a far less attractive marriage choice than children from a smaller estate who had fewer competitors for the patrimony.

Sons or daughters of farmers who were expected to take over the estate did not serve as farm-hands. This was in line with the logic of ultimogeniture, in connection with the custom to persuade a child to leave the farm as soon as the next child was old enough to take over his or her job. According to this logic, it was always the youngest son or daughter who stayed on the farm. In the region studied, the end of the period in which non-related farm-hands were to be found on major estates coincided with the end of the country's occupation by Soviet troops in 1955. Some farms still accommodate persons who work as *Knecht* (farm-hand) or *Dirn* (maid). In all of these recent cases, the persons concerned were unmarried siblings of the farming couple. Unmarried siblings of the farmer or his wife also frequently lived as farm-hands on large farm estates in the 1920s and 1930s. In this context, Regina Schulte observed the following with regard to rural Bavaria between 1878 and 1910: 'They cost less than outside workers, and because they had an interest in the farm, identified with it, and belonged to the family, they were also more serviceable than outside workers' (Schulte 1988: 79).

The cost-advantage argument was also raised in the interviews I conducted. A more important aspect, however, was the fact that a ceding heir or heiress could only assert a claim to inheritance, marriage portion or dowry if he or she married. Children who remained unmarried never received their share of the patrimony.

## Transfer of the farm

From the perspective of the retiring farmer and his wife, the local term for the transfer of property and all means of production to the next generation was 'handing over the house', whereas the young farmer and his spouse would 'take over the house'. This procedure usually takes place when the youngest son (or daughter) is able – permitted or forced – to get married. Shortly after the wedding, the farm is transferred from an older farming couple to a younger one. What we see here is an impartible pattern of inheritance, which provides for the transfer of property *inter vivos*. Decision-making power over all members of the family is linked to the status of ownership, which thus lies in the hands of the intermediate generation. Concentration of the means of production and full decision-making power held by the intermediate generation is quite customary in those parts of Western or Northern Europe where only one son or daughter is expected to take care of the 'house', maintain the size of the farm and run the business in the same manner as its previous owners (Sieder 1987: 65–72). Jack Goody pointed out that:

[W]here we find 'diverging devolution', vertical inheritance is combined with the non-sexlinked transfer of property; the inheritance goes downwards to children of both sexes, enabling them to maintain their status in societies where social positions depend to a significant degree on the ownership of property.

(Goody 1976: 89)

Roughly speaking, partible inheritance areas in Austria are found only in the extreme west and east of the country. In the greater part of Austria farms are transferred without partition, preferably to the eldest son. Ultimogeniture is common in Upper Austria and Lower Austria, with the exceptions of the Innviertel region and the wine-growing districts of Lower Austria, respectively (Kretschmer and Piegler 1965; Kathrein 1990; Kretschmer 1980). Unterweissenbach is located in an area where impartible inheritance patterns prevail and ultimogeniture is preferred. Nearly all of the farms in the area studied have been handed over in this way during the past seventy years. It must be noted, though, that this was always done on the basis of customary law, which has time and again come into conflict with statutory law (Kretschmer and Piegler 1965; Brauneder 1980).

Transfer contracts enabled the farm successors to take possession of their heritage before the testator's death. Moreover, it has been customary since the eighteenth century[16] for these contracts to enable the farmer to fend off attempts by the State to give preference to the eldest son. This is of particular importance in an area where the eldest son is generally viewed by the farming population as being unfit for becoming successor at the farm and where customary law would provide for the youngest son to be the obvious inheritor.

This divergence between State authority and peasant practice – between 'great' and 'little tradition' (Redfield 1956: 70) in regard to people's attitudes towards Government authority – is particularly well-illustrated by the following quote taken from an interview: 'It has always been said the older ones (will get the farm). But this has never been true. It is always the younger ones.'[17]

Transfer of the farm always takes place upon the wedding of the child who is expected to take over the farm (Gaunt 1982). The following passage (from an interview with a 68-year-old owner of a big farm) shows quite vividly, I believe, how clearly people perceive the link existing between transfer of the farm, wedding and ultimogeniture:

*Farmer:*    In the Gruber family, you know, Toni was the youngest son.
             And today, it is again the youngest one who gets the house
             because, after all, he got married at such a young age.
*Seiser:*    And in the old days, people got married later, didn't they?
*Farmer:*    Yes, of course, when the old ones did not want to hand over,
             they would not let you have it [the farm and a marriage].
*Seiser:*    And then you had to wait?
*Farmer:*    Yes, then you had to wait, that's right. Gruber got married
             at twenty-four, me at thirty-four, simply because, you see, at
             twenty-four, in 1951, my mother was fifty-one then and my
             father was fifty-eight. They would have chased me out of the
             house [if I had brought home a wife] at that age, you know.

The way in which ultimogeniture was applied cannot, therefore, be
regarded as a rule or norm proper, but rather as a practice that resulted
from the age structure of the persons living on the farm and from the
parents' 'willingness to hand over'. If, for example, the parents were
sick or their ability to work was otherwise impaired, it was possible for
them to express their readiness to hand over the farm before the
youngest child was of marriageable age.

The portion of the inheritance to which the other children were
entitled, which in the area studied was roughly the same for all regardless of sex, was given to them upon their marriage in the form of a dot
or dowry. If unmarried children were still living on the farm at the
time of transfer, provision was made in the transfer contract as to who
had to buy them out and what share they would get. If it was agreed
that this would be taken care of by the retiring farming couple, part of
the forest was excluded from the transfer assets.

Before the introduction of statutory old-age pension for farmers,
the retirement portion reserved for the elder farming couple, as well as
the 'buy-out payments', were due prior to the farm successor's
wedding. This made the starting position of the young couple rather
difficult (Gaunt 1982: 174–6; Planck 1978: 196). In the life of a
farmer, the several years immediately before and after the transfer of
the farm were the most difficult, economically speaking, because, as a
result of these payments, the farm was in a precarious situation with
regard to its substance and financial latitude.

The marriage portion of the bride (dowry) was, thus, attributed a
special value that was, moreover, laid down in customary law. This gave
rise to another characteristic feature of rural tenure that is reflected by
the possessory relationship between the spouses. As in most other rural

regions in Austria, the principle of community of property between spouses also applies to the study area. This means that the farm is co-owned by the two spouses. Unlike the situation prevailing in urban or aristocratic circles, the wife is much more closely involved in the fate of the estate (Brauneder 1980: 58–9).

In general, the farm-wife always has certain autonomous areas of work and authority on the farm (Planck 1978: 204). Despite a number of governmental rules (including, in particular, the legislation enacted under Emperor Joseph II, and, in the twentieth century, the German Reich's Farm Inheritance Act (*Reichserbhofgesetz*) of 1933,[18] which entered into force in Austria after the *Anschluss* in 1938), this type of 'spouse-owned farm' in combination with ultimogeniture has been preserved in the Mühlviertel region to this very day.

One prerequisite for the spouses to become joint owners of the farm is the wife's dowry, because without a sufficient dowry a transfer of the estate is not regarded as feasible, and would not be permitted by the farmer:

> Hans has already been urging me to hand over for quite some time now. Yes, I said, but first you need to bring home a girl, and then we'll have to see whether she has got property. For if she owns property, it goes without saying that the farm will be handed over. Whereas, if she has no property, she will have to content herself with having only you [i.e. both will remain without the farm].
>
> (60-year-old owner of a medium-sized farm)

Thus, the farmer announces that the farm will only be transferred on the condition that the son finds a socially acceptable spouse. He does not even consider the possibility of having her not entered as co-owner in the contract. This behaviour on the part of farming couples willing to transfer ownership also forms the basis for the important economic position that the young woman assumes in her husband's house, and creates in her a sense of independence, especially *vis-à-vis* her own children:

> No woman would accept not being entered in the land register. Because if I were not co-owner and something were to happen to my husband – like him having an accident with the tractor and being crushed to death or something like that – then I would lose the farm, for it would then already be the children who inherit the

house. The value of the property would then be estimated and shared among the three children. And me, I would then totally lose out on everything. But if something happened to him now, then everything would belong to me and I could do whatever I want with it. And that's the way it is done everywhere!

(55-year-old farm-wife whose children are aged twenty to twenty-eight)

My grandmother (on my father's side) had the same fear, and she kept telling me that, if my father died, my mother would immediately get married again and that the children from her first marriage, while still being entitled to being bought out under the rule of ultimogeniture, would lose their title to the farm. This had happened once to my grandmother, when her mother died after having delivered twins and there were several children in the house. Her father soon remarried, begot two more children by his second wife and was murdered two years later. The stepmother remarried right after that, and the children from the first marriage were accommodated with relatives. My grandmother was reared as a foster child by her godmother (and aunt on the mother's side). This important function of godparents in those unstable times brought about by high mortality rates is emphasised by Martine Segalen (1986: 33): 'If one of the two [parents] died, the other's children would be dependent on someone not related to them. Hence the need for arrangements for guardians and the importance of a system of godparents.' Later, my grandmother was no longer considered to have any inheritance rights whatsoever with regard to the farm her father had inherited, nor was she granted a portion of the inheritance when the farm was transferred. Her title to a dowry arose from her foster parents' farm, where she had worked until her wedding.

Mitterauer (1986: 312–15) relates the large number of remarriages in Austria to the strategies of landlords and the constraint of role substitution that would otherwise have decreased as a result of the disintegration of the system of landlord-rule. In my view, however, an investigation of the rationale for this behaviour must also take into account the strong position of peasant women on a spouse-owned farm. Bourdieu (1987: 281) notes that the relative strengths of the spouses in relation to each other is never independent of the economic and symbolic capital each partner owns or has brought into the marriage.

In the Wiesner family, it was not the son but his wife who took over the farm upon their wedding. He did not become co-owner on the grounds that he had a child out of wedlock with another woman. As a neighbour of the Wiesners stated, 'when a man had children out of wedlock, he usually did not become co-owner of the farm in order to avoid excessive payments'. This approach not only meant fewer alimony obligations, but was also designed to avoid having to pay the obligatory portion of the inheritance upon the next transfer of the farm. A child who did not live on the farm was not eligible for inheritance in the understanding of the rural population, and it was, therefore, not considered to be reprehensible to dodge alimony payments.

With the help of property transfer contracts, it was possible to circumvent the provisions of civil law, which relied on the notion of inheritance on the basis of biological descent. The rural concept of inheritance is derived from the principle of affiliation through services rendered.[19] The needs of the individuals capable of working on the farm at a given moment are crucial to the people's sense of justice. What is important is the farm and those who run it at a certain time. The idea of consistency over several generations is of secondary importance;[20] nor do ownership relations as such give rise to an imbalance between the sexes. It is true, though, that this traditional concept of justice is entirely incompatible with the notion or possibility of divorce, because the need for having to buy out one's co-owner in almost all cases would have meant selling, and thus losing, the farm. Here, we have an important parallel between Roman Catholic canon law and rural customary law. This did, however, not apply to other spheres.

As mentioned above, marriage was considered rather late in most cases, with men getting married between the ages of thirty and thirty-five and women between the ages of twenty-five and thirty. If the old farmer was not yet willing to transfer the farm, his son would attempt to force a marriage by making a socially acceptable prospective farm-wife pregnant. Almost all of my female interlocutors indicated that the underlying reason for their hasty wedding was the fact that they were already pregnant. I asked one of them, a peasant woman who came from a very austere Roman Catholic family, whether this had caused any problems with her father. Her response was, 'no, because I was already old enough'. Public opinion also found a way of reconciling this practice with Roman Catholic morals: 'People then used to say, well, it [the foetus] must have been growing faster.' My data do not enable me to comment on the situation of unmarried mothers who, as a result of such strategies, 'got stuck' with their children – as the local phrase cynically puts it.[21]

## The social practice of transfer

My interview partners were well aware of the economic transactions conducted in the wake of a marriage, since these events determine and define the future options and chances of all other members of the family. However, they did not think of marriage or inheritance patterns as rules, but rather as social practices or games of power involving various parties, interests or strategies, which the acting persons may either be aware of or that may be imputed to them. The old farmer and his wife are expected to be 'ripe', i.e. ready for transfer, but if they feel that they are in sufficiently good health they will try to delay transfer as long as possible. They see their preference for the youngest or younger child as a result of power interests and as a means of reducing tensions between the generations.

One farmer described the situation at the moment of transfer as follows: on the one side there are the parents (transferors) and siblings of one transferee (ceding heirs); on the other are the parents-in-law of the other transferee. The former try to exclude as much as possible from the transfer assets,[22] in order to preserve a certain room for manoeuvre in their old age. The siblings are also interested in their parents receiving a large retirement annuity upon transfer, as they also continue to benefit from these assets. The couple who take over the farm will try to minimise the sustained obligations that drain surplus earnings from the farm during the parents' lifetime. The parents of the prospective wife or husband of the successor support the young couple in their negotiations associated with the transfer of the farm. They make sure that the daughter or son be made a joint owner, and that the economic basis of the farm is not impaired by excessive demands on the part of the old farming couple.[23] I was informed of two methods by which the parents-in-law may exert their influence. These methods are, however, not mutually exclusive, but are usually applied in a serial order. Let me explain the procedure by using the transfer of the farm to a son as an example: Before putting up the banns, the bridegroom and his parents call on the parents of the bride. Then, the parents, parents-in-law, the bride and bridegroom negotiate the terms of transfer and the amount of dowry. Usually, all persons living in the bride's house are present at these negotiations. The negotiations as such are, however, conducted by the parents of the bride and bridegroom. I was informed of two instances in which the parents-in-law refused to 'give away' their daughter on the transfer conditions offered by the other side. Both cases became widely known because they eventually resulted in court proceedings. A common feature of both cases was the fact that the young couple and the parents-in-law successfully challenged the transferors. In the first case, the son waived his succession right on the ground that his parents declined to have his bride entered in the land register, and he sued his parents for payment of a remuneration for work performed on the farm between the ages of fifteen and thirty. In the second case, the problem was due to the fact that the young farming couple was to take care of a handicapped child of the transferors. The starting point for litigation in both cases was the round of negotiations between the parents prior to putting up the banns.

The second chance for influencing the process arises when the matter is subsequently submitted to a notary public. As a rule, the parents who are willing to transfer the farm will meet with the notary, inform him or her of their intention to transfer the farm and determine a date for an appointment at the notary's office. The current farm owners, the young couple expected to take over the farm and the parents of the bride are invited to attend that meeting. Shortly before the meeting, the parents of the bride will visit the notary and inform him or her of their requests and objections. During the transfer ceremony itself, i.e. when the contract is set up and entered in the land register, the father of the bride or, frequently, both parents are present. At several occasions, the reason for doing so was stated as: 'of course, they have to protect the rights of the young couple because the old farming couple will only try to defend their own interests'.

Serious conflicts may also arise concerning the exact date of the transfer ceremony at the notary's office, which should generally be scheduled after the couple have given notice of their intended marriage (approximately three weeks before the wedding), and no later than one month after the wedding. The date eventually agreed upon will allow the interested rural population to make estimations of the relative strengths of the two families involved. The farm transferors will try to insist on a date after the wedding, while the parents of the bride or, if the estate is to be transferred to a daughter, the parents of the bridegroom will argue in favour of a date before the wedding. The closer the date of transfer is to the wedding day, the more the neighbours and relatives will judge the transfer procedure to take place on an egalitarian and frictionless basis. If more than a week or two elapses between the two events, and if no generally accepted reason exists for that delay, this will give rise to a variety of rumours and speculations.

During the first interviews on the transfers of farm estates, I asked my interlocutors about the way in which the transfer procedure is usually conducted, and, at first, I interpreted their claim that they did not know as a refusal to discuss this delicate topic in the presence of a microphone. However, if one accepts the thesis that the negotiation aspect is crucial for the transfer of the farm, such refusals suddenly appear in a different light. For the persons involved, every farm transfer is a unique experience and the result of a constellation of forces that cannot be repeated. Therefore, it is possible for them to talk about individual cases, and to describe the initial circumstances, the parties involved and their respective interests, but they are unable to list specific rules.

What is referred to in the Austrian ethnological atlas as the 'area of impartible inheritance connected with ultimogeniture' and spouse-owned farms (Kretschmer and Piegler 1965: 2), and is classified as consisting of a compact area with uniform customary law, is viewed from an entirely different angle by the persons concerned. They are not aware of any rules that people would more or less comply with, but merely practices and strategies, which are 'habitual', 'customary' or 'traditional' by being negotiations following a particular logic of interests. It is the intentions and interests behind these strategies that make the results appear consistent, and not rigid rules that are meekly obeyed by the individuals affected. Another element I want to emphasise is the omnipresence of the principle of bilaterality. In contradistinction to the authoritarian patriarchal 'head of the house' who controls the fate of the 'whole house' (*das ganze Haus*), it is the wife and her relatives who again and again exert considerable influence.

## Ideology of descent versus ideology of the house

Primogeniture, which in rural Austria is always accompanied by the preferential treatment of sons over daughters, is governed by rules to a much greater extent. The first-born son will be treated as the future farmer from birth. He receives better care, and better food and clothing than his younger or female siblings (for example Sieder 1987: 44; see also Bourdieu 1987: 274–5). As far as ultimogeniture is concerned, nobody can know which of the children will be the last one; maybe the heir has not yet been born. In addition, there is another uncertainty: mortality rates in the adult peasant population were high. It is difficult to secure the continuity of succession within the same line of patrilineal descent if property is divided between the couple of the middle generation (i.e. the active owners), and, at the same time, there is always the danger that one of the parents might die. The surviving partner would then inherit everything and try to remarry as soon as possible, especially if there are small children to raise or if the farm is dependent on additional labour (Rosenbaum 1982: 69–70; Segalen 1986: 32–3). I was told of many cases of up to three remarriages within one generation. Primogeniture is also often associated with a pronounced patrilineal ideology and a genealogical memory of long standing. People take pride in the number of times it has been possible to pass on the farm within the same line of patrilineal descent. Under conditions of primogeniture, the remarriage of a widow will be avoided or will have no effect on the selection of an heir, because the offspring of the new marriage will have no right whatsoever to take over the farm.

Under the conditions of ultimogeniture and the considerable risk of dying before the farm is 'handed over' to the next generation, it is almost impossible to keep the farm in the hands of the same male line for several generations. This, in turn, correlates with a rather weak genealogical consciousness. To give an example taken from my survey, the term a peasant uses to designate his or her living father or mother is 'ancestor' (*Eihl, Ahl* [in German, *Ahne, Ahnin*]). Thus, after having 'handed over' their property, the retired parents also face a decline in social status. They seem to be at a great genealogical distance and, although still alive, slowly vanish into the general, anonymous category of (mostly dead) 'ancestors'.

While people generally attribute great importance to the continuity of the 'house', the genealogical continuity of the inhabitants of the 'house', or of any line of descent, seems to be of relatively little importance. This 'ideology of the house' also becomes visible in the local nomenclature. Peasants use the name of the 'house' to address each other. Thus, the name of a farm constitutes the decisive part of the term of address for its owners. The names of the different farms have remained the same throughout the centuries. Some of the names can even be traced back to the thirteenth and fourteenth centuries, when parts of the area concerned were cleared and cultivated. Family names, however, are passed on along patrilineal patterns and go from father to the children. Women change their names when they marry. In local dialect, family names are called 'written names', and these are known by only a few people. Terms of reference, as well as terms of address, usually consist of the name of the house followed by the designation of the position an individual person has in the house. The names of the farms and the relations of descent or marriage existing between individual houses are widely known.

Great emphasis is put on status endogamy. This means that the prospective farm owner is expected to marry a woman belonging to the same status group, and who will receive an adequate dowry. The dowry consists of money, timber and livestock, and is considered the payment for the wife's co-ownership of the farm after marriage. In this context, marriage is neither a matter concerning two individuals, nor is it one between two kin groups. The personal and economic conditions are determined by the economic situation, the social status of the 'house' and by the personal constellation prevailing within the households involved.

The value of the expected dowry depends not only on the size and wealth of the farm the bride or groom comes from, but also on the number, age and work ability of their brothers and sisters. The more siblings there are, the less each of them can gain from their parents' farm. This diminishes their chances to marry 'into' a house, as it is called. In order to keep the farm together, one unmarried sibling often works on the farm as a farm-hand. Even if they find work on other farms or in other professions, the siblings remain members of the house they were born in as long as they are unmarried. Only marriage can change their identification with a certain house. At the same time, marriage is the only reason for somebody to get his or her share of the inheritance. Therefore, this act is also called 'to buy somebody out of the house'. To pay the dowry to every member of a large group of siblings may diminish the value of the whole estate, and, as a consequence, its prestige. Many of my interlocutors openly told me about strategies that aimed at reducing the marriage chances of some of the children of the house.

In order to buy out the ceding heirs, and generally in situations where considerable amounts of money are needed at short notice, a special form of capital is used: the forest. Arable land and pastures constitute the permanent working capital of a farm, which yields income through work and thus secures the reproduction of the farm and its members. In contrast, the forest[24] constitutes a form of capital that will be activated predominantly in situations when alliances are formed between different houses. At the time when the farm is taken over by the young couple, this form of capital is very scarce, because the productive forest served to secure the dowry of at least some of the older siblings. At the same time, the dowry is used to compensate older siblings for the renunciation of succession rights, and constitutes the starting capital that enables them to marry into another house or to found a new household. In the winter before the planned marriage, the parents go to the forest, select an appropriate number of trees and fell them. Depending on whether the bridal couple plans to build a house of their own, to renovate the existing house or whether they need cash, the dowry is transferred to them either in the form of timber or cash.

The young forest now covering the clearance will be the starting capital for the great-grandchildren of the young couple. Thus, the different generations of trees growing in a forest represent an investment in different generations of descendants of a farm, and, at the same time, an investment in prospective marriage relations between individual houses. However, the forest in this context is not an inheritance or starting capital in the sense that the young adult may leave the farm at his or her own discretion to make a new life for himself elsewhere. Children who did not marry, or were not allowed to, did not get the opportunity to convert this form of immovable capital into movable capital. A peasant woman, in an interview dealing with marriage and the related customs stated in no uncertain terms: 'As long as a child does not marry, he belongs to the house, even if he has lived in a far away town for twenty years.' With marriage this unity dissolves; the married descendants of a farm now belong to a new house or to another house.

In this context, the dowry is no longer considered an anticipated portion of the inheritance but rather an 'admission fee' into a new house; this is a pledge, as it were, of a new alliance that will invest, in most cases, in the renovation and rebuilding of the farm and, thus, create improved economic reproduction capacities. The farms remain the fixed points between which people move. The forest guarantees this constant circulation. Consequently, women do not talk about marrying a certain man but rather about entering a certain house: 'Franz, of the Bauer-Haus, he would have liked me [for his wife], but I didn't want to go there [to his house], because his mother and his sister were known to be very quarrelsome people.'

In planning one's own future, considerations into which house somebody marries are more important than the future spouse. Once married, a woman is not considered the wife of Mr so-and-so but rather the peasant woman of a certain farm:

Once, Maria of the Müllerhof said to me, she would have become Wiesner [head of the Wiesner farm] had Hans of the Wiesner farm not died, because they were engaged, you know. Otherwise she would be on the Wiesner farm now, she would be the Wiesner wife now.

> (75-year-old former farm-wife who received
> the Wiesner farm from her parents)

On account of the rules and practices of impartible inheritance, the number of farms has remained nearly constant, with the children who did not inherit farms having to look for a livelihood elsewhere. Well into the 1960s, peasants tried to accommodate as many of these children as possible on other farms. A peasant (speaking about the rivalry between two brothers concerning their parents' farm) stated:

> Because, you know, everybody wanted to have the house, this increased your chances with women. Today, if you are the prospective heir of a house, this will diminish your chances with women. In those times, your chances were good because every father wanted to arrange for his daughter to marry into a house.
>
> (72-year-old former owner of a big farm)

A remarkable aspect of this statement is the dialectics between free will and paternal authority when it comes to selecting a partner for marriage: If a man has the prospect of inheriting a farm, this would make him more attractive to 'the women', but only on account of the fact that the woman's consent to marry him depends on her father's consent.

The more children there were on a farm, the more difficult, and, at the same time, the more desirable it was to marry the children off into other houses. The events in the first half of the twentieth century taught the peasants that the farm had not lost any of its importance as a basis for survival during the years of war and hunger. This experience, of course, cannot be generalised; it is the experience of a peasant population, which, by and large, was spared the direct consequences of the war, and which, nevertheless, succeeded in producing a surplus of food with very simple means of production and a high input of labour.[25] The debt crisis of the 1930s, too, has been perceived in a very specific way, insofar as the generation concerned laid down stipulations in the transfer contracts prohibiting the next generation to take up a loan or to sell the property.[26] The notion that it is possible to survive everything happening in the 'outside world' by a retreat into an extremely modest way of life has been expressed in all interviews with people over the age of fifty. The prerequisite for such a concept of survival is the existence of a farm with sufficient land holding; for those children who had to leave the parental house, marriage was the most important strategy to get access to the much wanted farm.

One important attribute of the prospective spouse – apart from the dowry he or she brings in – is his or her work ability, which counts more than non-material values such as descent. Untiring industriousness, demonstrated by helping on as many neighbouring farms as possible, considerably increased the chances of marrying into a house. The Müllerbauer, for instance, had many sons. He carefully saw to it that his sons worked as farm-hands or helped in houses or where there was a chance that the daughter would take over the farm. And, indeed, he was successful: three of his six sons married into other houses. Of his children, one inherited the farm of origin, three of them used the strategy of demonstrating particular industriousness and married into other houses, and, in the two remaining cases, the father used a different strategy that I will describe below. The marriages of his sons took place in the 1950s.

One of the two sons described the procedure of 'going marrying' very vividly. On a Sunday after church, his father had preliminary talks with the father of a prospective farm heiress, and a date was fixed for the 'inspection' of the farm. On the arranged day, father and son went to the farm of the peasants who were willing to marry their daughter to a son of another house. The opening phrase initiating the inspection and the subsequent negotiations was usually: 'I've heard you are looking for someone, and I have one here.' Then, they would inspect the fields, pastures, house and stables. Afterwards, they had a snack with schnapps, and the peasants discussed the expected dowry of the young man and the life annuity reserved for the retiring parents of the prospective bride. The young couple was physically present at the negotiations and also took part in the discussion; it would, however, not be admissible for the young people to openly reject the prospective partner. Refusal of the prospective partner was expressed by subsequent intervention with the respective mother who had to plea her children's cause *vis-à-vis* her husband and head of the farm.[27] Although both sons went through this sort of procedure several times, they eventually had their way and secured love matches with non-inheriting farmer's daughters.

The life stories and interviews show that – until the 1960s – peasant marriage was a matter concerning two houses, rather than two individuals.[28] The standard phrase 'I've heard you are looking for someone', refers to the house, i.e. to factors like land holding, labour force and material means of production (Inhetveen and Blasche 1983: 20), not to individual needs of the retiring peasant couple. Individuals had to subordinate themselves to the needs and requirements of the farm[29] in order to maintain the house as a basis of subsistence for future generations.

These close ties to the house were loosened only when other sources of income became available – especially for those who had left the rural world in part or for good. Inhetveen and Blasche describe the attachment of the peasant to his farm as follows:

> He feels and defines himself as part of his property; he is identical with his property in the sense that he derives his personal identity from his property. Any material loss reduces his personal substance; any danger of loss causes him to cling to his property even more ferociously.
>
> (Inhetveen and Blasche 1983: 23)

## The role of godparents

How are the interests of children protected if one of the parents remarries? Soon after the death of one parent, a notary public will draw up an inventory of all the property belonging to the farm. The godparents of the children are present as witnesses of this inventory, and it is their responsibility to protect the children's interests *vis-à-vis* the remaining parent. This is important with regard to the dowry due when one of the children marries. Furthermore, the statutory portion of the inheritance will be calculated on the basis of the inventory after the death of one parent. If the surviving parent wants to remarry, he or she has to ask the godparents of the children of the previous marriage for permission. The godparents cannot actually refuse permission, but they are expected to negotiate in order to achieve acceptable terms for these children. If there is a series of remarriages, or in cases of severe conflict, it may well be that the children move to the farm of their godparents.

Who are the godparents in terms of kinship with the godchildren and their parents, respectively? Usually, the children of the peasants have one married couple serving as their godparents. In ideal cases these will be a sister of the mother, and her husband. If there is no suitable sister, a brother of the mother, and his wife, will be the preferred relatives. Older peasants, in particular, explain this preference by the argument that the necessary emotional and economic support is guaranteed only by collaterals of the mother in case she dies. However, the godparents have to fulfil their obligations not only in dramatic situations such as cases of death. In everyday life they have to take care of the moral education of the children, and they should also defend the children's interests against other members of the family. They have to support those children who have not been 'bought out' of the house, especially in negotiations preceding the transfer of a farm.

## 'Marriage' and the 'house' today

What do modern, well-educated sons of peasants think about these issues? In 1993, I interviewed a 25-year-old farmer's son who was willing to take over his father's farm. Moreover, he was unattached at the time. I asked him what qualities he expected of a woman who was to be his wife and peasant woman on the farm. In his rather lengthy and roundabout answer he addressed the following issues one by one:

1  It is a problem for a farmer to find a wife nowadays. Women consider farmers 'poisonous'.[30]
2  If two people get along well and if the 'whole thing is meant seriously', he does not think it impossible to find a woman who is prepared to marry a farmer.
3  However, he would not want a 'total failure'. Alternatively, if you ask for too much, you definitely will not get what you want.
4  She ought to be a good cook – that is important. But if she's not, you cannot do anything about it.
5  She ought to have 'business sense' and an 'entrepreneurial spirit'. She should know how to work, of course, but first of all she needs business sense. She must understand that you have to earn money before you can spend it. When I asked him whether he meant thriftiness, he replied, 'no, not thriftiness, but business sense – because results of your labour you cannot sell are useless'.

The above young man knows Austria and foreign countries very well on account of his part-time job, and describes himself as modern and open-minded, yet is still influenced by the concept of the 'house'. A woman who is serious about him knows that he cannot be separated from his farm. If she loves him, she also loves his farm. This is his first fundamental statement. His second central statement concerning the requirements of the farm expresses the wish for a woman with business sense. He has understood the capitalist system and knows that labour you cannot sell is useless. Retreat strategies, as described by Chayanov,[31] are quite inconceivable given the present economic conditions and intricate, extensive trade links; this means that the important thing is to maintain the farm and its economic substance from generation to generation under the prevailing economic conditions. The farmer and his prospective wife have to dedicate all of their efforts to this task.

So, what does the 'house' offer to those members who will never get 'paid out'? Prior to the introduction of statutory old-age pension for farm labourers and peasants at the end of the 1950s, care for the sick and the aged was of great importance. It was an absolute obligation for the farming couple to implement the responsibility of the 'house' for all dependants. This responsibility included the retired peasant couple, unmarried sisters and brothers, and all children irrespective of their age. This responsibility was markedly less pronounced towards farm-hands and farm labourers. Thus, the social status of a house depends on its economic potential, but it is also a product of a moral discourse in a neighbourhood of peasants. The moral status of a house is determined, to a high degree, by the way the peasants treat their dependants.

Marriage is not only important with respect to the dowry, but it also marks the beginning of a long-lasting alliance between two houses that is characterised by mutual support in various social and economic spheres. The geographical proximity of the two farms in question is of great importance for this kind of support to work in everyday life to everyone's satisfaction. The local area of Hinterberg consists of twelve major single farms, which – with one exception – are all somehow associated with each other by multiple marriage, kin and godparent relations. In 1995, there was a double wedding in the village: the heir of the farm that constituted the one exception married the daughter of the neighbouring farm, while his sister married the brother of the bride who was the heir of the neighbouring farm. On the occasion of the party traditionally held a week before the wedding a large group of neighbours discussed at length the important event, and they agreed that 'it was high time, for it is not right that somebody should exclude himself from the community in such a way'.

## Conclusions

At this point, I would like to point out that – in contradistinction to Western bourgeois family ideology – we find here a widespread and clear consciousness that there are diverging interests within one household and also within the nuclear family. The system of godparent-hood indicates that parents and children have different interests, and the inheritance system reflects the various different positions of individuals within one sibling group. In addition, the system of godparent-hood strengthens the position of the peasant woman and her female relatives, as it gives them the formal right to interfere with internal family matters of other houses.

Furthermore, on account of the fact that social status largely depends on land holding, and only one person and his wife or her husband – respectively – may become successors to this economic and social position, this form of property transfer becomes a means of reproducing social inequality. The absence of any ideological justification, such as the 'natural' right of the first-born to become the successor in a system of primogeniture, coincides with the absence of definitions of rights and duties a person has by virtue of birth or as a God-given prerogative. But what is culturally defined are the legitimate interests of persons, and the rights and duties of support or intervention in other houses.

While social anthropology has discovered the benefits of the concept of the 'house' only recently (see Carsten and Hugh-Jones 1995), most social-historical and ethnological studies carried out in German-speaking countries have tended to overemphasise the importance of the 'house' and of individual households, and, at the same time, neglected the potential dividends of kinship relations between individual households. The most likely reason for this was the concept of the 'whole house' (*das ganze Haus*), formulated by Wilhelm Heinrich Riehl (1855), and further elaborated by Brunner (1978), Mitterauer (1990, 1992), Weber-Kellermann (1974), Sieder (1987) and Rosenbaum (1982).

The results of the 'Ethnologie de France', the studies of scholars such as David Sabean and my own fieldwork have demonstrated that it is imperative to study kin relationships in order to be able to understand and to describe social systems, including social systems existing in Europe. Therefore, I am convinced that the socio-historical analysis of the 'family' in German-speaking countries, or 'family history' as it is called, could benefit from a detailed and serious discussion of social anthropological approaches to the concept of kinship.

## Acknowledgements

I want to extend special thanks for comments on an earlier draft to Peter Schweitzer, Andre Gingrich and Mark Nemet; for the translation and for intensive periods of discussion I am grateful to Wolf Zemina.

## Notes

1   This chapter is based on a series of research projects and interviews about peasant economics and family structure conducted during the period of 1987–96 in the Lower Mühlviertel, Upper Austria. It has the character of an endo-ethnography (DaMatta 1994: 125), since I myself grew up in the region under social conditions similar to those being analysed in this chapter.

2   Henk de Haan (1994: 151–86) provides a summary of the diverse approaches employed in anthropological treatises of European inheritance patterns.

3   The authority of the head of the farm over his wife is considerably overemphasised by Brunner and Rosenbaum (see, for example, Sandgruber 1983: 138–40).

4   An English-language summary of the German debate about the household and the ideology of the house can be found in the monograph by Sabean (1990: 88–101).

5   For Ortmayr, it is the concentration of historical demography and of family history on certain written categories of sources, such as census lists, that is mainly responsible for the lack of any studies on social groups exceeding individual households.

6   One exception is the work by Ortmayr (1989).

7   However, there are some monographs and articles on a few French regions in which these questions are taken into account (see, for example, Segalen (1991) and Bourdieu (1987)).

8   For reasons of simplicity, I have focused on that segment of the population that actually engages in farming. Thus, the social stratification typical for the centre of the village – the townsfolk, craftsmen and workers – is not addressed, at least with regard to those who did not directly engage in the primary production sector.

9   Regarding the terms *ländliche Unterschicht* ('rural lower class') and *unterbäuerliche Bevölkerung* ('sub-peasant population') and a critical assessment thereof, see Mitterauer (1992: 33–41).

10   Since the size of land property itself – on account of varying altitudes (from 630 to 990 metres) and the different quality levels of grazing grounds and arable land – did not constitute a satisfactory criterion, local categorisation into social classes was based on the availability of draft animals:

   • on large farms (*grossi Baun*) horses are used as draft animals;
   • on medium-sized farms (*mittlari Baun*) four to six oxen are held as draft animals;
   • on small farms (*kloani Eachta*) milk cows are used for the same purpose;
   • on 'cow shacks' (*Kuahaisl*) one or two milk cows are held for one's own supply of milk, and these are also used as draft animals;

- on 'goat shacks' (*Goasshaisl*) a few goats and one or two pigs are held, but no draft animals;
- 'detached cottages' (*I-Haisl*) are found next to many large farms; these tiny huts are used by old farming couples that have been granted a life annuity (*Altbauern im Ausgedinge*). (If there is no retired farming couple on the farm, these shacks are sublet to poorer families (*Inwohner*), in exchange for a given number of working days.)

Farm-hands (*Deastleit*) were either male or female, and were, by definition, always unmarried. If they married, their social status changed and they either became *Inwohner* or they moved, through marriage, into a bigger house.

11 Handicapped people and people no longer physically able to work were handed on from farm to farm and received food and lodging for a limited period of time. The duration of their stay varied according to the size of the farm they were put up at (Ehmer 1990: 36–8). In the area studied, the local administrative authorities would assign farms and determine the duration of the stay for each of the individuals to be cared for as *Einleger*. Such persons were more frequently handicapped individuals than old people. The last *Einleger* in Unterweissenbach was taken to an old-age home in 1965.

12 Since children could be substituted by farm-hands – Mitterauer (1986: 261) uses the expression 'imperative of role completion'.

13 Here I am adopting the position of Jack Goody (1983: 19–21), according to which dowry to the out-marrying heirs at the time of marriage, the transfer of the farm during the parents' life-time and inheritance itself are merely facets of a single fact, i.e. the transfer of the patrimony to the next generation.

14 In this context, 'isogamy' refers to the selection of spouses from families of similar economical status; Weber-Kellermann (1974: 147) uses the term 'property-oriented endogamy'.

15 All family and farm names have been changed by the author.

16 At least since the issue of a patent by Emperor Joseph II on 3 April 1787, which ruled that the eldest son had to take over the farm (Kretschmer and Piegler 1965: 3; Brauneder 1980: 61).

17 Phrases such as 'it was said' or 'they said' might well be worth a separate investigation. They almost invariably refer to a normative instance when one ought to obey, but is unable to. It references an authority that decides what is to be done and which must not be questioned. These phrases relate to a code of local concepts that are characterised by an ambivalent relationship (both subordinate and rebellious) *vis-à-vis* the 'authorities'.

18 It contains an explicit ban of joint property held by spouses, which cannot be circumvented by transfer contracts (see Jagschitz 1980: 74).

19 Weber-Kellermann (1974: 151) concludes that to think in economic and labour terms is also reflected in the rural self-image of the family as a union of those persons who, through their labour and property, contribute to the individual farm estate.

20 Historical sources provide a number of examples for transfers of property to non-relatives in Austria. Ehmer (1990: 29), therefore, regards the

interpretation of the retirement annuity as a 'domestic form of old-age pension' as justified.

21  Ilien and Jeggle (1978) describe this mechanism – which often has severe consequences for women – using the example of a western German partible inheritance region, which, for a number of reasons, cannot be directly compared with the area under consideration.

22  The retirement annuity is known as *Ausnahm* (excluded property) in the village under study. It refers to those parts of forests, meadows, services and foodstuffs that the old farming couple has excluded from the assets upon transfer of the farm.

23  In this context, it must be noted that a lot has changed since the introduction of the statutory old-age pension scheme for farmers in 1959. Now the retired farmers have resources other than the farm estate at their disposal. The retirement annuity is typically limited to free food and housing, since major material allowances would reduce the amount of pension that can be claimed.

24  On average, one-third of the farm areas in the study region consists of forest.

25  In my interviews, there is ample evidence for this notion. As to the far-reaching effects of these conceptions, see the final chapters of Aistleitner (1986: 137–9) who, referring to the Mühlviertel, characterises the overwhelming majority of farming units forced to earn extra money as 'sweat shops' (*Schinderbetriebe*), since the families continued to operate the farms like full-scale units and tried to cover the deficit arising from the operation of the farm with income earned from non-farm work. If such an economic conduct is pursued over a period of twenty or more years, it certainly has to be motivated, to a large extent, by factors other than economic ones.

26  According to information I received from a civil servant working for the neighbouring community of St Leonhard, such stipulations were part of almost all transfer contracts concluded between 1945 and 1970. She knew of this fact because the signatures of the retired couple were required in order to obtain subsidised loans from the province or the community.

27  About a year ago, I told people approximately my age about this 'custom', which I had thought to be obsolete; they, however, reported a recent attempt to provide a 'sworn' bachelor from our village with a wife by this method.

28  Comparisons made in the literature between rural or pre-industrial marriages of convenience, on the one hand, and modern bourgeois marriages based on a 'love match', on the other, often simplify matters to such an extent that they lead to completely wrong conclusions, especially when they claim general validity. A good example is Shorter's (1978: 260) statement that 'on the farm husband and wife lived together in an atmosphere of silent hostility and aloofness'.

29  I assume that this subordination usually happened without friction, 'voluntarily' and with the consent of the persons involved. Given the fact that people only exist in social environments, 'free will' has to be defined in relation to the prevailing social organisation and its inherent contradictions.

30  Brigitte Menne (1994: 190) provides an in-depth discussion of the background and the reasons preventing women from giving in to 'love', if this

means accepting life-long hard work without income possibilities of their own, and without social or old-age insurance of their own, but with reduced mobility and limited social contacts.

31 In this context, Chayanov (Tschajanow 1923: 37–41) referred to survival strategies used by family farmers in situations of crisis, which consisted of efforts to increase work output and, at the same time, reduce the level of consumption and the needs of the family members.

# References

Aistleitner, J. (1986) *Formen und Auswirkungen des bäuerlichen Nebenerwerbs. Das Mühlviertel als Beispiel*, Innsbruck: Selbstverlag des Instituts für Geographie der Universität Innsbruck.

Bourdieu, P. (1987) *Sozialer Sinn. Kritik der theoretischen Vernunft*, Frankfurt am Main: Suhrkamp.

Brauneder, W. (1980) 'Die Entwicklung des bäuerlichen Erbrechtes', in A. Dworsky and H. Schider (eds) *Die Ehre Erbhof. Analyse einer jungen Tradition*, Vienna: Residenz Verlag.

Brunner, O. (1978) 'Vom "ganzen Haus" zur "Familie"', in H. Rosenbaum (ed.) *Seminar: Familie und Gesellschaftsstruktur*, Frankfurt am Main: Suhrkamp.

Burguière, A. and Lebrun, F. (1997) 'Die Vielfalt der Familienmodelle in Europa', in A. Burguière, C. Klapisch-Zuber, M. Segalen and F. Zonabend (eds) *Geschichte der Familie, Band 3: Neuzeit*, Frankfurt am Main: Campus.

Carsten, J. and Hugh-Jones, S. (1995) *About the House: Lévi-Strauss and Beyond*, Cambridge, UK: Cambridge University Press.

Chayanov, A. (1986 [1966]) *The Theory of Peasant Economy*, second edn, Madison: Wisconsin University Press.

DaMatta, R. (1994) 'Some biased remarks on interpretivism: A view from Brazil', in R. Borofsky (ed.) *Assessing Cultural Anthropology*, New York: McGraw-Hill.

Ehmer, J. (1990) *Sozialgeschichte des Alters*, Frankfurt am Main: Suhrkamp.

Gaunt, D. (1982) 'Formen der Altersversorgung in Bauernfamilien Nord- und Mitteleuropas', in M. Mitterauer and R. Sieder (eds) *Historische Familienforschung*, Frankfurt am Main: Suhrkamp.

Goody, J. (1976) *Production and Reproduction: Comparative Study of the Domestic Domain*, Cambridge, UK: Cambridge University Press.

—— (1983) *The Development of the Family and Marriage in Europe*, Cambridge, UK: Cambridge University Press.

Haan, H. de (1994) *In the Shadow of the Tree: Kinship, Property and Inheritance among Farm Families*, Amsterdam: Het Spinhuis.

Hettlage, R. (1989) 'Bauerngesellschaften. Die bäuerliche Lebenswelt als soziologisches Exotikum?', in R. Hettlage (ed.) *Die post-traditionale Welt der Bauern*, Frankfurt am Main: Campus Verlag.

Ilien, A. and Jeggle, U. (1978) *Leben auf dem Dorf. Zur Sozialgeschichte des Dorfes und Sozialpsychologie seiner Bewohner*, Opladen: Westdeutscher Verlag.

Inhetveen, H. and Blasche, M. (1983) *Frauen in der kleinbäuerlichen Landwirtschaft*, Opladen: Westdeutscher Verlag.

Jagschitz, G. (1980) 'Erbhof und Politik', in A. Dworsky and H. Schider (eds) *Die Ehre Erbhof. Analyse einer jungen Tradition*, Vienna: Residenz Verlag.

Kathrein, G. (1990) *Anerbenrecht*, Vienna: Manz.

Kretschmer, I. (1980) 'Verbreitung und Bedeutung der bäuerlichen Erbsitten', in A. Dworsky and H. Schider (eds) *Die Ehre Erbhof. Analyse einer jungen Tradition*, Vienna: Residenz Verlag.

Kretschmer, I. and Piegler, J. (1965) 'Bäuerliches Erbrecht', in Wissenschaftliche Kommission für den Volkskundeatlas (eds) *Kommentar zum Österreichischen Volkskundeatlas, 2.Lieferung, Bl.17*, Vienna: Böhlau.

Medick, H. (1978) 'Die proto-industrielle Familienwirtschaft', in P. Kriedte, H. Medick and J. Schlumbohm (eds) *Industrialisierung vor der Industrialisierung. Gewerbliche Warenproduktion auf dem Land in der Formationsperiode des Kapitalismus*, Göttingen: Vandenhoeck & Ruprecht.

Medick, H. and Sabean, D.W. (eds) (1988) *Interest and Emotion: Essays on the Study of Family and Kinship*, Cambridge, UK: Cambridge University Press.

Menne, B. (1994) *Wir Frauen am Land. Ergebnisse regionaler Kultur- und Bildungsarbeit im Mühlviertel*, Vienna: Wiener Frauenverlag.

Mitterauer, M. (1986) 'Formen ländlicher Familienwirtschaft im österreichischen Raum', in J. Ehmer and M. Mitterauer (eds) *Familienstruktur und Arbeitsorganisation in ländlichen Gesellschaften*, Vienna: Böhlau.

—— (1990) *Historisch-Anthropologische Familienforschung. Fragestellungen und Zugangsweisen*, Vienna: Böhlau.

—— (1992) *Familie und Arbeitsteilung. Historischvergleichende Studien*, Vienna: Böhlau.

Ortmayr, N. (1984) 'Beim Bauern im Dienst', in H.C. Ehalt (ed.) *Geschichte von Unten*, Graz: Böhlau.

—— (1986) 'Ländliches Gesinde in Oberösterreich 1918–1938', in J. Ehmer and M. Mitterauer (eds) *Familienstruktur und Arbeitsorganisation in ländlichen Gesellschaften*, Vienna: Böhlau.

—— (1989) 'Woodland peasants: Ecological adaptation in an Austrian peasant community 1870–1938', *Ethnologia Europaea* 19: 105–24.

Piegler, J. (1959) 'Die ländlichen Dienstbotentermine', in Wissenschaftliche Kommission für den Volkskundeatlas (ed.) *Kommentar zum Österreichischen Volkskundeatlas, 1.Lieferung, Bl. 5 und 6*, Vienna: Böhlau.

Planck, U. (1978) 'Die Eigenart der Bauernfamilie und die bäuerliche Familienverfassug', in H. Rosenbaum (ed.) *Seminar: Familie und Gesellschaftsstruktur. Materialien zu den sozioökonomischen Bedingungen von Familienformen*, Frankfurt am Main: Suhrkamp.

Redfield, R. (1956) *Peasant Society and Culture: An Anthropological Approach to Civilization*, Chicago: University of Chicago Press.

Riehl, W.H. (1855) *Die Naturgeschichte des Volks als Grundlage einer deutschen Social-Politik, Band 3: Die Familie*, Stuttgart: Cotta.

Rosenbaum, H. (1982) *Formen der Familie*, Frankfurt am Main: Suhrkamp.

Sabean, D.W. (1990) *Property, Production and Family in Neckarhausen, 1700–1870*, Cambridge, UK: Cambridge University Press.

Sandgruber, R. (1983) 'Innerfamiliale Einkommens- und Konsumaufteilung', in P. Borscheid and H.J. Teuteberg (eds) *Ehe, Liebe, Tod. Zum Wandel der Familie, der Geschlechts- und Generationsbeziehungen in der Neuzeit*, Münster: Coppenrath.

Schulte, R. (1988) 'Infanticide in rural Bavaria in the 19th century', in H. Medick and D.W. Sabean (eds) *Interest and Emotion: Essays on the Study of Family and Kinship*, Cambridge, UK: Cambridge University Press.

Segalen, M. (1986) *Historical Anthropology of the Family*, Cambridge, UK: Cambridge University Press.

—— (1991) *Fifteen Generations of Bretons: Kinship and Society in Lower Brittany 1720–1980*, Cambridge, UK: Cambridge University Press.

Shanin, T. (1987) 'Introduction: Peasantry as a concept', in T. Shanin (ed.) *Peasants and Peasant Societies: Selected Readings*, second edn, Oxford: Basil Blackwell.

Shorter, E. (1978) 'Bäuerliches Heiratsverhalten und Ehebeziehungen in der vorindustriellen Gesellschaftsstruktur', in H. Rosenbaum (ed.) *Seminar: Familie und Gesellschaftsstruktur. Materialien zu den sozioökonomischen Bedingungen von Familienformen*, Frankfurt am Main: Suhrkamp.

Sieder, R. (1987) *Sozialgeschichte der Familie*, Frankfurt am Main: Suhrkamp.

Tschajanow, A. (1923) *Die Lehre von der bäuerlichen Wirtschaft. Versuch einer Theorie der Familienwirtschaft im Landbau*, Berlin: Parey.

Weber-Kellermann, I. (1974) *Die deutsche Familie. Versuch einer Sozialgeschichte*, Frankfurt am Main: Suhrkamp.

Zonabend, F. (1987) 'Verwandtschaft in der anthropologischen Forschung Frankreichs', in I. Chiva and U. Jeggle (eds) *Deutsche Volkskunde – Französische Ethnologie – Zwei Standortbestimmungen*, Frankfurt am Main: Campus Verlag.

# Chapter 5

# Kinship, reciprocity and the world market[1]

## Jenny B. White

In working-class neighbourhoods of Istanbul, Turkey, kinship is meta-phorically conferred on those people who do what kin do: that is, participate in relations of collective reciprocal assistance with no calcu-lation of return. This 'fictive' kinship draws in resources, whether they be labour, goods, food, money, information or services from unrelated outsiders, and is crucial for the economic survival of the urban poor. 'Fictive' kinship has also been harnessed to the world economy by providing a model for relations of production between home-workers and home-work distributors producing for export. By constructing their piecework labour (production paid by the piece) as an expression of their social role – as a form of collective reciprocal assistance – rather than as 'work for pay', women avoid the onus of working outside the home or taking over their husbands' role as provider. The male distrib-utors also 'help' their neighbours by providing them with income opportunities. The relationship is couched in the language of kinship.

Kinship in this sense is not necessarily a correlate of biogenetic or agnatic ties, but rather a culturally defined domain. What is shared is not blood, but labour and obligation. In David Schneider's ground-breaking re-analysis of Yapese kinship, he demonstrated that what had initially been construed by anthropologists to be a social system grounded in patrilineal kinship, on closer inspection of the terminology and explanations of the Yapese themselves, revealed itself to be based on relations to a particular area of land and on exchange, rather than on genealogy. The right to play the roles that had previously been glossed as parent–child was earned by working the land properly and by engaging in constant exchange over a period of time. That is, Yapese kinship 'is more one of *doing* than of *being*. It is based largely on the interaction, the doing, of the exchange and less on the state of being, of having some substance, quality, or attribute' (Schneider

1984: 75; emphasis in original). Thus, a wife or child who fails to do the customarily expected work can be 'thrown away' (Schneider 1984: 29): that is, lose all rights of belonging and rights to and in the land and to the obligation of others.

In Turkey, kin (*akraba*) are at one level related by blood. These relations are mindfully sorted out at social functions and people interact with one another to a large extent on the basis of their biogenetic and agnatic relationships. However, a simultaneous pattern of kinship (*akrabalık*), which I call 'fictive' kinship, draws on the term's Arabic root meaning of 'close',[2] and colours and extends kinship beyond the domain of socially formalised relations. Furthermore, both domains of kinship are rooted in labour, and 'belonging-ness' in either can be modified on the basis of the member's contributions to the community. This means that such people as one's neighbours with whom one has long-term reciprocal relations of exchange and mutual obligation become *akraba*, with rights to one's labour and resources. In the same way, blood *akraba* who have not contributed their own time, labour and resources, while remaining kin, may be refused a share of a kin-member's resources.

These two domains of kinship, while discrete, overlap and share the hierarchical context of age and gender relations in Turkish society.[3] Not surprisingly, age- and gender-based roles, like kinship, for which they provide the relational vocabulary, are expressed to a large extent as labour given and received. Both kinship domains are also implicated in the unequal relations inherent in capitalist production. The form of economic activity described in this chapter, home production for the world market, exemplifies the intersection of the two domains of kinship with gender and capitalism. The home-work production system is based on a workshop generally organised around gender roles within a biological family. This system also incorporates unrelated neighbours as piecework producers within an idiom of closeness, represented as kinship. This measure of belonging gives *akraba* rights to the long-term assistance and support of neighbours, regardless of whether they are related by birth or marriage.

While home production is at base a capitalist relationship, and payment is eventually expected by the women for their products, the participants also absorb the labour and money involved in piecework into a cycle of reciprocal exchange that strengthens social bonds and creates ever new strands in the web of obligation that is the source of each individual's long-term security within the community. Ironically, insistence that the women's production activities are simply socially contributed labour (as expected among kin) facilitates the exploitation of that labour, since the women do not keep track of the time spent working or feel free to demand a higher price per piece. The money and labour involved in the short-term cycle of economic activity (which involves a desire for individual profit) is thus, through the alchemy of kinship, converted to serve the reproduction of the long-term cycle of social solidarity (where money and labour become morally positive (Parry and Block 1989)). This also reinforces traditional gender roles, despite women's income.

Forms of economic activity that are based on family and community ties act to build and maintain community, but are flexible enough to accommodate change. It is this flexibility, without loss of security, that makes such economic activities popular among the poor, for whom family and community provide the only buffer against failure. For women, this means being able to earn a wage without threatening their honour and reputation as good family and community members. However, economic activities where the division of labour is based on family and community ties also reinforce the power of the patriarchal family over women, even if they earn a substantial income, which is absorbed by the family.

Kinship in Turkey is widely characterised by patriarchy and the patterns of domination by age and gender that this implies. The ideological construction of labour as social identity (as modelled by relations within the family) and the relations of domination that underlie this construction can also be perceived in certain economic behaviour outside of the family. The ideology of labour is a mythical structure that makes relations of domination and exploitation seem a 'natural' part of the social and religious cosmology of Turkish life. At the same time, it provides the means for a long-term survival strategy within and around sets of institutions and material conditions that cannot be relied on to ensure reproduction of the basic social unit, the family.

The practical success of this scheme of perception and thought, which makes up the cultural understanding of labour, contributes to its reproduction through socialisation and to its naturalisation under new material conditions (such as those that have come about since the 1980s when Turkey opened its economy to the world market). Relations of domination that are learned and expressed within this ideology of labour are thereby transplanted (or grafted) to new economic conditions involving capitalist markets.

In Istanbul squatter areas, unequal relations, relations of domination and even exploitation within the family workshop and neighbourhood piecework projects, much as within the family itself, are euphemised as purely personal (although not necessarily individual) relations through which no profit is obtained by anyone, but rather labour, money and time are freely given and no immediate return is expected. The concept of the gift is thereby used to misrecognise both moral and monetary debts. Rather than seeking closure through counter-gifts, people try to keep relations open-ended: that is, to remain indebted. Both reciprocity and indebtedness are expressed and codified as social and religious moral imperatives.

## Patriarchy and the absorption of women's labour

The patrilocally extended household has generally been associated with the development and reproduction of classic patriarchy (Kandiyoti 1988). However, the actual structural arrangement of family life may vary without affecting the forms of control and subordination associated with the patriarchal family system. In the traditional family, the senior man has authority over all other family members, including younger men.[4] A girl is given in marriage into a household headed by her husband's father (through his physical presence or *de facto*). She is subordinate to her husband, his kin and her mother-in-law. A woman can establish her place in the patriliny and her economic security only by bearing sons. Kandiyoti adds that 'the patrilineage totally appropriates both women's labour and progeny and renders their work and contribution to production invisible' (Kandiyoti 1988: 279). The hardships that younger women endure are eventually superseded by the control and authority they exert over their own daughters-in-law. The cyclical nature of power through the life cycle encourages women to internalise patriarchal values.

The valuation of restrictions such as seclusion and 'veiling' as marks of status and honour further reinforces women's collusion in maintaining patriarchal practices. Seclusion deepens women's economic dependence on men because it blocks access to alternative economic practices such as trading activities[5] that involve movement outside of the domestic space (Kandiyoti 1988). In Turkey, seclusion is generally less strictly defined as the designation of arenas of activity appropriate to men and women. The complete seclusion of purdah is rare. Veiling also takes many forms, with various degrees and means of covering body, hair and face. Within a single neighbourhood it is possible to find a range of dress, from short sleeves and uncovered hair to body-enveloping coats and voluminous headscarves. Nevertheless, considerations of modesty and honour affect women's willingness to take employment outside of the immediate neighbourhood: they do so at the risk of their and their families' reputations.

Relations of domination within the family, such as those between mother-in-law and daughter-in-law or between husband and wife, are naturalised, in part, through their daily enacting in relations involving labour. A woman, for instance, often cleans her mother-in-law's home as well as her own. Generalised reciprocity – mutual assistance without calculation of return – is a crucial part of the definition of kinship, and for women kinship relations are enacted in large part through labour obligations.

Norms of reciprocity are embedded in family and other communal roles, including economic roles. Labour plays an important part in women's experience of reciprocity. Women's social and gender identity (their identity as good women, as good neighbours, daughters, mothers, wives or sisters) is very much tied up with labour and service. These are an important part of the socialisation of young girls, and women express and maintain their membership in family and community, in part, through contributing their labour and service to family and neighbours without expecting any specific return.

Young girls do housework, care for siblings and prepare elaborate trousseaux that involve years of skilled and intensive needlework, and many also do piecework or work in a workshop. At marriage a girl's labour is transferred to her husband's family, so her skills and industriousness are important considerations when a marriage is being negotiated. The girl's trousseau is displayed when she marries, so that people can form an opinion of her character from her skill.

A woman's role as wife and mother is also expressed through labour and service. While there is great social pressure to marry and to remain married, marriage is also an alluring prospect. A girl attains adult status through marriage. A married woman is a respectable woman, a person whose opinions carry weight among other similar women. A married woman has use of her own home and can receive guests (relatives or neighbour women) from whom she can take the status of serving them. 'To serve' (*hizmet etmek*) in one's own home is inextricably bound up with status; to 'be served' is an honour. Women serve their husbands, their children, in-laws and guests.

After marriage, a woman's ties with her natal family are generally expected to become attenuated, and her duties and obligations are transferred from her natal home to her husband's household and to his parents and other kin. However, even though a married woman owes her complete attention and labour to her husband, children and mother-in-law, the mother–daughter relationship remains important even after marriage. This results in competing demands for a woman's time and labour, which the woman (and her natal family) must negotiate carefully in order to avoid friction with her husband and his mother.

A married woman has many of the same responsibilities and duties as before marriage, just as a married man has many of the same privileges. A man is served by his wife instead of (or in addition to) his mother and sisters. A woman serves her husband, his relatives (particularly his mother), male children and their own guests, just as before marriage she served her parents, younger or male siblings and her parents' guests. A married woman's range of movement outside of the home remains constricted, just as it was restricted by her father and brothers outside of her natal home. She may, however, enter a cycle of visiting close neighbours and relatives that provides much movement outside the home, if not far afield.

The most important benefit of marriage (for both men and women) is children. The birth of a child marks the continuity of his family to the father, and the beginning of her family to the mother. Children represent many things: the conferring of true 'adulthood' on their parents; community respect and status; economic continuity and security; and, later, a sharing of labour and resources. Once a child is born, a woman's labour and responsibility increase, but this is seen as an investment in future *maddi* and *manevi* support: that is, the financial and labour contributions and moral support expected from one's children when they become adults. A son is the ripening fruit of a woman's labour, which binds him to her by means of an enormous reciprocal debt that can never be repaid. This sense of indebtedness to one's parents and especially of a man to his mother is commonly and openly expressed, as, for example, when a man chooses to heed the time or labour demands of his mother over those of his wife, explaining, 'I can never, never repay everything [my parents] did for me.' The debt of a child to its mother is also encoded in the 'milk debt' (*süt hakkı*),[6] a lifelong debt of service in return for the 'unrepayable' service and sacrifice of the mother, symbolised by breast milk. A mother can curse her son or daughter for disobeying her in a serious matter by saying she will never forgive the milk debt (*hakkımı helal etmem*). This is a severe curse and never used lightly. A mother provides for her son physically, emotionally and, if she is able, financially throughout his life. Even mothers who do not 'work' use their income from piecework or sell their gold bracelets (obtained as part of a woman's marriage portion) to meet a son's debt or help him set up in business or get married. Although mothers often help daughters financially as well, they are expected to be supported by their husbands.

## Kinship as metaphor

The expression of social and gender identity through labour is one aspect of a web of mutual support that characterises life in squatter areas and working-class neighbourhoods inhabited by rural migrants. It ensures that individual needs are met by the group and provides people with long-term security, which seems more reliable than economic investment or monetary savings under the given unstable economic and political conditions. This form of security is crucial for the working class and for women and children, who have fewer resources to fall back on.

Kinship and the group membership it confers are also metaphors that can be extended to non-relatives who do what kin do (visit; assist; give information, advice, loans, time or labour). They may be referred to by kinship terms and, most importantly, given the rights (and duties) of kin – and afforded the security of group membership. Such actual and 'fictive' kinship ties form the foundation for survival of the urban poor. Both real and 'fictive' kinship, expressed as generalised reciprocity, act as positive forces for economic survival, as metaphoric kinship ties pull in resources from unrelated others.

Mutual obligation or indebtedness is a kind of root paradigm (Turner 1974: 67): a cluster of meanings that acts as a cultural map and enables people to find a path in their own culture. This is not the same as an explicit custom. It is not written in children's schoolbooks, although it is omnipresent in admonitions to share, in instruction on how to be a good family member and on what it means to be a man or a woman. A root paradigm is more subtle than a rule; it affects the form, timing and style of people's behaviour. Mutual obligation and the assistance that flows from it are a cultural imperative: a structured disposition to behave in a certain way that is learned through daily practice, through the way people interact, use their bodies and use space (Bourdieu 1979). It is not a rule, but a disposition. People can break rules or bend them, but still be recognisable as members of their community because they share its root paradigm.

People participate in a web of mutual open-ended support that expresses and maintains their membership in family and community. They are constantly doing things for and giving things to others in their family and community without expectation of return from any particular individual. When they need something, someone in the group is expected to provide it. Mutual indebtedness means social relations are kept open-ended: that is, without expectation of closure by a counter-gift. This lack of specificity allows reciprocity to be constructed as a relationship between the individual and the aggregate social group, rather than just between two individuals, the giver and receiver. In this way, reciprocity not only provides access to the resources of a partner in exchange, but also to the resources of an entire group.

What emerges is a wide web of relations, based on obligation and generalised reciprocity. This web binds individuals to each other as a group and gives anyone in the family or community access to labour, goods, food, money, connections, useful information, partners in marriage and other necessities. Participation in such a web of reciprocal obligation creates long-term flexible networks of support and security that can be relied on over the long term, regardless of the ups and downs of the economy. Relations based on obligation and reciprocity, rather than simply on genealogical ties or economic contracts, are broader and more diverse. Such relations can be relied on for long-term commitment, yet are flexible in the face of unforeseen events.

## The business of reciprocity

An old man came into a small electric shop in a working-class neighbourhood on the European shore of the Bosphorus and gave the shopkeeper a fishing net he had repaired for him. He asked the shopkeeper for a length of electrical wire and left without paying. The shopkeeper told him the price as he walked out of the door. When I asked if the wire was in exchange for fixing the net, the shopkeeper was surprised and explained that the man bought on credit and paid once a month. Reciprocity is never immediate and cannot be seen to be a measured payment for a measured service. Reciprocity by nature is open-ended; otherwise, it is business. The shopkeeper thought it outrageous to even consider 'payment' for a (reciprocal) service like fixing a net.

Since neighbourhood business transactions in Istanbul sometimes lack the markers we associate with business in the West – set prices, the open exchange of goods for money, impersonal service, immediate or scheduled payment – it is easy to confuse business with reciprocal relations. Both appear to be personal relations bound up with sets of mutual obligations (I feel guilty if I patronise a different grocer). Such business transactions have elements of continuity as a result of the 'gentle economic violence' (Bourdieu 1979: 192) that secures long-term clientele through an indebtedness not related to money.

Such business relations differ from non-business reciprocal relations perhaps only in terms of ultimate closure. Business transactions are in one respect temporally complete – selection is followed by payment that, if not immediate, is at least within a specified time. Otherwise the relation is endangered; time, services and credit may be withdrawn. Reciprocal relations depend on lack of closure. Hospitality, labour and services are donated. As Bourdieu pointed out (1979: 183), while return is expected, it cannot be a conscious expectation.

This contradiction of business relations requiring closure while also – as reciprocal relations – requiring open-endedness is resolved (or at least hidden) by the studious avoidance of dwelling on economic symbols such as money or bills of sale during the transaction. However, the difference, as the shopkeeper demonstrated, is clear to everyone. Blurring the boundaries by being too personal in business relations and/or by being too business-like in personal relations is frowned upon.

There are gradations in the amount of profit allowed and the extent of the openness of the business over the reciprocal content of a transaction. These gradations are based on the degree of closeness of the partners in the transaction. Degree of closeness is not necessarily measured in structural terms such as kinship proximity, although this may be an important element, but rather is an expression of a reciprocal debt already built up that has been continually renewed over a long period of time. The reciprocal content of the transaction must appear paramount. While this type of business relation may not be based on kinship or even be expressed as 'fictive' kinship, it is nevertheless an extension of the principles of mutuality and obligation underlying these.

It puzzled me that the vegetable shop owner I usually patronised in my neighbourhood insisted that I pay for my purchases at a later time, when I already had the money to pay him in my hand. At first I refused and pressed him to take the money, because I was afraid that I might forget the amount that I owed him and also because I felt that, if he wouldn't let me pay for my purchases, I would be too embarrassed to shop there any more. It took a long time to overcome my anxiety over what I perceived from my own perspective to be an intrusion of the personal side of our relationship into the business side, thereby endangering the latter. It was only when I noticed the same behaviour – asking me to pay later – on the part of other shopkeepers whom I visited regularly that I realised its significance. By putting off payment, the open-ended (reciprocal and therefore personal) nature of the relationship was highlighted.

Among those 'close' to one another, whether as kin, 'fictive' kin or in 'personal' business relations, the emergence of money and profit too close to the surface of the transaction or relation causes anxiety. The introduction (or recognition) of a naked profit motive may endanger or even end the relationship. If it is necessary for money to change hands between friends or relatives, it must be done accurately and personally, with no apparent profit on either side by giving too much or too little. What is said and not said about the business aspect of a transaction can cause anxiety or shame, and can be manipulated to be an insult. Talking about or disputing money openly implies that the relationship has closure and is therefore business only, as between strangers. Time is a crucial element; if payment is immediate, the transaction loses any social value since the reciprocity on which social relations rest can be neither created nor maintained.

This is not the case with a gift (*hediye*: present), which is often immediately reciprocated to show that it is appreciated. This is much to the dismay of the Western gift-giver in whose own culture gifts must be returned after an interval of time has elapsed, so as not to give the impression that one gift 'buys' the other. What is exchanged in a reciprocal relation in Turkey are not gifts (presents), but debts, the indebtedness calling forth feelings of guilt and obligation to cement a sense both of solidarity (as family, friends, acquaintances or non-strangers) and dependence. It is not surprising that the ritual exchange of gifts (as in the sense of a birthday or anniversary present) is not common, given the widespread and continuous circulation of goods and labour that characterises working-class Istanbul society.

Van Baal (1975), in his review of theories of the gift, argues that while goods exchanged as gifts aim to strengthen social bonds, the goal of trade is fundamentally different. The goal of trade is a balanced reciprocity of direct exchange, although sometimes with the possibility of delayed requital. Trade, in this view, is impersonal, ideally balanced and a matter of bargaining rather than gift exchange, the parties dispersing afterwards without any further obligation to one another (Van Baal 1975: 39). Extrapolating from the difference between Trobriand *gimwali* trade and other forms of Trobriand exchange, he writes, 'Even in the case of traders who deal regularly with each other (not uncommon in economically more advanced societies) the relationship remains commercial, distinct from the personal ties that may have developed in the course of prolonged contacts' (Van Baal 1975: 42). Trade, however, may be facilitated by being associated with, or situated within, a ceremonialised environment that assures peace and increases contacts. 'The occasion to trade, if it does not present itself by chance, must be purposively created' (Van Baal 1975: 42). Van Baal gives the example of the institution of trade-friendship in New Guinea, where trade-friends are 'like relatives', who exchange presents and help each other acquire desired commodities. 'The trade-friendship is a mutual gift-relation that promotes opportunities for commercial barter' (Van Baal 1975: 42).

According to Van Baal, then, trade differs fundamentally from gift-exchange (although the latter can function to facilitate the former) in that trade 'does not have, nor is it meant to have a unifying effect' (Van Baal 1975: 43), whereas the purpose of gift-exchange is to establish or strengthen a relation between the persons making the exchange. Trade relations in Turkey's poor urban neighbourhoods, however, evince a more intrinsic link between the development of social relations through reciprocity and the exchange of commodities through bargaining. The giving of personal information and assistance, time and tea, as well as the insistence on 'paying later', are all aimed at developing social bonds along with their attendant reciprocal obligations. This search for open-ended reciprocity, even in what is clearly understood to be trade (with ultimate closure), is not merely designed to enhance the loyalty of customers or to facilitate trade. Rather, trade relations, like all reciprocal relations, foster the social solidarity and mutual dependence that are the bedrock of social identity in Istanbul squatter areas and provide strategies for the practice of survival.

## The morality of debt

It is precisely the putting-off of the counter-gift (I include here labour and other services) that joins people and groups in elastic but durable relations, creating both solidarity and dependence in social relationships ranging from those within the family to those in the market-place. The counter-gift is delayed indefinitely or temporarily, depending on the relative personal/business content of the relation. In a sense, it is less an exchange of gifts than an exchange of debts. Children are bonded to their mothers by the unrepayable milk debt that is predicated, in large part, on the labour their mother has expended for them since their birth. In business transactions among friends, money debts are desirable (if temporary) markers of a willingness to become personally indebted that is the hallmark of friendship.

While indebtedness is intrinsic to reciprocity and necessary for maintaining the open-endedness of the social relations upon which social solidarity (and consequent security) rests, there is also a strong moral imperative to release the other person from reciprocal obligations. This is done in a ritual fashion in order to avoid the suspicion that favours have been done in order to get something in return: that is, to incur unlawful profit – profit that has been obtained through coercion. The avoidance of apparent profit in personal relations is codified as a ritual verbal exchange between people who have been together, for example, as friends or as business associates, and who are parting. Each person says to the other '*Hakkın kaldıysa helal et* ', which can be loosely translated as 'If any unjust profit (from our relationship) remains with you, give up your lawful claim to it', or 'If you retain any (reciprocal) moral debt (to me for things I have done for/given to you), let (the profit) be religiously lawful. I have given it to you with my heart and of my free will.' The phrase '*Hakkını helal et* ' is difficult to translate exactly because the words that comprise it have multiple meanings; *Hak* means right, justice and law as well as share, due, remuneration and fee. *Helal* means canonically lawful. When combined with the verb 'to make' (*etmek*), it means to give up a legitimate claim to another and not to begrudge something done or given.

Reciprocal relations between people, as well as business relations involving money and profit, are understood, then, by reference to a religious ethic wherein profit is unlawful unless that which has profited the person was given freely and fairly. If person A has done more for person B than person B has for person A, person B remains under a moral obligation (*manevi borç*: literally 'moral debt') to person A. This means that person A has more *hak*, more right. Upon parting, such an imbalance must be corrected because otherwise person A has done more good (deeds) and could remind person B of them. This means that person A has not done these things from the heart, but wanted something.

The ritual forgiving of moral debts does not imply a disapproval of indebtedness or a desire for closure in the relationship, but rather a fear of making conscious what must remain hidden (or misrecognised) in order that reciprocity continues to be seen as a social relation devoid of naked economic (unlawful, profit-oriented) motives. This ritual abnegation of the profit motive points up the importance of maintaining the personal (and reciprocal) nature of all transactions, be they between friends or between business partners. Only among strangers is a market transaction allowed to be nakedly economic (and profit-oriented): that is, featuring immediate payment for measured goods or services. There is, after such a transaction, no further expectation, no debt and no personal relation. Only after repeated transactions of this kind between the same people does a reciprocal relation begin to emerge, as the 'buyer' has shown loyalty to the 'seller'. After someone has established a pattern of patronising the same shop, the 'buyer' can expect to be extended credit, given a reduction in price, offered tea and conversation – all markers of a reciprocal relation. These can be seen as offers of indebtedness to create a personal/business bond. As the history of reciprocity in the relationship accumulates, the business relation takes on elements of personal obligation (for example, to buy from a particular shop). The naked economic aspects of the relation (buying, selling, money and profit) become euphemised as personal relations of loyalty, trust and membership in a group as friends or symbolic kin.

Whether the relation is purely personal, as within a family, or relatively impersonal, as between almost-strangers, the exchange of debts allows each person to partake in the solidarity, mutual dependency and consequent survival of the group as a whole. Each person in Istanbul working-class society belongs to and is busily developing and strengthening membership in many such groups. As a consequence, outsiders find it frustrating to attempt even such relatively simple projects as having a telephone connected or picking up a parcel from the post office, because the outsider does not have access to the chain of people linked through reciprocal indebtedness that ordinarily eases access to these goods or services.

When two strangers meet, often the first thing they do is to verbally sift through a list of people they might know in common. They are looking for a reciprocal link on which to base a personal relationship. Reciprocity, then, not only gives access to a particular group, but also to a varied web of relations, which are linked through reciprocal indebtedness between people that the individual may not know directly. Before attempting any project or major purchase, a person sifts through all of the connections at his or her disposal and sets in motion one or more relations (calling in a debt, so to speak, thereby creating a new debt) to activate the strands to which they are connected, with the ultimate purpose of getting as close as possible to the source of the desired service or product. To connect a telephone, the ideal contact is a friend or 'friend of a friend' (*torpil*: push, influence) who works for the telephone company. The service is thereby made possible (at the time of my research, it could take up to six years to have a phone connected without a *torpil*), or the product acquired more cheaply.

Debt exchange creates a web of relations in which every individual has access to different strands of debt-based relations. The strands available to an individual are constantly being added to and sometimes being blocked as new relations are formed and old ones cut. Like gifts exchanged, debts are created by individuals meeting face-to-face. Debt-exchange differs from gift-exchange, however, in that debts can be called in from individuals that one has never met through a reciprocal strand. Thus, to have a telephone installed, a person may activate a strand of many people that begins with a friend and ends with a complete stranger who is employed by the telephone company and who facilitates the installation.

Gift-exchange may involve chains of people, as in Malinowski's classic description of the Trobriand Kula ring (1922). Nevertheless, it ultimately takes place between two people: the gift giver and the giver of the counter-gift, with the ball being, so to speak, in one court or the other. The gift is always followed by a counter-gift (Van Baal 1975: 23). In debt-exchange, on the other hand, the ball is always in play. That is, while gifts must be returned, debts can be passed on. The individual's position in a family web and community web of reciprocal debt is continually shifting and being renegotiated. There is no closure and no final and direct return of a gift (except in an exchange of presents).

The currency of negotiation among women is primarily labour. Women's preparation of food for other women's weddings, engagements, birth celebrations and other ceremonies, for example, is not so much a gift of food as a contribution that assures that those women are included in the web of mutual support that provides for the redistribution of necessities of life such as food, labour, information, children in marriage and so on. Food preparation is not a gift that must be reciprocated in kind at a later time, but one of many varied means of access to a web of indebtedness that underlies the process of survival.

Membership in relations of indebtedness involves one in relations of power and domination. Bourdieu writes that 'giving is also a way of possessing (a gift which is not matched by a counter-gift creates a lasting bond)' (Bourdieu 1979: 195). He argues that this is a form of reconversion of economic capital into symbolic capital – a source of power. Power, in this case, is not a male–female construction, nor is it related to public/private contexts. It is, rather, an individual mobilisation and strategic manipulation of the reciprocal social web within which power is distributed. While public and private spheres do act in working-class Istanbul as strong ideological (and physical) constructs that reinforce gender and age role differences, all members of society have access to some degree of power through the manipulation of reciprocal debts. Individuals are usually both dominated and dominant depending on their position in the strands of reciprocal relations that have been activated.

Relations of domination, then, in the sphere of economic behaviour as well as within the family, may be euphemised as relations of kinship, 'fictive' kinship or as an extension of principles of reciprocity undergirding them. The coercive power of economic relations is misrecognised as reciprocal obligation, just as within the family labour exploitation is misrecognised as obligation inherent in the role identity of family members. In both cases, power and domination are played out simultaneously at multiple levels, whereby an individual can be both dominant and dominated at the same time.

Power is a process encoded in the shifting web of family and social relations. That is, power is created by all members of the society through the manipulation of reciprocal debts, but is at the same time limited in its potential practice by this very definition. Power can be practised only within the parameters of a social web from which there is no escape. Reciprocity and the exchange of debts (and attendant obligations) are a source of power and thus domination (and exploitation) in society. Within the family, exploitation is euphemised as obligations embedded in role identity. In economic behaviour, business and the extraction of profit are euphemized as obligations inherent in kinship, 'fictive' kinship and friendship.

## Informal economics

Piecework is a production system based on both the assimilation of labour obligations into women's identity within the family, and on the euphemisation of business as 'fictive' kinship. Piecework and family labour are one way in which the web of reciprocal obligations and relations of indebtedness provides support to individuals within groups and within society as a whole in what appear to be insupportable economic circumstances. The labour of women and children is associated with their identity as group members and is consequently devalued as a resource. The labour relations themselves are generally

euphemised as (actual or 'fictive') kinship. This supports the suggestion of Friedmann (1986) that the deployment of resources within
small-scale commodity production under capitalism is governed by a
kinship logic. I would add that in the Istanbul squatter and working-
class districts this kinship logic extends to persons who are not kin but
who are in a reciprocal relationship with one another, regardless of
whether this relationship involves services, labour or money (as in the
exchange of labour for money in piecework production). These are
often incorporated in the production system as 'fictive' kin.

Family labour or home-work in Istanbul is organised in a number of
different ways. Small-scale production using family labour in its least
complex manifestation can mean simply an individual producing articles in the home that have been requested by and are sold to friends
and neighbours. An individual (male or female) works at home – knitting, sewing, stitching, filling car batteries, doing repairs, woodworking
and so on – for neighbours or for friends. A family might also co-
ordinate production by neighbours to fill an order for items requested
by a merchant from outside of the neighbourhood. The transition to
piecework production is fluid because the middleman is often a relative
or a neighbour who acts as a central conduit for materials and orders
obtained from outside of the neighbourhood, and for collecting and
delivering the completed products and obtaining payment for them.
Some of this money is then distributed among the neighbours at a set
rate per piece produced. The rest is retained by the family of the
distributor and is generally used to buy status items such as a video
recorder or a car, or to add another storey to the family house. The
family might co-ordinate the production and sale of these articles from
their home or might operate out of a small workshop. In some cases
the workshop is a room set aside within the home or a room built on
to the house especially for this purpose. This type of production is
locally based and risk-averse. Family and 'kinship' labour keep costs
down.

More formally organised types of small production take place
entirely on workshop premises, using family labour but also incorporating apprentices and salaried assistants. Such workshops are generally
situated on premises away from the home, are registered as small businesses and pay taxes. This particular form of organisation of small
production, therefore, has been more accessible to researchers and
government enumerators (see, for example, Çinar, Evcimen and Kaytaz
1988; UNIDO 1987; Ayata 1982). Piecework workshops, in contrast,
involve less financial investment and a workforce that can be expanded

or contracted as needed. Financial risk is further avoided through a number of strategies: the person who orders the item often supplies the materials or prepays part of the cost so that materials can be purchased; alternatively, the producer may lay in a stock of materials. In the latter case, however, only those materials that are certain to be used (for example, white wool) are bought in any quantity. Other materials that reflect the requirements of a particular order (wool of a certain colour) are purchased in quantities sufficient to meet that order. Production is expanded only in response to larger orders. Using family and 'kin' labour also keeps costs down.

Piecework and workshop are well suited to organise women's labour in the poorer districts, because the women are able to reconcile earning additional income with traditional role constraints that discourage women leaving the home, having contact with strangers and taking over the male role of provider. The workshop allows the women to maintain the connection between their labour and their identity. Thus, while a woman is working at home, producing for pay a product often destined for the local or world market, she is encouraged to see that labour as part of her role as woman, as family member and as neighbour. She is encouraged to do so both by the attitudes of the other women and by her employers, all of whom entwine the woman's labour with the other social activities that bind them together. Thus, a woman knitting a piecework sweater will generally do this in the company of other women or even in the home of the woman who is organising the piecework.

The labour relation is euphemised as a social bond. The relation of labour to identity is maintained and work is seen to be an expression of the individual's role as group member. While this seems clear in the case of unsalaried family labour in family workshops, it is more difficult to demonstrate with the labour of unrelated women who are given piecework by a neighbourhood family.

Over half of the population of Istanbul has migrated from the countryside and lives in squatter neighbourhoods. In the 1980s, in these neighbourhoods, piecework production for export became widespread, as it has in other industrialising countries in the wake of the globalisation of industry. Government incentives encouraged exporters to commission products for the world market, especially textiles – one of Turkey's major exports. Many export firms subcontracted production to small workshops that used family labour and pieceworkers. Textiles and clothing lend themselves particularly well to subcontracting, in part because of premium prices paid in industrialised market countries for hand-crafted products, and in part because of the large reservoir of female labour skilled in knitting, sewing, stitching, embroidery and so on. In the 1980s, subcontracting and piecework became very well established and successful, in part for structural reasons such as government incentives, but also because of the particular conjunction of traditional ideology and capitalism described here.[7] In the 1980s up to 60 per cent of women in Istanbul squatter neighbourhoods were employed as poorly paid pieceworkers or as unpaid labour in family workshops (Üşümezsoy 1993; White 1994). By contrast, women's participation in wage labour outside of the home in Istanbul squatter areas was estimated to be as low as 5.5 per cent in 1976 (Şenyapılı 1981). In 1988 only 16.9 per cent of all urban women in Turkey were employed (SIS 1990).

Piecework can be done on an individual basis for friends and neighbours, or can be more structured, with whole neighbourhoods working for a particular middleman, making products that are then often exported. It is practised mainly by women and children, and involves items that can be produced or finished by hand.

One widespread form of piecework was set up as follows: within the community, neighbours brought in orders and materials from outside merchants and distributed materials and patterns to neighbour women, who worked in their homes. Payment trickled down to the women through a subcontracting pyramid. The women stitched decoration on to shoes and clothing, they knitted sweaters – by hand or by machine – and they sewed clothing for export. They also assembled, among other things, cardboard boxes, containers of pencil leads, necklaces, prayer beads and doorbells. The distribution of piecework materials by the workshop owner usually took place in co-operation with other family members and was organised by gender. The person dealing with the world outside the neighbourhood was usually a father or other male relative. He obtained the orders and materials and brought them into the neighbourhood. His wife distributed them to their female neighbours and collected the finished pieces. The women were only paid after the distributor himself received the money from the merchant for the finished products. If there was a delay, the women sometimes had to wait for months to be paid. Piecework rates were very low, especially considering the complexity of some of the work. The work was burdensome, time-consuming and often bad for their health.

Although some of the women did piecework forty to fifty hours a week, they denied that their production activities were work (as in work for pay). Instead, they represented their labour as an expression of their gender roles and a marker of community membership. Representing labour (even when it is exchanged for money in a capitalist relationship) as an expression of family and community obligation did not allow for it to be evaluated in terms of market value. That is, the women did not keep track of the hours they worked or ask for a higher piece rate. In effect, the women were investing in the long-term security of group membership at the expense of short-term monetary gain.

In the family workshop, women's and children's labour is seen as a 'natural' contribution to family life, not as work for pay. It is surprising, however, to find that clearly capitalist relations among non-kin, such as those in piecework production, are also expressed as social reciprocity – as the obligations of community members to one another – and not as work for pay. The notion of kinship is used by the pieceworkers as a metaphor that extends the requirements and benefits of reciprocity beyond the family and actual kin to a group of unrelated individuals who do what kin do: they participate in relations of collective reciprocal assistance with no expectation of return.

## Workers as kin

The squatter district of Yenikent is situated on a bare hill overlooking the Bosphorus, up a steep hill from a relatively affluent neighbourhood along the shore. In 1986 the neighbourhood was a welter of cement block houses in various stages of completion. There was one main road, unpaved, leading down the hill through areas of open land to the older neighbourhood by the shore. Hatije and her husband Osman, in their mid-thirties, were owners of a workshop that produced vests made of leather strips knitted together, and matching tops and skirts made of large diamond-shaped patches of very fine leather attached by means of crocheted panels of shiny yarn. Almost all of the products of the workshop were exported or sold to merchants catering to tourists. Hatije and her family made up samples and Osman brought them to shops and middlemen to see if they wanted to place an order. Alternatively, a merchant or middleman brought in an exemplar and placed an order. If the merchant did not provide his own materials, Osman bought the materials himself with money given to him in advance for this purpose.

The family, with the assistance of a young neighbourhood girl, prepared the leather, cutting it into shape and making the holes, and then gave the materials to neighbourhood women with instructions.

The women came into the workshop to look at the models. For the knitted leather vests, the women took the leather scraps home and cut them into strips there. Osman had a book of women doing piecework. Each woman had a page on which he noted what she took and what she brought back. The women, he explained, were mostly married women and a few young girls. Güllü, his daughter's friend, added, 'Young girls don't have time because they are making their trousseaux.' Osman had up to forty women a month working for him.

Some of the women did a lot of piecework; some less. One industrious woman did four skirts and sixteen tops in one month. If one calculates five hours labour per piece, this means that the woman worked 200 hours that month – more than forty hours a week. For this she earned 42,000 TL ($47). The minimum wage at this time (April 1987) was 41,400 TL ($46),[8] although it was raised two months later to 74,250 TL ($82.50) (Çinar 1989: 19). Osman, however, did not increase the amount he paid for the women's labour. Indeed, the piece rate was raised only minimally during the entire year.[9]

The women worked, Hatije said, because they needed money. She explained that 'if the husband's salary is too low, for example if he is a worker in a factory or in construction and gets 80–90,000 TL a month, the women work more then. The women working for us have husbands who make anywhere between 80–150,000 [$54–60] or 200,000 TL [$134].' Sometimes children worked 'to pay for amusements' or to contribute to the household. The women did the work, she said, in the 'empty hours' after their housework was finished, while sitting with their husbands at night. They were paid once a month or every fifteen days. The unmarried teenage girls either gave the money to their mothers or used it to purchase materials for their trousseaux. The women's income was used in traditionally female ways: for example, to complete the inventory of such household items as pots and pans, carpets and certain furniture items that are traditionally the responsibility of the women's side of the family at marriage, and which they were perhaps too poor to afford at the time. The women also used their earnings to purchase food and clothing for their children and perhaps to pay for school supplies. The women felt they were primarily responsible for their young children – for their health, upbringing and education.

Likewise, the income earned by the workshop was generally used by the middleman to improve the status of his family through purchase of large consumer items such as a video recorder, car or better housing, all of which are traditionally the responsibility of the husband. The workshop's income could also be saved to expand the premises or change the location of the workshop. This was often related to an improvement in housing for the family.

The women who did the work were generally neighbours, although some women came from other nearby neighbourhoods. Anyone was free to come in and look at the exemplars to see if they could do the work, Hatije explained. A neighbour who ran his own piecework workshop added, 'They are stranger women (*yabancı kadın*) but they are *para ile akraba olanları* (ones who have been made kin through money).' When I asked Osman what this meant, he explained:

> If you give money to someone, they become kin. In Anatolia there is something called *imece çalışma*,[10] or *bedelsiz*.[11] Or you can also say *ırgat*[12]. You do something for me; I do something for you with no expectation of return. For example, in the villages they do this with gathering fruit, sowing and harvesting so that the things won't dry up. For example, Güllü[13] punches holes in two of these outfits a day and then takes them home, without pay.

I asked why. 'Because she likes us.' I asked if he was joking with me. 'No joke', he insisted. His daughter tried to clarify things by stating, 'She's my best friend'. Güllü, looking serious, added, 'We're sisters'.

In their explanation, Osman and the others did not differentiate between donated labour such as Güllü's and paid labour such as that of the women who came from another neighbourhood to get piecework. In their view, the women are *akraba* (kin) by virtue of their participation in the exchange of labour for money, providing of course that this was done in the spirit of *imece*: that is, as collective reciprocal assistance with no expectation of return. Although the relation between Osman and the women from another neighbourhood was based on a commercial transaction (payment for labour), it was euphemised as a kin relation (involving open-ended reciprocity). Güllü's donation of labour without pay to the workshop was also explained in kinship terms: she was Emine's 'sister'.

Kinship is metaphorically conferred, then, on those people who participate in relations of collective reciprocal assistance with no expectation of return. These relations may or may not involve payment for labour, but the payment of money for labour has the same role as an exchange of labour or services in terms of participation in a reciprocal relationship. Indeed, money *makes* them relatives. In other words, these 'fictive' kin relations are constructed in the same way as actual kin relations, which are expressed and maintained through participation in a web of reciprocal obligation and indebtedness. Women participate primarily through labour.

Money as kin-maker is patently a myth, since the women generally do expect to receive money for the sweaters they knit. However, money in this situation has become a thing or a service, emptied of its capitalist and market content. Money is a thing that can be freely given, just as labour (within this mythic refraction of meaning) is freely given. Even when money is given as money – that is, having a market value – loans and debts among kin are not openly expected to be repaid. Repayment need not necessarily be in the form of money; certainly it should not be immediate.

It was Osman, the workshop owner, who insisted on the mystical power of money to make strangers kin: that is, to bind them to him in relations of open-ended reciprocal exchange of labour for money, thing for thing, service for service. I do not know whether the 'stranger women' from another neighbourhood also thought this way about their relation with Osman. I would doubt this, judging from the attitudes of women in another squatter area who worked for a middleman who was a stranger to the community. The 'stranger middleman' perceived the women who worked for him paternalistically as children for whom he was responsible. The women, however, saw him as a source of money for labour and did not express any kinship-related attitudes towards him. The larger piecework workshops were often set up by outsiders who came into a neighbourhood and rented a storefront to pass out materials and collect the finished products, sometimes hiring hundreds of women. These distributors generally had few ties to the community and did not live there. In such cases, distributors and producers related as patrons and clients, rather than as 'fictive' kin. The paternalistic overtones to their relationship remained, however.

The expectation of a 'kin' type relation – that is, one of reciprocal obligation – seemed to be an intrinsic part of the middleman's relationship to the women who worked for him, since it provided the ideological foundation for the organisation of (and rate of payment for) the women's labour; however, it was not necessarily reciprocated. Women or girls from the community did not donate labour without pay to the workshop of the 'stranger middleman', nor would the 'stranger women' have donated their labour to Osman's workshop. However, in those piecework workshops where the middleman and the women who did the piecework were neighbours, the relation of labour for money on both sides was overlaid with feelings of group solidarity. Labour, whether paid or unpaid, was seen as part of the obligation for mutual assistance that is required for group membership.

When business was slow, Osman said he employed only women from his own neighbourhood and not from any other neighbourhood. He did this because he felt he should employ his neighbours first. 'First those close to you, close neighbours.' Then, if there was more work left over, he employed women from other neighbourhoods. This was because 'you know your own neighbours and they're close by to pick up and deliver'. I asked whether he felt an obligation towards his neighbours, and he agreed that it was shameful (*ayıp*) to leave neighbours without work.

## Conclusions

Individual production, piecework and the family workshop are organised in similar ways. Production is passive, done only in response to orders from outside of the community or from abroad. Risk is avoided at all stages of production and sale. The structure of each of these types of organisation of labour is fluid. Women who do piecework or who produce individually in their homes may also at the same time organise other women's labour on a piecework basis or subcontract to other women. The physical location of these activities is also fluid: production may or may not take place in the household or it may occupy various locations at once (for example, the household and a detached or semi-detached workshop for different stages of production involving the same people). A workshop may subcontract to another workshop, so actual production may take place in a different part of town.

However, regardless of the specific spatial and structural configuration of production, one element common to individual production, piecework and workshop work in the squatter areas of Istanbul is the use of family labour. If the labour is done by non-kin, the relations of production are euphemised as kin relations, emphasising the parties' participation in the collective reciprocal exchange of labour, services and money that characterises kin relations in Turkey. When middlemen and producers are strangers or relative strangers and of different classes, the relations of production are disguised as paternalistic concern for the welfare of the producers.

As a result of this ideological filter, both the women themselves and the middlemen undervalue the women's labour and do not consider it to be 'work' having a market value, although income may be derived from it. As an outsider middleman put it:

> Knitting sweaters is small work. Some say it's an art, but I don't see it as that. It's easy work. These are things women can do. It's merely tradition. Our women love to knit. They also need money. If we don't have them do it, they'd do it for their children and for themselves anyway.

The women themselves insisted on this distinction between labour and 'work' (in the sense of work for pay or alienated labour).[14] In their own words, they 'do' (*bunu yapıyoruz*) this labour, and they 'give (the product) out' (*dışarıya veriyoruz*). They do not 'work' (*iş yapmak, çalışmak*), although the noun 'work' (*iş*) may be used to describe their activities. This is a general noun also used to describe activities such as housework or even activity or business in general, as in *işim var* ('I am busy').

Despite the devaluation of their labour as 'not work', the women did occasionally ask for a higher piece rate. This was more often the case when the middleman was somewhat of an outsider to the community and hired a large number of women. His relationship with the producers lacked much of the sense of mutual obligation that disguised economic activity between neighbours and kin. Among themselves, however, the women kept to the fiction that they were not 'working', only 'doing' and 'giving out' to the middleman. This allowed them to avoid the onus of being considered a woman who had economic dealings with strangers, a woman who had to 'work', demonstrating that her husband was not able to support his family financially. The latter would dishonour the family as a whole, including the women. In this way, the organisation of women's and children's labour in family and neighbourhood workshops and as piecework constructed and reaffirmed their roles as members of these social groups: that is, as daughters, wives, mothers, neighbours and so on. This allowed them to contribute financially, while remaining reconciled with the moral standards of the traditional family. This conflation of capitalist labour with women's traditional activities, and of labour relations with kinship obligations, was what kept production costs low and profits high for middlemen, exporters and merchants. Thus, while reciprocity in production contributed to solidarity, these same production relations also supported both patriarchal norms about women's role and capitalist forms of labour exploitation.

Interestingly, in recent years, in order to deal with the reoccurring problem of quality control, several local piecework distributors set up 'work rooms' in the middle of the neighbourhood, where women could knit without smearing egg or leek on the product, as often happened when women at home combined knitting with such household tasks as cooking. An unanticipated effect of such central work spaces was a public acknowledgement of the fact that these women were working, without negatively affecting their reputations. Before long, the women began to ask for a higher piece rate. The logic and naturalness of the hierarchies implicit in the overlapping domains of biological and 'fictive' kinship are made real 'through the institutional arrangements and discourses people encounter in everyday life' (Yanagisako and Delaney 1995: 12), in this case the institution of home-work for the world market. However, kinship as metaphor for economic relations requires that relations of domination appear 'natural'. To that end, the expectation of return for labour must remain unspoken (as in relations between kin) and thus the possibilities for resistance unthought.

## Notes

1   This discussion is based on two years of fieldwork in Istanbul in 1986–8, sponsored by Fulbright-Hays and the National Science Foundation. A fuller account of this research can be found in White (1994).

2   The Turkish word for kin, *akraba*, originates in Arabic and its etymology provides a broader set of meanings within which proximity, relationship and kinship are given equal place. *Akraba*, which means kin or relative in Turkish, is derived from the Arabic root *qaruba*, meaning 'to be near'. Another form of the same Arabic root is *qurba*, meaning 'relation, relationship or kinship'. Yet another form of the root is *aqrab*, meaning 'near, nearest'. The plural of this can be *aqarib* or *aqrabun*, both of which mean 'relations, relatives'.

3   Carol Delaney (1991) describes in great detail the multiple levels of closeness and belonging implied in Turkish kinship, and how these are expressed in the context of gender and age in an Anatolian village.

4   Kandiyoti's description of the conditions of classic patriarchy is a generalisation that, as such, does not take into account such individual conditions as spatial proximity, health, ethnicity and religious beliefs that may ease or deepen patriarchal vectors of control. Nevertheless, as a general concept, it accurately portrays the basic expectations of family life in the urban working-class areas where I conducted my research, even if those expectations were not always met.

5   Women in sub-Saharan Africa, for example, engage in trading activities that give them some autonomy in countering male attempts to control their labour and appropriate their production (Kandiyoti 1988).

6   This term has generally been translated as 'milk right'. The term *hak*, however, as it is used in other related verbal formulas, discussed elsewhere in this chapter, implies a moral debt.

7   Piecework declined in the 1990s when government incentives were withdrawn, trade regulations governing export (particularly to the European Union) became more complex, and textile and clothing imports from other cheap-labour countries, like those in Asia, competed with Turkey in the European and other markets.

8   The dollar equivalents reflect changes in the exchange rate during the fieldwork period.

9   Çinar (1989: 19–20) also notes that, while subcontracting (piecework) wages in Istanbul and Bursa were on a par with the gross formal sector minimum wage, when the minimum wage was raised there was no corresponding increase in subcontracting wages. This discrepancy is exacerbated by the fact that formal sector employment also provides health, pregnancy, vacation and retirement benefits that are not available in home employment.

10   *Imece çalışma* means work done for the community by the entire village or by the united efforts of the community (*Redhouse Turkish–English Dictionary* 1983). In a broader sense, however, the phrase means work done as enduring, collective (*ortaklaşa*), reciprocal assistance (*karşılıklı yardımlaşma*) (cf. Eyuboğlu 1988).

11   *Bedelsiz* means without equivalent value expected in exchange.

12   The *Redhouse Turkish–English Dictionary* (1983) defines *ırgat* as day-labourer or workman. Eyuboğlu (1988) gives the Anatolian usage of the word as a worker who subsists on agriculture. In the context in which it is used by Osman, it may mean agricultural labour to meet a social or financial obligation or perhaps agricultural labour given with no return.

13   His daughter's teenage friend whom I had seen on various visits punching holes in leather pieces. Later in the year, as production increased in response to larger orders, she began to work in the workshop regularly and received a small wage.

14   Berik (1987: 3) described a similar attitude among Turkish women carpet weavers in rural Turkey who regarded weaving as 'an integral part of their lives as "peasants", farmers and women, and did not consider themselves to be "workers"'. Carpet weaving in the home was interpreted by the community and by the weavers themselves as a leisure activity, even though it may have been a full-time money-making activity.

# References

Ayata, S. (1982) 'Differentiation and capital accumulation: Case studies of the carpet and metal industries in Kayseri (Turkey)', unpublished Ph.D. dissertation, University of Kent.

Berik, G. (1987) *Women Carpet Weavers in Rural Turkey: Patterns of Employment, Earnings, and Status*, Geneva: International Labour Office.

Bourdieu, P. (1979) *Outline of a Theory of Practice*, Cambridge: Cambridge University Press.

Çinar, E.M. (1989) *Taking Work at Home: Disguised Female Employment in Urban Turkey* (Loyola University of Chicago Business School Working Paper No. 8810), Chicago: Loyola University.

Çinar, E.M., Evcimen, G. and Kaytaz, M. (1988) 'The present day status of small-scale industries (Sanatkar) in Bursa, Turkey', *International Journal of Middle East Studies* 20(3): 287–301.

Delaney, C. (1991) *The Seed and the Soil: Gender and Cosmology in Turkish Village Society*, Berkeley: University of California Press.

Eyuboğlu, I.Z. (1988) *Türk Dilinin Etimoloji Sözlüğü*, Istanbul: Sosyal Yayınlar.

Friedmann, H. (1986) 'Patriarchal commodity production', *Social Analysis* 20: 47–55.

Kandiyoti, D. (1988) 'Bargaining with patriarchy', *Gender and Society* 2(3): 274–90.

Malinowski, B. (1922) *Argonauts of the Western Pacific*, London: Routledge & Kegan Paul.

Parry, J. and Block, M. (eds) (1989) *Money and the Morality of Exchange*, Cambridge, UK: Cambridge University Press.

*Redhouse Turkish–English Dictionary* (1983), Istanbul: Redhouse Press.

Schneider, D. (1984) *A Critique of the Study of Kinship*, Ann Arbor: University of Michigan Press.

Şenyapılı, T. (1981) *Gecekondu: Çevre İşçilerin Mekanı*, Ankara: Middle East Technical University, Department of Architecture.

SIS (Turkish State Institute of Statistics) (1990) *Household Labor Force Survey Results*, Ankara: SIS.

Turner, V. (1974) *Dramas, Fields and Metaphors: Symbolic Action in Human Society*, Ithaca, NY: Cornell University Press.

UNIDO and Organisation of Islamic Conference SESRTCIC (1987) *Small and Medium Sized Manufacturing Enterprises in Turkey*, Ankara: Organisation of Islamic Conference.

Üşümezsoy, B. (1993) 'Women's informal-sector contribution to household survival in urban Turkey', unpublished Ph.D. dissertation, Istanbul: Marmara University.

Van Baal, J. (1975) *Reciprocity and the Position of Women*, Amsterdam: Van Gorcum.

White, J.B. (1994) *Money Makes Us Relatives: Women's Labor in Urban Turkey*, Austin: University of Texas Press.

Yanagisako, S. and Delaney, C. (1995) 'Naturalizing power', in S. Yanagisako and C. Delaney (eds) *Naturalizing Power: Essays in Feminist Cultural Analysis*, New York: Routledge.

# Chapter 6

# Is blood thicker than economic interest in familial enterprises?

*Antónia Pedroso de Lima*

This chapter is an attempt to consider the dividends of kinship relations in the context of large Portuguese family firms. I will centre the debate on the research I have been carrying out on high-status Portuguese families[1] who own large familial enterprises that have been in existence for at least three generations and which are on the list of the 100 most important Portuguese enterprises. As in every family business,[2] in these large companies the familial and professional relations of the people involved are continuously interchanged. In fact, social relations engaged in this context are constructed on several different levels, occur in diverse contexts of action and are based on various kinds of interests. In the context of large familial companies we find that, both in the area of family relations and in the context of the enterprise, there is an underlying conflict between the universe of those who constitute the family and those who are partners. I believe that it is this permanent combination, of two very distinct forms of operating in these different domains, that makes this social context a particularly interesting one for anthropological reflection on kinship and family relations in Western societies. This is because the analysis of large family firms forces us to 'read across the boundaries' (Yanagisako and Delaney 1995: 12), as it clearly reveals that familial relations cannot be analysed as if they were mere kinship relations and, simultaneously, demonstrates that business decisions are not based exclusively on strict economic rationality. In fact, in this social context, family relations are built around a web of economic interests that bind people together whose interests in the enterprise are often opposed. In the course of my research I have found that the formal organisation of these big family companies, which are vast and complex institutions, is built according to the best organisational models and with the most competent professionals, but it is also built around a web of affective familial relations that unite shareholders. In fact, familial values – the ways of being and living in a family – are crucial elements in defining the ways in which the economic group works and continues through time.

By pointing this out I do not want to revive the crystallised frontiers that David Schneider has labelled as 'the quartet of kinship, economic, politics and religion in anthropological theory' (Schneider 1984: 181), calling our attention to the analytical problems they cause in anthropological studies. I am pointing this out because in this particular ethnographic case the static separation between the domain of economics and that of kinship is an emic problem. In fact, these wealthy Portuguese families who own large enterprises live with a profound sentiment of contradiction that, I think, is shared by a major part of Portuguese society. It is generally accepted that business activities should not be mixed with familial relations because they are two kinds of relations that are very different in their essence (economic interest and common substance, respectively) and in their objectives (profit and disinterested solidarity, respectively). The existence of a family business inevitably brings together these opposing interests and realms of action. While this does not necessarily constitute a cultural problem in the area of small family firms, in the domain of large national companies it is seen almost as a contradiction, causing some form of cognitive discomfort among these wealthy élite families. As a consequence, we observe a constant concern on the part of the people involved to construct these two domains of interest as separate areas of action in order to resolve the contradiction of values in which they live. I will argue that this emic contradiction is overcome by an enormous investment in the professional training of family members who work at their companies and that, at the same time, this professional training guarantees the reproduction of their economic and social prestige in contemporary Portuguese society.

A general characteristic of these entrepreneurial élite families is their attempt to maintain a joint ownership of valuable assets over several family generations. In order to preserve their family cohesion, family-based companies try to maintain family members in top decision-making positions in their firms, and this implies the creation of forms of family succession in business. In this chapter, I will argue that this is the specific basis upon which familial relations are built and is what distinguishes the kinship relations of this social group from other Portuguese social contexts. This difference leads to important characteristics in the way these people manipulate national hegemonic cultural symbols of family and kinship. I will demonstrate that this is because these people are united by a common economic project, and that, because the enterprise is family owned (with their efforts geared towards maintaining the collective familial property), this creates a solid base for the conscious maintenance of active familial relations in the universe of extended kin. It is this that opens the way for the formation of dynastic families. Furthermore, I will show that, in the context of large Portuguese family companies, the enterprise itself becomes a cultural symbol of kinship. Its effectiveness in bringing people together attributes greater power to the enterprise by maintaining active kinship relations than to the sharing of a common substance: 'blood' – one of the most important Portuguese cultural symbols of the family.[3] Finally, I will risk making some conclusions on how this social context can be especially relevant in promoting new insights into kinship in Western societies. The complexity and multidimensionality of such social contexts mean that we have to produce new conceptualisations that allow us to think about kinship without the straitjacket of blood. In his stimulating critical reflections on the universal basis of kinship, David Schneider has demonstrated that blood is the main cultural symbol of Western kinship rather than its universal constitutional element (Schneider 1984: 119–126, 165–180). In this chapter, I will try to follow his suggestion and look for the diverse cultural symbols and their meanings as used by élite Portuguese families in their discourse, values, rules and practices regarding kinship and family relations.

The combination of theories of kinship relatedness and of entrepreneurial growth in large family firms obliges us to study both the family and the enterprise's developmental processes as integral parts of the socio-economic national context in which they take place. This is particularly relevant in Portugal, where the political transition from a dictatorial regime to a democratic one in 1974 caused a great deal of change in the national economic, political and social order. This had far-reaching implications for the developmental processes of those enterprises (and their dynastic families) that constituted, and once again constitute today, the core of the Portuguese financial élite.

It is worth noting that, until 1974, Portuguese economic life was dominated by a small number of economic emporia. These were, in reality, family-based economic groups. The families who owned these economic groups had enormous social prestige and a significant, yet indirect, amount of intervention in national politics. The Salazar dictatorial regime, under which Portugal lived from 1926 to 1974, depended upon what he believed to be the most important national

values: 'God, Nation, Family and Authority'. Obviously, this constituted the ideological basis for the legitimisation of the fact that the
core of Portuguese economic groups were family owned. As a result of
the democratic revolution in 1975, the financial sector was nation-
alised, as were other sectors of public interest. These processes took the
control these families had over their own businesses. At the same time
the privileged conditions, in which those families had lived before the
revolution, collapsed. Therefore, the new social and political conditions of the revolutionary period forced most of the members of these
families to leave the country (mainly to Brazil, the United Kingdom
and Switzerland), leaving behind the majority of their material goods
and investments. Abroad, they restarted their economic activities and
quickly rebuilt their economic empires. At the end of the 1980s, when
the Social Democratic government began the process of re-privatisa-
tion, they returned to Portugal to buy back their old enterprises. Since
then, we have witnessed the rapid growth of these firms, reflecting the
great dynamism demonstrated by the new leading generation of this
financial élite (the fifth generation in most cases). They have managed
to buy back their enterprises and rebuild their economic emporia in
such a way that they once again constitute the core of the Portuguese
financial and industrial élite.

## The family company as a kinship symbol and the formation of the dynastic family

Although the families that I am discussing form a self-conscious social
group, they are in no way a neatly defined community. The members
share interests, ideals, ways of life, attitudes, forms of behaviour, ways
of being, acting and dressing, and they form a close web of relations,
into which it would be very difficult for any outsider to enter. The
primary context for the production of these defining characteristics is
the area of domestic relations, as it is mostly here that the codes,
values, attributes and attitudes specific to this socio-cultural-economic
group are perpetuated. In relation to the rest of Portuguese society,
these Lisbon élite families have adopted forms of self-representation
that are consciously conceived of as 'conservative': for example, family
values – which are now clearly on the wane among other Portuguese
social groups – such as patriarchal authority, seniority, birth order,
gender belonging and a profound adherence to Roman Catholicism.
In fact, as they neither form a 'culture', nor even a 'sub-culture', they
have to use the language of the general Portuguese bourgeoisie,

adapting it to their interests. In this way they manipulate not only relationships, but also the concepts and values that are part of the 'general ideological tool kit'[4] of the Portuguese historical cultural legacy.

Generally, members of this social context make a decided investment in familial relations. They live together, work together and socialise together. Family permeates their existence in a way that creates an intense feeling, which is crystallised in a sense of sharing something in common: a family name, a history, ancestors, family houses and farms, titles of nobility, coats of arms, a network of enterprises and, most importantly, a common aim – to perpetuate all of this. The preservation of these 'conservative values' is a primary factor in the perpetuation through time of extended family ties and the legitimisation of the 'dynastic sense' of these families. In fact, they are permanently dealing with the problem of 'how do I keep my family as a corporate entity?' The ideological tools generally available within Portuguese culture that best assure the pursuit of their interests are those that are least 'individualistic' and, therefore, least 'modern'. In this way, they find the response to their problem in the ideological remains of an old aristocratic tradition, and so have revived the largely deceased language of aristocratic corporateness.

In this chapter I will use George Marcus's and Peter Hall's notion of dynastic families, in which a family dynasty is 'as much a family, as a fortune, as a class desire. … It is a formal organisation of an extended family, a corporate' (Marcus and Hall 1992: 7). They also state that a 'distinctive feature of the stronger families is a dynastic tradition or ideology that seems to have an emotional and cognitive hold on descendants' (Marcus and Hall 1992: 86–7). The group of Lisbon élite families that I have been studying constitutes dynasties in this sense because they share the specific aim of perpetuating themselves as a defined social unit made up of those who share the same blood (in the sense of the same substance), the same family name, the same ancestors and the same family history. These dynastic families have a detailed knowledge of their family genealogy and their family history. For example, a summer holiday on a family farm is an important family reunion for one of the families I have been working with. Almost 200 individuals are present, divided into nine houses – one for each branch of the founder's descendants. Siesta time and evenings are passed recounting old family stories, which call for sharing sentiments, explaining famous family objects and showing family pictures to the younger members. These moments are a powerful way to embody in these young family members a base on which to build a sentiment of belonging, on which family identity is in turn rooted.

Families guarantee the continuity of their status and privilege by means of their children's socialisation. In this way, children succeed their parents in social practices and social relations as much as in their family enterprises. Socialising children as followers in the collective project is a central factor in guaranteeing the continuation of the social group, as it ensures the active participation of the next generation in the family project.

The family-owned enterprise is felt to be a collective project in which almost every family member is involved, personally investing a great deal of energy in what is everyone's primary source of social prestige and economic income. This becomes very evident when we analyse the narratives of the firm's history as produced by the owners. Such narratives revolve around the legends of the dynamic family members who were personally responsible for its foundation and development. So, family narratives and the enterprise narrative mix, and are related to each other, in such a way that it becomes difficult to differentiate between them. The family enterprises are, therefore, part of the shared whole that symbolises the family and guarantees the continuity of its unity. In fact, the enterprise becomes, in this context, a most important symbol of family identity: its continuity and success are a necessary stimulus for the continuity of family relations.

Let me illustrate this argument with an example. The Mendes Godinho family company was founded in 1917 by a dynamic farmer and tradesman of the small city of Tomar. By 1930 the company had reached a level of local importance and, by the 1960s, it had launched three industrial enterprises in Portugal. These went on to become leaders in the national and international market in their respective areas of activity: red ceramics, and the transformation of oleaginous and wood agglomerates. The board of administration of the family enterprise has always been composed exclusively of family members. At the time of the death of the founder, the presidency was assumed by his eldest son. As the result of the latter's sudden death, his own eldest son took over the leadership of the group of enterprises. Later, a brother-in-law succeeded him and, later still, his nephew. Nowadays, the central enterprise of this group has been confiscated by the bank that was its major creditor. This economic failure has been attributed by many observers to an excess in family spirit, which dictated that only family members could assume roles of leadership within the family businesses. This ideal was so strongly rooted that it was not given up, even in moments when it clearly led to the breakdown both of the firm and of family relations. It must be noted that this extended family has had very hostile relations ever since the founder's sons took control of the presidency in 1923. In spite of this, its members have stuck together because of their common business interests. One of them once told me, 'my family doesn't meet at Christmas or at weddings. Perhaps, at funerals ... but the big family rituals are the general assemblies of the family enterprise. There we all meet, but it is to fight with each other.'

This example shows us that, in this social context, the maintenance of family relations is primarily due to the existence and the continuity of family enterprises. It is the common familial project – the enterprise – that creates the conditions which maintain active family relations within the larger kinship universe. In fact, as a family grows into the third and fourth generation, its several branches form a very large group of people, some of whom are so distant that, if it were not for the fact that they share something in common, they would most likely not even know each other. Here, however, we witness a generalised tendency for the various branches of descendants of the business founder to keep their relationships alive throughout the generations. This is, I believe, a result of the fact that they share a link that they do not want to lose – the family enterprise, which is the source of wealth and social prestige. It is interesting to note that even though not all family members are business associates (as not all of them possess shares in the family companies) all of them benefit from its social prestige because they carry the family name. Thus, the enterprise is a patrimony that is valued by all, even for those who do not receive direct economic income from it. In this way, the family firm becomes an integral part of the family and, therefore, one of the primary reasons for the continuation of familial relations – the *raison d'être* of the family. It engenders a sentiment of union – a sentiment of family as shared substance – that guarantees its continuation through time. The enterprise becomes the reification of the family's unity and the symbol of its identity.

Family and enterprise can be seen as one; they form what Marcus and Hall call 'family-enterprise formations' (Marcus and Hall 1992: 15). What defines the identity of these families and what they want to transmit to their future generations is not one but three things: a family, a fortune and a successful enterprise. In *Lives in Trust* Marcus and Hall argue that it was a collectively shared fortune that promoted the dynastic sense of the families they studied in Galveston, Texas:

'There is no compelling reason for descendants to maintain other than casual relations, *but* for the fact their reified shared wealth intrudes constantly into their mutual relations and individual lives' (Marcus and Hall 1992: 56). In Portugal I believe that the enterprise itself promotes a dynastic sense within the members of old, wealthy entrepreneurial families. Among Lisbon's contemporary financial élite, the reason for the appearance and reproduction of dynastic family formations is that relatives are business associates rather than shareholders of the family fortune, and do not necessarily share the family's cultural constitutional values – like blood, sentiments or a shared past. Shared kinship is not what sustains active kinship relations in these dynastic families. It is the successful family-owned company that keeps them together.

Rather than being a case particular only to Portugal, I believe this is a general attribute of large families who own important enterprises. The perpetuation of the familial firm over several generations creates a particular situation in the family that contributes to the preservation of close relations between members of the large universe of kinship to which their family belongs. In families with considerable patrimony, to transmit across generations the emphasis on a lineal perpetuation of identification is clearly perceived. This could explain why it is common to find large extended families functioning in a relatively cohesive way among wealthy entrepreneurial families – something quite unusual in Western bureaucratic societies. Marcus and Hall note the very same occurrence in American dynastic families. They have argued that these families 'have achieved durability as descent groups in a bureaucratised society by assimilating, rather than resisting, characteristics of formal organisation which are usually assumed to be antithetical to kin-based groups' (Marcus and Hall 1992: 15). So, it is possible that we are witnessing a phenomenon with wider socio-geographic implications associated to these large family-enterprise formations. If this is so, whenever an economic project owned and ruled by one family gets to reproduce itself over decades with considerable success, in both economic and social domains, it promotes the maintenance of kinship ties in the extended family and opens the way for the existence of large dynastic families in Western industrialised societies.

## The importance of sharing blood and of carrying on the family name

The analysis of strategies of ensuring perpetuation through time is of central importance to understanding Portuguese financial élite families.

The production of legitimate descendants is a major element in the accomplishment of this primary family aim. Thus, matrimonial alliances are very important as they create the basis for the maintenance of the family as a continuing social unity. This explains why there is such a tendency for endogamy among the Lisbon financial élite families. Whether these matrimonial alliances are the origin or the result of economic alliances is not an issue worthy of discussion. What is relevant, from an analytical point of view, is that through these alliances families with economic relations consolidate their ties. This is done, it must be noted, by a most sacred commitment (a sacrament) and not merely through economic alliance. In fact, among Portuguese Roman Catholics marriage is not primarily seen as a legal contract: it is a sacred act.[5] As João de Pina-Cabral puts it:

> it is not a mere cultural fact imposed by law: it is something much more fundamental, which mediates between nature and culture. The association God creates when He unites man and woman is not only insoluble, it corresponds to a creation of consubstantiability.
>
> (Pina-Cabral 1991: 207)

In this way, by means of marriage, these élite families unite their descendants in a most effective way. But these matrimonial alliances also consolidate anterior family ties as they reinforce the relations of the families involved. By systematically marrying inside the same group of families, the Lisbon élite strengthens its ties of solidarity, which work both on a social and a financial level, and which have wider repercussions within the larger social group. Later on, the birth of children will further fortify these unions, ensuring the legitimacy of the families' fusion. A common substance has been produced, and the creation of consubstantiability legitimates the continuation of both families through time. This is central, as the continuation throughout successive generations of the same blood (in the sense of family substance) is one of the most important Portuguese cultural symbols. Thus, the power of blood as a family symbol is strengthened even though we are dealing with a social context in which, as we have seen, the family enterprise is the principal force of kin congregation.

This point can be further clarified by using another example. The Espírito Santo Group belongs to the family with the same name. It is the second largest Portuguese economic group and its national and international sphere of activity is extremely influential and diversified:

six banks (two in Portugal, two in Brazil, one in Luxembourg and one in the United States), three insurance companies (two in Portugal and one in Brazil), real estate, telecommunications, agriculture and cattle raising. Their first bank was founded at the end of the last century by J.M. Espírito Santo, who started his career in Lisbon as a poor but daring businessman – he was middleman for the Spanish lottery in Portugal and in Brazil. In only two decades he made a large fortune, acquired important social relations and gained considerable respectability. He fathered five children, and through their successful business activities father and sons built a formidable international web of business and friendship relations. At the end of the 1960s Espírito Santo Bank was the major Portuguese bank. In 1974, the democratic revolution and the process of the nationalisation of banks and insurance companies forced a majority of the members of this family to flee to Brazil, the United Kingdom or Switzerland. Abroad, they established a new and soon powerful financial group, with international associate partners, while still maintaining the family majority. Their international professional prestige and their influential social and financial relations in the international world of finance were central to this new beginning, as their financial rebirth required considerable financial credit and powerful associate partners. In the mid-1980s, when the reprivatisation processes began, they started a slow return to Portugal, and bought back their old enterprises. Now they have fully regained their place in Portuguese economic life and recovered their family firms.

The founder's three sons succeeded him at the presidency of the bank by birth order. When the last of them died, it was not clear who should succeed. Although the eldest son of the founder's first-born son was the vice-president (and thus, according to the bank's statutes, the legal successor to the presidency), no one wanted him to assume the presidency. At that time, the group's senior member was C.R., husband of a daughter of the founder's second son, who had changed his military career for a second distinguished one in his father-in-law's enterprises. But, as he did not have the family name, he could not succeed. A member of the bank's administration explained it to me in the following way:

> You know, people have trust in our bank, in our family. To put someone outside the family in the bank's leading position, even an old and important partner such as C.R., would separate the image of the bank from the trust given to our family, it would betray our clients' confidence.

So, the eldest son of the deceased president, M.R. Espírito Santo, who had the skills and the Espírito Santo family name, was chosen. In this succession situation between two very skilled men, blood spoke louder than business seniority. M.R. Espírito Santo was a very favourable and agreeable person, who had been thoroughly trained by his father to become the president of the bank and the family's patriarch.

In August 1991, however, the important choice of a new president for the bank was required, because of M.R. Espírito Santo's death. This time the presidency was assigned to C.R., who had previously been passed over. What had changed? By 1991, the long period of living abroad after the democratic revolution had changed the forces within the family, mostly as a result of two factors: on the one hand, the way each family member was dedicated to the rebuilding of the economic group; and, on the other, the amount of shares each had managed to acquire in their new group. Two other factors, however, were of primary importance: first, the new democratic social order installed in Portugal after the 1974 revolution; and, second, the fact that the Espírito Santo Group was now no longer exclusively family based. Thus, in 1991, in spite of not bearing the family's name, the presidency was given to the only living member of the older generation – C.R. This was done, clearly, as a way of symbolising the continuity of the old family project.

Such is the argument as presented by the family. I found out, however, that in the 1972 succession crisis the branch to which C.R. was linked was not sufficiently powerful to compete for the role of president, as it was formed only by Espírito Santo women and their husbands. This fact was felt to be such a disqualification that, in his will, R. Espírito Santo – C.R.'s father-in-law – gave all his bank shares to his grandchildren, granting his daughters only the usufruct, until such time as his grandchildren reached maturity. By 1991, however, C.R.'s branch had acquired sufficient power to capture the presidency of the group (expressed in the significant amount of shares of the new Espírito Santo Group they possessed and in the occupancy of top executive positions in the administrative boards of their firms). This family branch had invested great effort in the professionalisation of their members (now the fourth generation of the family) and had clearly proved their excellent managerial and leadership qualities, with their central contribution to the rebuilding processes of the economic group abroad and the restoration of the family's old business in Portugal. Now C.R. is the president of the Espírito Santo Group, and his eldest nephew in his family's branch, R.S. Espírito Santo, is the executive president of the group, as well as the president of the first Espírito Santo Bank.

This case shows us that blood is, in fact, a central element in defining kinship relations in the context of the Portuguese financial élites, and a powerful symbolic item of social integration. The fact that blood is the primary basis of leadership positions in large family companies is clearly seen in the immense importance attributed to carrying the family name. In fact, in the context of family business, being a good professional is not good enough: you must carry the family name (and name of the firm) because central symbolic importance is given to the fact that family members occupy top leadership positions. However, blood, and its external reification – the family name – is not a sufficient criterion, because at this high level of economic relations family members are very conscious that the stakes of poor decision-making are substantial, and they know that their future, the future of their families and of their associated partners depends on good leadership choices.

## Gender bias among the Portuguese financial élite

Although descendants are fundamental to the continuity of the family it should be noted that in the social context of élites, descendants are not all equally valuable as family perpetuators. Although equally loved, boys are more desired than girls as they are the ones who can continue the family. As we have seen, it is important to carry the family name and, because the transmission of family names favours agnatic continuity in Portugal, boys have a symbolic value of central instrumental importance, as they guarantee that the family's name will survive across the generations by means of legitimate heirs. No daughter and no son-in-law, as good as they may be, are able to do it. So, the family's survival depends on the existence of male descendants in every generation, because the family's continuity depends on the transmission of its name. Here again we witness the evident influence of an aristocratic ideological value. Indeed, it should be stressed that, although there is an agnatic tendency in the transmission of family names, Portuguese law is not restrictive in this respect.

This fact opens the way for a great number of different legal combinations in Portuguese family names. João de Pina-Cabral has argued that, in this flexible legal context, the choice of which family name people give their children when they are born or which they use in their daily life – which are not necessarily the same – thus depends mostly on the social prestige attributed to the family name of their father and of their mother (Pina-Cabral 1991: 174–6). This means that if they were not deeply interested in reproducing *a varonia familiar* (the male family line and a central term of aristocratic succession), they would be perfectly able to transmit the family name through women. And in fact they do. All the sons of Espírito Santo women carry the Espírito Santo family name. If we were dealing with a patrilineal system they would, of course, use their father's family name. So they manipulate the flexibility of the Portuguese family name transmission law in accordance with two of their most valued ideals: the importance of passing the family name along the generations and their patriarchal view of the family. The idiom of the family name is, thus, an extremely elastic instrument in the manipulation of legitimacy. What is most important is to ensure that men in future generations will be able to use the family name, even if this is accomplished by manipulating the transmission of the family name through the female line. So, it is clear that we are not in the presence of a patrilineal descent system. The frequent need to manipulate the 'normal' formation of a child's family name reveals, instead, that we are in the presence of a cultural system that attributes symbolic primacy to men. This is a most important point, as it reveals the effectiveness of the symbolic power of the family name in the context of the Portuguese financial élite and, as a consequence, attributes a totally different status to boys and girls. When a member of the administration board of the second most important Portuguese bank was making a list of his brothers and sisters at my request, he referred systematically to the latter by the family name of their husbands, as if they were no longer part of his family.

This gender distinction is also neatly perceived in the different participation men and women have in the family enterprises they both own. In this social context, business is clearly men's business. It is only in today's generation that we can find some shareholding women working at their family firms. Normally, however, they are in positions of reduced responsibility. A 55-year-old Espírito Santo woman once told me that when she was young she wanted to have a college degree but her parents were adamantly opposed, defending their idea of what a girl in her position should do. This includes preparing herself to be a good wife, with enough cultural knowledge to be an interesting and educated hostess for her future husband's business and social needs. So, after leaving the Convent of the Sacred Heart in Brighton (United Kingdom) where she attended high school, she went to Florence

(Italy) for two years to study art history in a college where she met a great number of girls of her age, who belonged to the European social and financial élite, and who are still some of her best friends.

This woman, however, is an exception. Most of the women of these families do not evince any desire to acquire professional knowledge, or to hold a job at their family's enterprise. Having been socialised in patriarchal and male-centred family values, they are the first ones to defend the importance of their exclusively familial role. As Sylvia Yanagisako noted about northern Italian industrial families, 'this does not mean assuming that women have no desires, but rather assuming that their desires are shaped by dominant ideological representations of gender' (Yanagisako 1991: 334). Women from these social contexts are not supposed to work in the same way as men. The work they are expected to do is to look after the well-being of their family health, both their nuclear family and their universe of near kin. Their fundamental efforts are dedicated to the proper education of their children, and to the maintenance of active relations with close relatives and family allies. Women are expected to co-operate in family business on a different level from men. They must look after their family homes, which are the visible and public images of their collective prestige and where they maintain social contacts with the most prestigious families of the financial world. Women are also expected to guarantee the crucial activities of organising the social events that support their husbands' and brothers' business arrangements. In fact, in this social group, a woman with high personal prestige is one who has raised a perfect family, and who is beautiful, educated and a good hostess. To be *uma Senhora* ('a lady') they must stick to the cultural symbols that define a proper woman, not those that attribute value to men. Being a good professional would not be the proper characteristic for a proper lady. In fact, the women I interviewed often responded with vague irritation when I asked them if they had ever wanted to work at their family enterprises. Work, in the traditional economic sense of the concept, is something that these women do not need and do not want to do. Notwithstanding, through the performance of these strictly female activities that normally occur at their homes, we can see how women play a fundamental role. Indeed, this is quite evident in the words of one of my interviewees when asked about her daily activities: 'We can say I am a family manager.' Their seeming 'invisibility', therefore, only partially reflects reality, and, of course, in the public eyes of the press they are supposed to be seen. In fact, it is through women that family relations are kept alive in these large dynastic families. It is by means of the intense and frequent uxorilateral relations, which unite mothers, daughters, sisters and grandmothers, that they can create solid familial ties. In fact, women are the ones who maintain up-to-date information about the relatives of every branch of the extended family and the ones through which men relate to each other and are kept informed about their relatives.

We can see here another dimension of gender differentiation in Portuguese élite contexts. The hegemonic cultural patterns and symbols identify Portuguese men as family heads, particularly in the conservative and Roman Catholic context we are dealing with, where the ideal model of family is a patriarchal one. However, uxorilateral relations have enormous influence and power in family practice and in the daily structuring of Portuguese families. This can be found across class and regional differences.[6] In this élite context, they seem to have an even more powerful effect, as women dedicate almost 100 per cent of their time to their family project. In fact, the extra-domestic familial networks of social relations have a strong uxorilateral leaning and I believe that it would not be possible to understand Portuguese familial relations if we did not pay attention to the practices and meanings that they generate. There are a number of female daily practices that are accepted by everybody and which belong to this uxorilateral world, such as mutual help between female relatives (for instance, child-minding), which have become recognised as customs. In this way women create an informal web of relations that becomes a central part of family life, but which is difficult to identify because they do not have an ideology or a formal structure associated to them. Here we can follow João de Pina-Cabral's suggestion that social and cultural life 'is composed by daytime aspects, legitimised by the operation of symbolic power, and by night time ones, which exist in the penumbra of marginality' (Pina-Cabral 1996: 40). We can see that although uxorilateral relations are not hegemonic cultural patterns of Portuguese family relations, their extreme frequency and daily practical importance have an evident structuring effect in the way Portuguese families are organised and how their projects are defined. In spite of being unstated, these contra-hegemonic aspects constitute an integral part of cultural life. Although they are 'night time aspects of action', uxorilateral relations are, therefore, a central element in the understanding of Portuguese family relations.

In this social context, sons are seen as successors to the business and daughters as family keepers. This distinction is very obvious from childhood. This was clearly evident in the interviews I carried out about childhood memories. The men's favourite topics were the visits they made with their father, when they were young boys, to the enterprises or their holiday work in unskilled jobs in one of their companies. A parallel occurred with women. They talked about helping their mothers or grandmothers to organise important tea parties, or dinner parties, learning which china to use on which occasion, which table-cloth would be more appropriate or where to seat people at the table. Boys and girls are treated differently and are thought of differently because their families want them to have distinct roles in the destinies of their family and their family's enterprises.

And yet, Portuguese inheritance law makes men and women equal beneficiaries to their fathers' fortunes. This legal disposition dictates an absolute egalitarian distribution of family wealth among descendants, whatever their gender or birth order, but it also creates a space for the development of familial strategies of sibling differentiation. So, if élite family leaders want to make sure that boys will be the ones who will actively participate in their family companies' future development, and that girls will continue to be the guarantors of the stability of their family dynasties, they must transmit to them different values for their different items of property, as well as different cultural and patrimonial values and expectations.

To be able to work at the enterprise is the first step to eventually getting a leadership position in the family firm. Therefore, by excluding daughters from the possibility of acquiring the kind of knowledge needed to work there, family members have a most effec-tive way in ensuring that women will not be potential successors to leadership in the firm. Thus, socialising young girls in the cultural values that associate men with business and women with family is of central importance, as it guarantees that women accept their own exclusion from the command of their family companies, and that they will reproduce these cultural values as they become mothers. Therefore, the combination of cultural values regarding family and gender with the practice of transmitting gendered knowledge is a very effective way of forming men as successors and of excluding women as potential ones, by promoting them as family keepers.

However, in these families and in these enterprises, not all men are equal. Among them, one will be the leader of the economic group. In this social context there is an overall tendency for primogeniture: it is generally expected that the eldest son will succeed his father in the presidency of their family companies. Although there are many variants in the application of this tendency, it essentially depends on the existing family alliances and on the respect, trust and professional training each person manages to acquire. We have seen that it is by blood that one belongs to the family, and that it is by means of this substance, reified in the carrying of the family name, that one acquires the right to accede to top positions, both in the family and at the enterprise. After that, however, other factors assume importance, as only a few who share the substance and carry the family name will make it to leadership positions. These factors are: family alliances, the respect and trust each person manages to acquire and the professional training and competence they demonstrate in their business activities. To assume a leading position in the family firm, men have to distinguish themselves from their relatives by their personal relations in the family context and, most importantly, by their professional competence.

## Knowledge as the major legacy of the senior generation for the formation of successors

We have seen that the maintenance of familial control over the enterprise is a central family issue that requires a considerable investment by family leaders. In fact, to guarantee the continuation of family members in executive leadership positions from generation to generation, actual family leaders have to attract competent young family members into the business and prepare them for future senior management. They can not simply follow a filial descent process of succession – the demands made on a leader at the high national and international level of economic dealings in which they act being too high. In fact, if members of the senior generation are to guarantee economic growth, credibility and trust from public investors in their family companies, they must develop and train potential successors to be top-grade professionals. To ensure that they have the best managers at the enterprise's key executive positions, in a professional context ruled by competence, they have to adhere to strict principles of equal opportunity and of meritocracy. They have to fulfil their companies' needs through the open processes of selection.

This seems to be the central reason why these families make such a great investment in their male descendants' academic training: to give them the best possible professional skills. With these skills, even in a situation of public competition, they can always be the professionals who are best prepared to occupy the central decision-making places at their family enterprises. So, to qualify for leading positions in their own company, family members must be able to demonstrate publicly that they have the knowledge, the ability and the interest to contribute to the company's development. In this social context, family successors who make it to top executive level truly have to earn their positions. However, it should be noted that, in most cases, the children of these families do succeed to their parents' posts. This is clearly the result of the great investment made by these families in the formal education of their children. But, this is also the result of the privileged social and economic positions of these families and the benefits of being a closed élite group. Furthermore, through the investment these families make in the academic preparation of their younger generations, they also guarantee one of the most powerful bases of the reproduction of their rather closed social group. In fact, the children of these families usually go to the same schools and, as they grow up together and become colleagues and friends, they perpetuate in future generations the web of their parents' economic and social relations and commitments.[7]

I believe that professional training is the most important legacy that these families grant to their future generations, and that professional training and managerial experience make all the difference between close male kinsmen. In fact, among these wealthy families who own large companies, not even the first-born male son is the natural successor to his father. Although he may be in the best position to occupy the place, he must prove that he is the most competent and best qualified to do so. Successors must be produced by the commanding generation. More than money, family name or social status, the best formal education is what distinguishes family heirs, transforming one or two of them into potential successors to the patriarchal role both in the family and at the firm. At the same time, it is this particular investment in professional training and knowledge transmission that guarantees the reproduction of this social group as an élite. It is due to the fact that these families have significant financial capital that they have access to the best schools, where they can guarantee the best cultural and professional capital for their children, as their own fathers did for them. So, it is by the reproduction of the restricted access to these assets that this small group of families, which constitute the Lisbon financial élite, reproduce their access to high managerial positions and thus, informally, deny outsiders access to these places. It is by means of their financial power that people in this social group guarantee almost exclusive access to the best professional training in the best schools in the world.[8] But the fact that, theoretically, these are open schools creates the illusion that the whole system is based on meritocracy. Meritocracy in this professional and social

context is, therefore, the result of the economic power of these families, their powerful social relations and high social prestige. Through
the process of the reproduction of their social group they reproduce
inequality in the wider social system. In this way, the élite succeed in
informally closing their frontiers in a formally opened democratic social
system and, at the same time, become able to recruit their own people
under strict principles of equal opportunities. According to Abner
Cohen, these processes are two of the most important characteristics of
élite groups (Cohen 1981: 220).[9]

## The myth of the three generations in family firms: the Portuguese case

Top professional training is of particular importance in Portugal, where
it is not common to find large family firms in control of the sort of
professional administrators whom Marcus and Hall call 'fiduciaries'.
According to these authors, fiduciaries are professionally trained
administrators who have imposed themselves as central figures in
North American family-enterprise formations where family members
are generally not professionally trained managers. Therefore, fiduciaries
have a 'central role in the perpetuation of both fortunes and families as
corporate organisations [in the United States]' (Marcus and Hall
1992: 54). Their relative absence from the Portuguese scene is probably due to the recent political history of our country.

As I have suggested before, both the inner process of development of
these Lisbon family companies and their family cycles were vigorously
shaken by the 1974 democratic revolution and by their consequent exile
in foreign countries. Because of the loss of control of their enterprises
resulting from nationalisation processes, these families had to restart
their economic lives. For that purpose, they relied on two fundamental
things: their solid family ties, which gave them the emotional and
practical support for starting life in a new environment, and their excellent international social and business relations, because they needed
associated partners and financial credit. With the nationalisation of their
firms these families did lose a great deal of their commodities, but they
did not lose their most valuable assets: their social prestige, their
international good name and their place in the world's financial élite.[10]

So, as we can see, to rebuild their economic power and to get back
their enterprises, the men of these families could not rely on any kind
of fiduciary. They had to do it on their own because their most valuable assets were not transmissible. And after they had accomplished

their objectives – to rebuild their economic empires and to recover their leading positions in Portugal's economic scene – they were so proud that they wanted to show the world they were still the rulers of their enterprises. For this reason they did not want to give the command of their firms to a fiduciary. This may be a symbolic act, but it also demonstrates that they are good professionals, and that their great investment in professional skills and experience, allied with their social position, are a most powerful combination. So, Portuguese financial élite members kept the ruling and executive places of their firms for themselves.

This situation obviously goes against the famous theory in family enterprise studies[11] which states that family firms collapse at the third generation. Portuguese large family–economic formations are now at their fourth or fifth generations, and there is no evidence either of near collapse or of the introduction of fiduciaries to the executive positions of their firms. The personal investment Portuguese élite members commit to their professional training can be seen as a consequence of the changes that have taken place in the Portuguese economic and social order introduced by the democratic revolution. The new social and political order in which we have lived since 1974 created very special conditions for the managing period of the third, fourth and fifth generations. Individuals of these generations arrived at the top positions of their family firms in the late 1980s with an unusual dynamism and strength. Far from being able to rely on formerly acquired glory, they have had to prove their capacities to return to Portugal and to repurchase their enterprises and regain their position as rulers of the Portuguese financial élite. And, as they want to keep their ruling places, they have had to provide themselves with the best professional skills. As we can see, to provide the next generation with the same patrimony is the most powerful weapon to legitimise managerial succession in Portuguese family-owned businesses.

The myth of the 'three generations of family firms' seems to be related to the notion that economic and family domains are separate and irreconcilable. This supports the idea that the internal logic of these domains – one based on emotional ties and the other on profit motivation – is expected to result in the recruitment of personnel on the basis of kinship criteria alone in an economic environment where recruitment should have been made on the basis of professional competence. The analysis of large Portuguese family companies clearly shows that this is not necessarily the case. In fact, we have seen how these families create a strategic production of professionals that transforms blood criteria into professional competence. The Lisbon large family enterprise shows that, in this context, economic interest is thicker than blood and so, to keep their businesses, these families have to create ways of guaranteeing that, in spite of being based predominantly on economic and professional criteria, the ones who share the same family substance get to succeed one another in their common family project. The successful succession of family members to top leading positions in family enterprises is a clear demonstration of the cultural importance of blood as a Portuguese symbol of family and kinship unity. So, the understanding of its symbolic power is very revealing, even in a social context where its influence can be unexpected. In this way, we can see that these large familial enterprises constitute a social context where kinship and economics are not two social dimensions, but form a unique multidimensional context where family relations and economic interests are always present. If this were not the case, then it would not be necessary to engage in the process of training future generations to be competent professionals. They would contract external professionals to do the job and there would be no need to transform filial descent into meritocratic professional achievement, since leading positions would simply pass from father to son. Likewise, it would not be important to carry on the family name, and any good professional could do the job. However, in the case of Lisbon's entrepreneurial élite, it is the economic interest of the people involved that explains the complex processes of manipulating kinship relations. We have seen how economic interest is what keeps the family together. So can economic interest be classified as a pattern of kinship?

## Economic interests are thicker than blood in large familial enterprises

In Western society the separation between family and economics has been so strongly built, both culturally and theoretically, that it is difficult to think about them as a combination of two social dimensions. In their reflection on David Schneider's contributions to cultural analysis, Sylvia Yanagisako and Carol Delaney call our attention to the fact that one of the things that contributes to the difficulty in understanding these two cultural domains of social action is the fact that 'cultural domains usually come with prohibitions against reading across them' (Yanagisako and Delaney 1995: 12). This is clearly felt in the analysis of the context of large companies owned by Portuguese élite families. Contemporary anthropology has not produced an analytical framework to adequately understand the complex social domain of family firms in Western bureaucratic societies. As a consequence, there are no analytical instruments to conceptualise the diversity of levels in which these people live, nor theoretical concepts to understand their overlaps. However, this is also a cultural problem and it can be clearly witnessed in the families I am working with. My interviewees get very upset when I suggest that economic alliances have anything to do with familial relations. In a world of meritocracy, the financial élite can not afford to give the impression that it is perpetuated by blood criteria.

Throughout this chapter I have argued that large family enterprises, which want to continue to be run by family members, have to introduce strict economic and competence criteria in the selection of family successors if they are willing to continue their top national and international positions. Such enterprises face a permanent challenge to their aim of continuation: they have to co-ordinate their family motivations and desires for direct succession with the rational and objective logic of economic management. In this social context, succession to leading positions in the family company can not be seen as a simple process of filial descent. In fact, even traditional processes of succession – like primogeniture or male transmission – are not applicable to top positions because there are, on the one hand, legal demands for the equal treatment of heirs and, on the other, the need for economic competence. Yet, the visible process is one of passing the position from father to son, brother or nephew. I have demonstrated how, in the context of the Lisbon financial élite, there are no natural successors to leadership positions. Family successors have to conquer their way to the top by means of personal merit. Nevertheless, this merit is mostly a result of their parents' conscious investment in their training. The most valuable patrimonial transmissions that are made from parent to child are the family name and the professional preparation. Without them, these men would not be sure of making their way to the top. Through this process, these families have created the conditions that guarantee their own reproduction, ensuring that they are able to pass the leadership of the firm, as well as the consequent gains in wealth and in social prestige, from generation to generation. We can put this another way: by playing the meritocratic game, they succeed in developing what looks like kinship transmission.

I have also argued that it is through these processes of the production of successors that the Lisbon financial élite became a rather closed social group. They have the financial means to best prepare their children, to 'earn' their leading positions by personal merit. As they marry

élite have significant influence in Portuguese national life and, consequently, they have a significant voice in international economic and
political Portuguese relations. By being part of the major national
enterprises, and with their influential national and international web of
personal relations, these people have an informal control over some
sectors of public life. If this is so, their personal relations have large-
scale repercussions. We are, therefore, at a level of reflection where
personal relations can acquire importance as a dimension to understanding some global phenomena, usually studied in macro-economics,
but to which anthropology has much to say, as it uncovers the central
importance of small-scale relations.

## Acknowledgements

I am grateful to João de Pina-Cabral and Manuel Pedroso de Lima for
their stimulating comments on a first draft of this chapter.

## Notes

1   The investigation presented in this chapter is part of a larger project enti-
    tled 'Grandes famílias, grandes empresas' ('Major families, major
    enterprises'), co-ordinated by Professor João de Pina-Cabral and financed
    by JNICT under the number PCSH/C/ANT/851/95. This research has
    been carried out since September 1994. We have been working with eight
    families who own large Portuguese companies. For each of these economic
    groups we have conducted extensive interviews and gathered family stories
    (from the founder of the firm), along with the elaboration of histories of
    their companies or economic groups. This procedure has enabled us to
    gain access to information about the developmental processes of the family
    and of the enterprise, combining the information about both of them:
    about the family members who worked in the family firms and which jobs
    they occupied; about the ways in which the familial strategies are structured
    by the economic project; and the ways in which the enterprise strategies are
    influenced by family projects. Throughout the research we have gained
    insights into the common strategies of the different family-based
    Portuguese economic groups, as well as their characteristics. It has also
    given us the opportunity to analyse the history of these family-based
    economic groups in the light of the recent history of our country.
2   It is worth noting that we are not dealing with the usual universe of small
    family enterprises, where the family owns the totality of the firm and where
    the employees and the administration board are mostly composed of family
    members. The universe of companies I am dealing with is constituted by
    large important companies, some of them well-known multinationals,
    which are the property of different shareholders, from the family of the
    founder or not, but where the sum of the family members' shares gives
    them the majority of votes. Of course, to analyse these multinational firms,

among their own social group, they further close their invisible
tiers and contribute to the reproduction of the privileged cond
Privilege is, thus, passed from generation to generation and thro
these families guarantee a legitimate system of maintaining the su
sion inside their rather small social group. They have created a
process of succession, based on modern economic and meritoc
rationality, which substitutes the traditional filial succession pro
without losing their main family ambitions: to reproduce their co
tive economic project; to maintain the social prestige associated
their family as an entity; and to preserve for themselves the lea
management positions in their family firms.

Through the ethnographic examples presented in this chapter
have also seen how economic relations are embedded in kinship re
tions in such a way as to make it hard to distinguish which is t
prevalent one. However, what seems central to the anthropologi
study of kinship is that, although blood is an important symbol
Portuguese kinship, it is not the only one (cf. Pina-Cabral 1989). F
this reason, we can not think of kinship relations based only on bloo
criteria. Like Yanagisako and Delaney suggested, I believe that in orde
to analyse family relations among the Portuguese financial élite w
should 'read across the boundaries', in order to be able to understand
'the local patterns of meanings in practice' (Yanagisako and Delaney
1995: 13, 14). 'While institutions and cultural domains of meaning
have a profound impact on shaping ideas and practices, people do not
necessarily organize their everyday actions according to these divisions.
Rather, people think and act at the intersections of discourses'
(Yanagisako and Delaney 1995: 18). I suggest that we refer to them as
'economic-based kinship relations' or as 'kinship-based economic relations', depending on which context of social action we are
emphasising. Through the use of these concepts I believe we can better
describe the multidimensional social relations that characterise these
financial élite family companies. Through this chapter we have seen
that there are considerable economic dividends in these kinship relations. However, the example of the Portuguese financial élite also
highlights the familial dividends of economic privilege.

Finally, I also want to suggest that the study of large family enterprises foreshadows how important a contribution anthropological
analysis can make to élite studies and to kinship theory. In the social
domain of an international financial élite, the world economy is related
to the face-to-face relations of this group of people. In fact, the family-
based economic groups that form a significant part of the Lisbon financial

with hundreds or thousands of employees and complex shareholding structures, implies a different perspective in classifying these companies as family
firms. I use the concept of family firms to classify these companies because
they have been founded by a member of the family who has kept the
majority of shares and maintained control of the administration boards over
more than the last two generations. Although we can find an enormous
amount of literature on small family firms, since it has been a common
topic of research for sociologists, economists and historians, the analysis of
these large family-owned enterprises is much rarer, particularly in anthropology.

3  On this topic see João de Pina-Cabral (1991: 128–34).
4  I want to thank João de Pina-Cabral for this expression.
5  Although I am not going to discuss it here, it is worth noting that divorce
   is a very frequent practice among these Roman Catholic élite families.
6  João de Pina-Cabral has noted the same occurrence in the bourgeois families of Oporto (1991) and in peasant families in Minho (1989).
7  Jean Lave calls our attention to the extremely important contributions of
   the 'Oporto British School' in the successful formation of successors
   among the English élite families of Oporto (Lave 1997).
8  See, for instance, the work of Jean Marceau (1989) on the management
   training of an international school, INSEAD in Fontainebleau, which she
   characterises as the locus of the foundation of a European business élite.
9  In his study of the Creole élite in Sierra Leone, Abner Cohen has brilliantly
   shown how it is through informal relations of kinship and amity that this
   élite group closes its frontiers and thus reproduces its privileged social position. He also gives an excellent example of how they create a formal
   meritocratic system over an informal system of recruiting their own people.
10 Compare, for instance, the example of the Espírito Santo family: it was
   through the direct influence of Giscard D'Estaing, then president of
   France, and of MacNamara, then president of the World Bank, that the
   revolutionary government of Portugal released the six members of the
   Espírito Santo family from prison in 1975. In the same year, at the first
   meeting of the Portuguese government with the World Bank, MacNamara
   invited M.R. Espírito Santo to sit at his right, as his private guest, to
   publicly show to the new Portuguese democratic government whose side
   he was on.
11 For more on this issue see, for instance, the works of Gary McDonough
   (1989), George Marcus and Peter Hall (Marcus and Hall 1992) and Kelin
   Gersick (Gersick et al. 1997).

## References

Cohen, A. (1981) *The Politics of Elite Culture: Explorations in the Dramaturgy
of Power in a Modern African Society*, Berkeley: University of California
Press.

Gersick, K.E. *et al*. (1997) *Generation to Generation: Life Cycles of the Family
Business*, Boston, MA: Harvard Business School Press.

Lave, J. (1997) '(Re)serving succession in a British enclave', paper presented at the 'Leadership and succession in elite contexts' workshop, Lisbon, October 1997.

McDonough, G.W. (1989 [1986]) *Las Buenas Familias de Barcelona. História Social de poder en la era Industrial*, Barcelona: Editiones Omega.

Marceau, J. (1989) *A Family Business*, Cambridge, UK: Cambridge University Press.

Marcus, G. and Hall, P.D. (1992) *Lives in Trust: The Fortunes of Dynastic Families in Late Twentieth-Century America*, Boulder, CO: Westview Press.

Pina-Cabral, J. de (1989 [1986]) *Filhos de Adão, Filhas de Eva. A visão do mundo camponesa do Alto Minho*, Lisbon: D. Quixote.

—— (1989) 'L'Heritage de Maine: Repenser les catégories descriptives dans l'étude de la famille en Europe', *Ethnologie Française* 19(4): 329–40.

—— (1991) *Os contextos da Antropologia*, Lisbon: Difel.

—— (1996) 'The threshold diffused: Margins, hegemonies and contradictions in contemporary anthropology', in P. McAllister (ed.) *Culture and the Commonplace: Anthropological Essays in Honour of David Hammond-Tooke*, Johannesburg: Witwatersrand University Press.

Schneider, D. (1984) *A Critique of the Study of Kinship*, Ann Arbor: University of Michigan Press.

Yanagisako, S. (1991) 'Capital and gendered interest in Italian family firms', in D. Kertzer and R. Saller (eds) *The Family in Italy: From Antiquity to the Present*, New Haven, CT: Yale University Press.

Yanagisako, S. and Delaney, C. (1995) 'Naturalizing power', in S. Yanagisako and C. Delaney (eds) *Naturalizing Power: Essays in Feminist Cultural Analysis*, London: Routledge.

# Chapter 7

# 'Philoprogenitiveness' through the cracks

## On the resilience and benefits of kinship in Utopian communes

*Christoph Brumann*

---

> Whether there is a complete correspondence of the fortunes of these several Communities to the strength of their anti-familism, is an interesting question which we are not prepared to answer. Only it is manifest that the Shakers, who discard the radix of old society with the greatest vehemence, and are most jealous for Communism as the prime unit of organization, have prospered most, and are making the longest and strongest mark on the history of Socialism. And in general it seems probable from the fact of success attending these forms of Communism to the exclusion of all others, that there is some rational connection between their control of the sexual relation and their prosperity.
>
> (Noyes 1961 [1870]: 141–2)

> Of course we shall not be understood as propounding the theory that the negative or Shaker method of disposing of marriage and the sexual relation, is the only one that can subordinate familism to Communism. The Oneida Communists claim that their control over amativeness and philoprogenitiveness, the two elements of familism, is carried much farther than that of the Shakers; inasmuch as they make those passions serve Communism, instead of opposing it, as they do under suppression. They dissolve the old dual unit of society, but take the constituent elements of it all back into Communism.
>
> (Noyes 1961 [1870]: 142–3)

## Oneida Community

The preceding quotes are taken from one of the first contributions to the research on Utopian communes, *History of American Socialisms*. Its author, John Humphrey Noyes (1811–86), was the charismatic leader of what he was writing about — one of the most radical social experiments in American history, namely Oneida Community in upstate New York. Educated as a Protestant minister, Noyes converted to Perfectionism, a dissident creed that found numerous adherents in the religious excitement that welled up in the New England of the 1840s. According to Perfectionism, the Second Coming of Christ and the Advent of the Millennium had already occurred so that it was within the reach of true believers to lead a sinless life. Moreover, Noyes's idiosyncratic exegesis of Matthew 22: 30 – 'For in the resurrection, they neither marry nor are given in marriage, but are like angels in heaven' – convinced him that in the millennium, celestial love was no longer bound by the shackles of monogamous marriage. In a private letter, he wrote:

> The marriage supper of the Lamb is a feast at which every dish is free to every guest. ... In the holy community, there is no more reason why sexual intercourse should be restrained by law, than why eating and drinking should be.
>
> (quoted in Parker 1973: 44)

Understandably, these convictions – although he presented them guardedly at first – provoked resistance, and Noyes lost his pulpit and retired to his family's holdings in Putney, Vermont. Among the small band of followers he assembled there, he felt particularly attracted to one Mary Cragin. In 1846, he decided to put his ideas into practice and convinced Cragin's husband and his own wife to start a four-person marriage. Gradually, the other followers joined in this arrangement, and 'complex marriage', as Noyes termed it, was born. This alliance was not to be confounded with unrestrained free love, however, since men were to practice 'male continence' or *coitus reservatus*. Thereby they spared their supply of semen, which Noyes equated with life force, and saved the women from unnecessary childbirths – Noyes's wife had had four stillbirths. It supposedly also contributed to a purer sexual experience – suffused with the spirit of 'amativeness' – which could even serve as an instrument for the veneration of God. Sexual activity was closely monitored by the group, and any exclusive attachment ('special love') between two particular members was punished by their separation.

In 1848, the group moved to New York State where it merged with another Perfectionist community that had settled in Oneida County. After two more years membership exceeded 200 persons, never to fall below this number again. The Oneida Perfectionists built themselves the impressive, still existing Mansion House and subsisted on the manufacture and sale of animal traps, soap, silk, fruit preserves and a host of other products, becoming prosperous enough to employ many outsiders in their factories. It was only in the 1870s that religious enthusiasm cooled and Noyes's leadership capacity dwindled, although membership continued to grow until 1878 when it peaked at 306. The experiment ended in 1881 when the commune was transformed into a joint-stock corporation based on the private ownership of shares. Yet for many members, the Mansion House remained the hub of their social life during the following decades (Carden 1969; Dalsimer 1975; Kern 1981; Parker 1973; Robertson 1972, 1977, 1981; Thomas 1977).

Except for a brief celibate interlude, complex marriage was continued throughout the more than three decades of Oneida's existence. 'Male continence' worked reasonably well at first, with on average less than two children born annually (Carden 1969: 51) in a community of around 200 adults. Since experiences with outside recruits left something to be desired, however, 'stirpiculture' was introduced in 1869, meaning that, henceforth, member couples matched by the group for their spiritual quality were to produce offspring for the community. From these unions, altogether fifty-eight children were born (Carden 1969: 63). They were raised in a children's house, and while their relationships with their parents were severely restricted, those with other adults were actively encouraged. 'Philoprogenitiveness' – Noyes's word for nepotism (Robertson 1981: 75–6) – should thereby be eradicated, or, rather, transferred from the family level to that of the entire commune. Uncommon though this arrangement appeared to contemporary observers, it apparently worked to the satisfaction of the members. This is attested to not only by the long duration of the community but also by the fact that more than 80 per cent of the adult founding members either died in the community or stayed with it until the end (Carden 1969: 77).

## Commune and family: born rivals?

As demonstrated by Oneida, intentionally formed property-sharing communes are not always bound to immediate failure – contrary though this may seem to those that expect our egoistic nature to thwart all well-meant attempts towards voluntary sharing.[1] And neither must communes collapse quickly if they try to suppress monogamous marriage, family and kinship. Oneida's group marriage, however, is not the only way to do so; more impressive still are the achievements of a number of communes of male and female celibates. Harmony was a group of German Separatists that, after several clashes with State authorities and Lutheran orthodoxy, emigrated to the United States in 1804. They built up thriving communities at three successive locations in Pennsylvania and Indiana, basing themselves on agriculture and some industry, and did not disband until 1905 (Arndt 1965, 1971). A whole century longer still is the history of the Shakers (or United Society of Believers). This off-split of the English Quakers formed around the charismatic Ann Lee and then emigrated to New England where it gathered adherents and became communal in 1787. Also supporting themselves with agriculture, handicrafts and industry, the Shakers lived in up to eighteen communal villages throughout New England and the Midwest. Although the Shakers are often regarded as a thing of the past – and are remembered warmly for their outstanding material culture – their history of more than 200 years has by no means ended, since there is one last village in Sabbathday Lake, Maine, which still functions (Brewer 1986; Stein 1992).

But does the success of group marriage and celibate communes mean that doing away with family and kinship is the only path to communal longevity? A number of scholars have argued so, most notably sociologist Rosabeth Kanter in her seminal *Commitment and Community* (1972). Following in effect the zero-sum logic implicit in Noyes's argument, she sees family and community as antagonistic units competing for members' loyalties. What is accorded one of these units in terms of attachment cannot go to the other, so that the family must be weakened if the commune is to be strong. For this purpose, celibacy and group marriage are functionally equivalent since they both elimi- nate the family (Kanter 1972: 82, 87, 92). This line of reasoning has found wide support (e.g. Barrett 1974: 42; Coser 1974: 137; Muncy 1973: 229–31) and has been questioned only haltingly (Lauer and Lauer 1983: 56; Oved 1988: 413; Wagner 1986: 176), with more emphatic rejections restricted to Shenker's (1986: 220–7) and Van den Berghe and Peter's (1988) remarks. What follows is an attempt towards a more comprehensive reappraisal.

## Longevity reassessed

When juxtaposing Utopian communes that were unequivocally mono- gamous with those which in some way tried to do away with monogamous marriage, the latter ones appear more successful at first sight (see Table 7.1). Among the fifteen longest-lived communes encountered in my research – all with life-spans greater than sixty years – only five are monogamous. While monogamy thus beats group marriage, for which Oneida's thirty-seven years have already set the record, the celibate suppression of family ties has on the whole led to the most impressive durations.

Table 7.1 Life-spans of the most durable communes

| Name | Start | End | Duration |
| --- | --- | --- | --- |
| **Shakers** | 1787 | | 212 |
| Hutterites | 1874 | | 125 |
| **Abode of Love** | 1840 | 1958 | 118 |
| **Harmony** | 1804 | 1905 | 101 |
| **House of David** | 1902 | | 97 |
| **Snowhill** | 1798 | 1889 | 91 |
| **Amana** | 1843 | 1932 | 89 |
| Kibbutzim | 1910 | | 89 |
| Ittô-en | 1913 | | 86 |
| Atarashiki mura | 1918 | | 81 |
| **Zoar** | 1819 | 1898 | 79 |
| Bruderhof | 1920 | | 79 |
| **Koreshan Unity** | 1880 | 1947 | 67 |
| **Ephrata** | 1732 | 1797 | 65 |
| **Woman's Commonwealth** | 1877 | 1940 | 63 |

Note: Somewhat consistently with their character, the non-monogamous communes are printed in bold type and the monogamous communes in ordinary type. Where no end date is given, the respective case continues to exist at present. The Hutterites have repeatedly abandoned community of goods during their history of almost five centuries. The date given refers to the last communal period beginning with their migration to the United States. Some of the dates for the remaining communes also deviate from those given in other accounts. This is because when the adoption of communal property did not coincide with the founding of a settlement, I chose the former date. Also, the date of dissolution is difficult to determine in some cases, especially in those that 'died out'. Here, I chose as the end date the earliest year when community of goods clearly must have been abolished. In Woman's Commonwealth, the third to last member died in 1940 (Kitch 1993: 110) so that what one can meaningfully call a communal *group* ended at this time. For a detailed discussion of the dates given, see Brumann (1998: ch. 2).

This is relativised, however, if one takes a closer look at how these durations were achieved. The Shakers still exist today as a commune, but only one of their villages has survived. Even back in 1874 they were described as 'a parcel of old bachelors and old maids' (Stein 1992: 230), and membership has hovered below one-tenth of the former maximum for more than eighty years now, with only eight Shakers remaining in 1992 (Stein 1992: 252, 435–6). In Harmony as well, decline set in after no more than thirty years. When sixty years had passed membership had already fallen below one-sixth of the highest number, which supposedly was between 750 (Carpenter 1975: 163) and 1,050 (M.R. Miller 1972: 42–3). After eighty-six years the less than twenty members that were left – most of them rather aged – needed more than 300 outside employees to run the communal enterprises in their stead (Arndt 1971: 189; M.R. Miller 1972: 66–7). Both communes would have ended much earlier if they had not been able to live off the lasting fruits of initial prosperity. The other celibate communes – with the exception of Amana and Zoar (see below) – show a similar pattern. It is obvious that they continued until they virtually died out. At that time, however, they had been reduced to faint shadows of their former glory, and the ageing members had abandoned all hope for continuity decades before (cf. McCormick 1965: 149–69 for Abode of Love; Treher 1968: 84–103; Fogarty 1981: 120–8; Landing 1981: 13–14; Kitch 1993: 110–12).

The five monogamous communes present a different picture. First of all, they still exist today whereas, apart from the Shakers and House of David, none of the celibate cases do. Moreover, while Ittô-en and Atarashiki mura seem to have passed their prime (Brumann 1992, forthcoming), the Hutterites, the kibbutzim, and the Bruderhof communities continue to prosper and exhibit no signs of imminent decline. These three cases are in a better shape at present than any of the celibate communes were after an equal time span, so they can be assumed to continue as communes for at least several decades. Taking the diverse modes of communal survival into account, then, leads to a different result from a rank order based on sheer duration alone. There seems to be an advantage for monogamy within Utopian communes, so that a closer look at the three most successful cases is in order.

## Hutterites

The Hutterites arose as a part of the Anabaptist movement of the Reformation. Founded in the sixteenth century in Bohemia, they were subject to century-long religious persecution and forced migrations as far as the Ukraine, and repeatedly abandoned communal property in the process. In 1874, most Hutterites migrated to the United States and, afterwards, also to Canada, where they have prospered ever since by supporting themselves with large-scale agriculture. Their austere, conservative life-style is based on a literal understanding of biblical requirements and is opposed to most North American mainstream values; moreover, their German dialect sets them off ethnically. Presently, there are about 30,000 Hutterites living in some 400 colonies (Hartse 1994b: 110; for general descriptions see Bennett 1967; Hostetler 1974a; Peter 1987; Stephenson 1991).

The Hutterites believe in the sanctity of the indissoluble mono-gamous marriage bond. Divorce is not allowed, and extramarital affairs are regarded as a grave sin (Hostetler 1974a: 146). Average marriage age has risen in recent years but still not yet beyond the mid-twenties (Stephenson 1991: 107; Peter 1987: 161). Less than 5 per cent of the adults over thirty have never been married (Hostetler 1974a: 203). Men and women work on separate assignments, and communal child care leaves most of the women free for other tasks. Families, however, are the habitual units for distributing allowances and for leisure activities. Marriage ties are also acknowledged when filling positions of responsibility: the wife of a Hutterite colony 'householder', the economic manager, often holds the highest female office of head cook (Bennett 1967: 145–6). There are limits to familism: when being baptised, Hutterites have to promise to place loyalty towards the commune over that of family members (Peter 1987: 39), and they have to participate in sanctions such as ostracism against family members (Shenker 1986: 224). However, there is no principal restriction of family ties, and members are also free to choose their own marriage partners. Because of decreasing colony sizes, nurseries and kindergartens are now discontinued in some Hutterite colonies, with the mothers taking care of their smaller children. Signs of declining discipline have been reported and have been attributed to this development (Peter 1987: 65–6), but the evidence so far does not appear conclusive enough to predict a negative effect.

Beyond this emphasis on families, Hutterite society is densely inter-woven by wider kin ties – a situation caused by endogamy and the fact that the colonies have attracted only a minuscule number of converts from outside. All present-day Hutterites are descendants of the 443 individuals who emigrated to the United States in 1874 (Sato *et al.* 1994: 422), and they were already well connected themselves, going back to ninety-two individuals who had been cut off from external marriage relations since 1760 (Peter 1987: 128–9). Although first-cousin marriage is avoided, the average married couple in the 1970s was more closely related than second cousins (Hostetler 1974a: 265). Because of virilocal preferences, colonies often consist of only a few sets of brothers with their families (Bennett 1967: 108, 119, 121), and in extreme cases an entire Hutterite colony of between sixty and 180 people can be made up of a single ancestor couple, its descendants and their spouses alone (Bennett 1967: 116).

Kinship provides an important resource for individual agency. Personal help is first sought among relatives (Bennett 1967: 131–2). Kin groups, especially groups of brothers, often form factions that try to corner important offices in the communal hierarchy (Peter 1987: 45–6, 80; Bennett 1967: 257). Inheritance of such positions from father to son is not uncommon (Shenker 1986: 225–6). Even deviance seems to be kin-based when specific families are regarded as especially vulnerable for defection to outside society (Hostetler 1974a: 273). Strong kin ties between some members might alienate those who are not so deeply enmeshed, but it has been observed that colonies with many kin groups are more prone to factionalism on the basis of kinship than those with just a few kin groups (Peter 1987: 62). Marriage ties also strengthen inter-colony bonds since they often go along with economic co-operation (Bennett 1967: 124–5; Hostetler 1974a: 241, note 9). Furthermore, male members from culturally deviant or economically weak colonies will have difficulties in finding marriage partners (Hostetler 1974a: 271; Shenker 1986: 164). Although the refusals are informal and based on individual decisions, they work as a powerful sanction, forcing the respective colonies back into line. Case studies of one colony in crisis (Peter 1987: 146–8) and of another one that has been excommunicated (Holzach 1982: 174–7) show that the impossibility of finding wives is one of the harshest consequences that deviant colonies have to face. Moreover, family and relatives are usually what Hutterite defectors miss most and are what brings many of them back into the commune, often in spite of serious doubts about the way of life and religious practice. Many more members supposedly refrain from leaving for the same reason (Peter 1987: 106–7; Shenker 1986:162, 227).

Finally, offspring is important for the maintenance of the colonies and for their spectacular expansion pushed forward by the planned division of colonies. The Hutterites once were the fastest growing human population with annual increases of more than 4 per cent around

1950 (Peter 1987: 154). While these rates have declined considerably (Nonaka *et al.* 1994; Sato *et al.* 1994; Peter 1987), they still lie around 2 per cent at present (Peter 1987: 155–6), with the natural growth far exceeding the increasing, but still small, number of permanent defections.[2] The Hutterites were thus able to increase the number of colonies by more than a hundred times and the number of members by almost seventy times, simply by retaining their own offspring.

## Bruderhof communities

The Bruderhof communities model themselves closely on the Hutterites, not so much on the contemporary ones but on the idealised Hutterites of sixteenth-century Bohemia. There are important differences between the two groups, however, and the mutual relations have been rocky at times so that I consider it justified to treat them separately. The first Bruderhof community was founded in Germany in 1920 by the Protestant theologian Eberhard Arnold (1883–1935) who had converted himself to Anabaptism. When he learned about North American Hutterites, he paid a visit to them and had his community acknowledged as a fourth branch alongside the three traditional branches, or *Leut*, of the Hutterites. Arnold's unexpected death in 1935 and forced migrations (first, from Nazi Germany to England; then, in 1941, from there to Paraguay) provided a serious challenge to the commune, followed by a new crisis around 1960 that resulted in the shifting of activities to the United States. Today there are about 2,500 members in eight 'bruderhofs' – six in the United States, two in England – where they produce toys and equipment for handicapped children. Bruderhof members are no less committed to biblical precepts than the Hutterites, but, compared with their forerunners, they have placed a greater emphasis on unity with the Divine Spirit than on established rules and rituals. At present, relations with both Hutterites and a network of former members are strained (Eggers 1985; Mow 1989; Zablocki 1973; see also the Bruderhof website at http://www.bruderhof.org).[3]

The status of monogamous marriage among Bruderhof members is similar to that of the Hutterites. Here as well divorce and extramarital affairs are anathema (Zablocki 1973: 117), and the remarriage of divorced people entering the commune is also prohibited (Zablocki 1973: 119; Eggers 1985: 69). In the absence of precise figures, it nonetheless appears that the emphasis on marriage is equally intense. Single adults are incorporated into families with whom they share leisure time, meals, celebrations, etc. (Zablocki 1973: 122). While concrete family limits are thereby blurred, the status of the family as the normal and natural living unit is emphasised. As among the Hutterites, the wives of Bruderhof office holders (such as 'servants of the word', 'witness brothers' and 'stewards') are often 'housemothers' – the only office open to women (Zablocki 1973: 203). While being separated during daytime, families live together in the same apartment and receive their allowances as a unit (Zablocki 1973: 26, 43, 128–9). Furthermore, they have breakfast and several other meals together (Zablocki 1973: 46–9), in contrast to the Hutterites where all meals are eaten in common. As among the Hutterites, the loyalty towards the commune should in principle be greater than that towards one's family (Zablocki 1973: 267), and the more severe sanctions separate a member from his own family (Zablocki 1973: 196–9). But as long as family life does not deviate from the commune's standards, the commune is in principle not expected to interfere with it.

Detailed kinship data on the Bruderhof communities are not available, but endogamy, the importance of the nuclear family and the high number of children (discussed below) make it very likely that the group is also cross-cut by many kin ties. While nepotism is officially frowned upon (Zablocki 1973: 28, 228), it has been reported that the family members of office holders often receive privileged treatment, even against their own wishes (Pleil 1994: 57, 226, 267; Zablocki 1973: 271). Kinship has also played a crucial role in the succession of the group's leadership. The charismatic founder, Eberhard Arnold, died early and suddenly in 1935. A power struggle ensued, with Eberhard's three sons pitted against their two sisters' husbands. The in-laws prevailed at first and went so far as to temporarily expel the sons from the commune. But the sons had their comeback and took over the leadership in a tumultuous, drawn-out crisis accompanied by substantial purges around 1960. Unbridled by accusations of instituting a 'royal family' (Mow 1990: 305), the founder's son, Heinrich Arnold, became the new 'elder' of the commune, whereas his main opponent was charged with adultery and expelled (Zablocki 1973: 104–12; Mow 1989: 109–51). When Heinrich died in 1982, his son, Christoph, succeeded him, again after a crisis (Eggers 1985: 160; Mow 1989: 289).[4] All these events were clearly disruptive for the Bruderhof communities, and one may question their functionality for the survival of the communities. It has been observed, however, that these crises resulted in greater unity among those members who stayed (cf. Zablocki 1973: 111). Moreover, the Bruderhof has always been suspicious of fixed rules and procedures, and instead emphasises harmony with the Divine Spirit, so that, repeatedly, basic policies have been completely revised. It can therefore be argued – and has been argued also by an author sympathetic to the Bruderhof (Goeringer 1995) – that the Arnold patriline has provided the crucial element of stability when almost everything else was subject to change.[5] As with the Hutterites, it can be suspected that relatives are an important motivation to staying in the commune. Defectors suffer from being separated from their relatives, and re-establishing contact with the latter is a prime objective pursued by the dissidents' support organisation (cf., for example, Sender Barayán 1995).

Finally, members' children are also a crucial source of recruits for the Bruderhof. Precise demographic data are not available, but birth control is not practised (Zablocki 1973: 115, 117; Eggers 1985: 145), and large families of eight to ten children were fairly common at the end of the sixties (Zablocki 1973: 115, 117) and continue to be so today (Bohlken-Zumpe 1993: unnumbered page, opposite 1; Pleil 1994: 277, 279, 291). According to a former member, women are encouraged to have many children (Pleil 1994: 225, 362–3). Until 1965, 75 per cent of the children stayed in the commune as adults (Zablocki 1973: 268), and, nowadays, it is still one-half (Kruse 1991: 22) in a period when growth is steadier than in past decades. The reliable source of new members that their own children provide enables the communes to follow a rather rigorous policy of temporary and permanent expulsions of deviant members without endangering organisational continuity. While these sanctions can – repentance provided – always be reversed, the Bruderhof communities have never hesitated to make use of what seems to be an important means of keeping their spiritual balance.

## Kibbutzim

In contrast to these two Christian communities, almost all[6] kibbutzim are secular and socialist in orientation and have made a point of rejecting the religious ingredients of Jewishness (Bowes 1989: 129–41). The kibbutzim were a product of the migration of European Jews to Palestine where the first kibbutz was founded in 1910. Ardently patriotic, they played a pioneer role in the establishment of the state of Israel. Since its foundation in 1948, however, they have occupied a somewhat uneasy position within Israeli society and have repeatedly been haunted by slow growth rates and feelings of crisis.

Currently, there are around 270 kibbutzim with almost 130,000 members (Malan 1994: 121) that engage in a wide range of agricultural and industrial enterprises. With regard to age, gender and leadership positions, the kibbutzim are a great deal more egalitarian than the two preceding cases, although by no means perfectly so (Ben-Rafael 1988; Bowes 1989; Melzer and Neubauer 1988a; Spiro 1972; Tiger and Shepher 1975).

Despite many important differences from the two preceding cases, however, marriage, family and kinship are no less salient in kibbutz life. Kibbutzniks marry early, and people still single at the age of twenty-five are already considered problematic (Bowes 1980: 672–3).[7] According to older data, less than 5 per cent of all adults never marry (Tiger and Shepher 1975: 223). Singles are socially marginal (Bowes 1989: 85–6), and leadership offices are usually filled by married members, and, at least in one kibbutz, often with both partners of a married couple (Rayman 1981: 138). Divorces are permitted, although older rates were low, as compared to Israel in general (Tiger and Shepher 1975: 220–1). Extramarital affairs do occur (Bowes 1989: 91), yet despite some early sympathies for free love and contempt for the institution of monogamous marriage (Bowes 1989: 122–3; Blasi 1986: 25; Spiro 1972: 112–13), the alternatives, group marriage and celibacy, have never been seriously considered. Children are taken care of collectively, and the gender division of labour is no less pronounced than in Hutterite and Bruderhof communes. But families live and pass their leisure time together, and allowances are now increasingly distributed to families as a unit rather than to individuals (Liegle and Bergmann 1994: 33).

This has not always been so: strong sentiments against the bourgeois family held sway in the beginning, and when children were born they lived and slept in children's houses, meeting their parents for not more than a few hours on weekends. Thereby, they were educated as children of the entire kibbutz. However, a daily 'hour of love' in which parents could visit their children was instituted in the 1960s (Spiro 1972: 278; Tiger and Shepher 1975: 227), and in the 1980s and 1990s the children's houses were discontinued in almost all kibbutzim so that children now sleep in their parents' homes (Melzer and Neubauer 1988b: 30–1; Liegle and Bergmann 1994: 33). The necessary extensions to apartments have plunged many kibbutzim into heavy debts (Melzer and Neubauer 1988b: 30–1), but other than this no negative effects on their social fabric have been reported so far. Interestingly, kibbutzniks may take in their ageing parents or relatives

even when they do not want to become full members, so that the legitimacy of family ties superseding kibbutz loyalties is acknowledged
(Anonymous 1982: 170–1).

Kinship beyond the nuclear family has also grown in importance,
especially in the older kibbutzim, where large groups of relatives
numbering up to twenty-five serve as power blocks lobbying for the
interests of their members (Bowes 1989: 102; Maron 1988: 225; Tiger
and Shepher 1975: 40; Liegle and Bergmann 1994: 32). There is even
a special word for these kin groups: *hamula* – interestingly, an Arabic
word for patrilineally extended families (Tiger and Shepher 1975: 40).[8]
Among kibbutzniks, the presence of family and relatives is one of the
most important reasons not to leave the commune (Shenker 1986:
227; Spiro 1972: 227). In a 1993 opinion survey, almost 90 per cent
of the members gave as a reason to stay the opportunity to enjoy one's
family life, whereas only about 50 per cent mentioned official values
such as co-operation and equality (Liegle and Bergmann 1994: 33–4).
It seems that family and kinship are about to replace ideology as the
central motivation to be a kibbutznik, or, rather, that it is no longer
controversial to admit this openly, even if nepotism is not encouraged
on an official level (Blasi 1986: 112).

Most kibbutz families reach three or four children (Ben-Rafael
1988: 4) and the average in 1975 was 2.8 (Tiger and Shepher 1975:
223). Among the Jewish population of Israel, the kibbutzim had the
highest birth rate of 1.8–1.9 per year in 1980–5 (Van den Berghe and
Peter 1988: 526), and, generally, the birth rate has gone up since children have returned to their parents (Maron 1988: 227). While the
proportion of children that leave for good has now increased to more
than one-half (Ben-Rafael 1988: 131; Liegle and Bergmann 1994: 73),
those remaining often bring in marriage partners from the outside
(Ben-Rafael 1988: 4). About two-thirds of new members have grown
up in the kibbutz (Van den Berghe and Peter 1988: 526), so that
without this supply total membership would have long since been on
the decline.

## Monogamy and communal success

None of these three most successful present-day communes espouses
nepotism as a value: officially, all members are to be treated alike. In
practice, however, families are taken as the natural building blocks for
the wider commune in a quite matter-of-fact way, and what efforts
there were to suppress 'philoprogenitiveness' among kibbutzniks have

been abandoned, finding their most vociferous opponents in precisely those second-generation mothers who had experienced children's houses for themselves (Fölling-Albers 1988: 106). Wider kinship is also clearly important in all three cases. Furthermore, the three communes depend on natural growth to an astonishing degree. Finally, where changes have occurred, these were more in the direction of familism rather than less. It must be concluded, then, that Hutterites, Bruderhof communities and kibbutzim benefit from their monogamous family and kinship patterns, very likely more so than if they were to follow their anti-nepotistic official precepts more determinedly.

A number of other, younger, present-day communes provide further support for this argument. Shinkyô (founded in 1939) and Ô-yamato ajisai mura (founded in 1946) in Japan, Koinonia (founded in 1942) in the United States and the Arche communities (Communautés de L'Arche) in France and neighbouring countries (founded in 1948) will very likely exist for longer than, for example, Woman's Commonwealth. While they seem to have a larger propor-tion of singles and fewer mutual kin ties among their members than compared to the three most successful communes (personal visit to the Japanese communes; Day 1990: 119; Lee 1971: 172–3; Lanza del Vasto 1978: 205–6; Popenoe and Popenoe 1984: 141, 143), they also rely on monogamous marriage and the family, and do not implement alternative versions of communal family policy. Obviously, the presumed loyalty conflict between family and commune does not reach a dys-functional level in any of these cases.[9]

## Celibate communes

Even some of the communes that officially favoured celibacy were not so different from the aforementioned cases. Of the ten cases listed above, five are included among the nine nineteenth-century communes that Kanter regards as successful in her study (1972: 248–9), in which she gives celibacy as one reason for their longevity (1972: 82, 87, 92). At least for two of these cases, however, this argument appears highly dubious. Zoar, a settlement of German immigrants adhering to Protestant Separatism, was fully celibate until 1828 or 1830 (Randall 1971: 20), and members paid lip service to the supremacy of celibacy until the dissolution (Carpenter 1975: 205; Nordhoff 1960: 108). The majority, however, lived in monogamous families, and the children's houses that had been introduced were closed in 1845 (Randall 1971: 46). The Inspirationists of Amana, also German and Protestant in origin, had much respect for celibacy in the beginning, when an unusually large portion of members remained single and when leadership positions were preferentially filled from their ranks (Andelson 1974: 439–42). Almost until the end, members were temporarily demoted in rank after marriage or childbirth (Andelson 1974: 202–3), and elders and school teachers had to remain unmarried if that was their status when nominated (Andelson 1974: 164, 341). The majority of members, however, did marry and lived and received their allowances as families (Andelson 1974: 44, 107–8). There is ample evidence for the importance of wider kinship (Barthel 1984: 43–5), e.g. in the choice of marriage partners (Yambura 1961: 176–7) and the allocation of influential positions (Andelson 1974: 64–9, 171, 176–8). Thus, Amana was much closer to the kibbutzim and the Hutterites than its official preference for celibacy would suggest. Moreover, in both Zoar and Amana it was the children and grandchildren of founding members who lived in the commune in its later years and kept it going (cf. Andelson 1974: 329, 448–9; Nordhoff 1960: 108; Randall 1971: 48). A comparison between Amana and the strictly celibate Harmony is instructive: Harmony's absolute duration is twelve years longer, but Amana was far more successful in remaining a stable and 'healthy' communal institution. Its population did not fall below 90 per cent of the former membership maximum in more than 70 years and never fell below 75 per cent (cf. Andelson 1974: 326, 329), and none of the seven villages had to be closed prematurely. In contrast, Harmony had to live with less than 20 per cent of its former maximum for its last forty years, needed throngs of outsiders to keep up its economy and was dissolved when there were only three members left. Clearly then, compromising with celibacy improved the survival chances of those communes that praised it but stopped short of its strict enforcement.[10]

Moreover, even in some of those communes that were strictly celibate, nepotism played a role at least for a while. In the early years of the Shakers, numerous large, often extended, families (Brewer 1986: 23, 31–2, 35–6; Paterwic 1991: 27–8, 29–30) joined the communal settlements. Some of the primary living and property units – which were called 'families' – numbered between thirty and 100 people and almost half of each unit's members had the same family name (Brewer 1986: 69). This suggests that families were not separated after joining the commune. Families also rose together: several family names appear with significant regularity among prominent Shakers of the first period (Stein 1992: 92), for example the related Wells and Young families whose members held many important positions (Stein 1992: 31–2, 54). For a while, the two male members of the 'central ministry', the supreme leadership body, had the same family name (Stein 1992: 92, 122) and may have been brothers. According to Brewer, '[t]he stability that these kinship networks provided was considerable, and was a key factor in the early success of the sect' (Brewer 1986: 23). She also believes that kinship was more important in the past than can be demonstrated with the remaining sources (Brewer 1986: 36), at least until the recruitment of entire families became less significant after the 1840s (Brewer 1986: 138). The other major historian of the Shakers agrees that '"natural relations" … still counted in the world of Believers' (Stein 1992: 92).

## Group marriage communes

It might be expected that the more unconventional option of doing away with family and kinship that was chosen by Oneida should lead to more substantive results. However, even here family and kinship feelings were not entirely eradicated, and the commune may have profited in the end. John Humphrey Noyes made his first and most loyal converts among his own siblings (Carden 1969: 18–19, 21) and initiated marriages between these and other important but unrelated followers (Dalsimer 1975: 33; Parker 1973: 93, 95). It was only after having consolidated the group that Noyes introduced 'complex marriage' (Robertson 1981: 75–6).

Less successful were Noyes's much later attempts to institute his son, Theodore Noyes, as his successor. Theodore proved incompetent for the leadership position and also held grave doubts about his father and his religion, and the ensuing opposition contributed to the demise of the commune a few years later (Robertson 1972). Yet 'John Humphrey Noyes believed sincerely in the superiority of his family line' (Carden 1969: 63), which made him sire nine (Parker 1973: 257) or ten children instead of the one or two that were permitted to the other male participants in the 'stirpiculture' programme (Carden 1969: 63). It is apparent that Noyes's own unacknowledged nepotism blinded him to his son's shortcomings. Ordinary members found it no less problematic to refrain from 'philoprogenitiveness'. In documents of the commune, repeated injunctions are made against too narrow relationships between mother and child (Robertson 1981: 317–8, 319–20), and Theodore Noyes's attempt to take the right to care for their own children's clothing away from the mothers was answered with stern refusal (Dalsimer 1975: 147). There are numerous hints suggesting that the commitment of many members towards the commune as supreme educator was at best half-hearted, so that a good number of mothers, children (Dalsimer 1975: 168–82; Robertson 1981: 14) and fathers (Wayland-Smith 1988: 43) suffered from the arrangement.

Finally, the break-up of the commune was preceded by a surprisingly swift and easy return to monogamy. After John Humphrey Noyes had suggested abolishing the experiment in 1879 (Carden 1969: 103), members formed thirty-seven monogamous couples in addition to those that had existed previously and were now revitalised. Most of the marriages took place within the next three months (Carden 1969: 103–4, 118–19; Parker 1973: 286; Dalsimer 1975: 282), although – because many adults had children with more than one partner – sixteen women, twelve of them mothers, remained single (Carden 1969: 119). Even when the uncertain prospect of an unmarried future is taken into account, it is still significant that after more than thirty years of complex marriage, returning to customary practices was not beyond the powers of most members.

An interesting modern parallel is provided by the AAO ('Aktionsanalytische Organisation'), an Austrian group marriage that became communal in 1973 and built up branches in several European countries. Its charismatic leader, the former teacher and performance artist Otto Mühl, looked down with contempt on the '*KFM*' or '*Kleinfamilienmenschen*' (small family persons) of bourgeois society and denounced them as '*Detis*' (short for '*denkende Tiere*', i.e. thinking animals). Nevertheless, the women of the group sought status by being his sex partners and giving birth to his children (Schlothauer 1992: 90–1, 106, 128). When the commune disbanded, genetic testing prescribed by legal authorities showed Mühl to be the father of only eight children and not the twenty to thirty that had generally been assumed (Schlothauer 1992: 171), meaning that there must have been social advantages that encouraged the mothers to report the leader as the father in case of doubt. In the commune's last years, Mühl tried to build up his infant son Attila as his successor and also legally married the child's mother (Schlothauer 1992: 125–6), causing considerable estrangement among the members who finally demoted him in 1990 and disbanded shortly after.

## Alternatives to strict monogamy

It would go too far, however, to assume that familism and nepotism are the 'natural' destiny of all communes. For one, in the celibate cases not hitherto mentioned, they were apparently even less consequential than among the Shakers. And there are also monogamous communes where the bonds of blood and marriage hardly play a role, with some of them being candidates for life-spans similar to the cases listed above. One of these is Twin Oaks, a rural commune in Virginia founded in 1967 (Kinkade 1973, 1994; Komar 1983; http://www.twinoaks.org/tohome.htm). Most of its members come from the alternative segment of the educated middle class and hold critical attitudes towards many establishment concepts and institutions. With regard to partnership and family, they are generally more tolerant and flexible than average Americans. Owing to the egalitarian nature of the commune, '[i]f any one constant does exist, it is that the absence of even a subtle group pressure allows everyone the freedom to explore their sexual natures more fully than most other contemporary settings' (Komar 1983: 262–3). Within the last decade, children have never amounted to more than one-fifth of the membership (Fellowship for Intentional Community 1995: 208; Kinkade 1994: 2; McLaughlin and Davidson 1985: 117), and families with children have been few in number throughout (personal communication from a Twin Oaks member). Despite some homosexual and occasional multiple relationships (Kinkade 1994: 177, 180), the majority of members live in stable heterosexual couples (Komar 1983: 264; information from Twin Oaks). Nevertheless, legal marriages are rare (Kinkade 1994: 117), and the ideal of a life-long relationship plays only a minor role for many members (Kinkade 1994: 177, 183–4; Komar 1983: 268). Members' love lives are regarded as their private affairs (Kinkade 1994: 177, 186). 'People do what they can for themselves, and government keeps its hands off', as one member states (Kinkade 1994: 186).

The special needs of members with children are acknowledged when educational costs up to a set limit are paid by the commune (Kinkade 1994: 146–7; information from Twin Oaks) and caring for one's children is at least in part creditable to one's personal workload (Kinkade 1994: 152). Communal child care, however, stopped a few years ago (Kinkade 1994: 143–52) and there are only few among the several households that will accept children (Kinkade 1994: 152). Despite explicit efforts towards integrating families, Twin Oaks remains a commune primarily of and for singles, and the latter often choose communal life as an alternative to ordinary family life on the outside. This is rarely a terminal decision since in spite of a growing determination on the part of many members to stay (Kinkade 1994: 294), the average time lived in the commune has not yet risen above 5.5 years (*Leaves of Twin Oaks*, January 1993: 8). Thus, communal membership is not more than a life cycle stage for many and may be preceded or followed by family life. Twin Oaks has never attempted to raise its children as future members, and, so far, only one child that grew up in the commune has joined it as an adult (*Leaves of Twin Oaks*, Winter 1995: 15). This means that any investment in child care and education would hardly contribute to institutional survival since the continuity of the commune so far has depended on its capacity to attract single adults.

Riverside, an agricultural commune in New Zealand, presents a similar picture. It was founded by Christian pacifists in 1941 and prohibited divorce for a long time (Rain 1991: 51–2, 56, 94–5, 143; Popenoe and Popenoe 1984: 263). In 1971, however, the former religious fundaments were dropped, and most new members in the following years came from hippie and alternative backgrounds. While marriage and family are still more important than in Twin Oaks, single and single-parent households have become the majority (Rain 1991: 143; personal communication from a Riverside member), and the general attitude towards partnership and family life increasingly resembles that of Twin Oaks (Rain 1991: 95, 143–4, 153, 156, 160; Popenoe and Popenoe 1984: 258). My more fragmentary information about younger, yet also stable and promising, communes such as East Wind (founded in 1973) and Sandhill Farm (founded in 1974) in the United States (Federation of Egalitarian Communities n.d.; http://www.eastwind.org); and Niederkaufungen in Germany (founded in 1986; personal visit) hints at a similar situation.

All these groups tolerate partnership and family arrangements that would be unthinkable among Hutterites and Bruderhof members and would still be controversial in the kibbutzim. But nevertheless, members of Twin Oaks, Riverside and the other communes I mentioned are still mainly – though often serially and not always legally – monogamous, and none of these cases prescribes any specific practices, so that the patterns imported from counter-cultural 'peer segments' in outside society remain largely unchanged. Thus, communes must not be strictly monogamous and family-orientated if they are to remain in good shape for a long time, and as long as they stay close to the established practices of the members' cultural background.

This is corroborated by the only well-described commune from a non-monogamous setting. Aiyetoro in Nigeria was formed by a splinter group of an indigenous Yoruba–Christian church and became a communal settlement in 1948. Located on the coast, it supported itself with fishing, ferry services and small-scale manufacturing. Owing to its syncretist Christian background, members were to live in strict monogamy while the polygynous marriages of the Yoruba ambient society were reserved for the leadership alone (Barrett 1974: 24, 1978: 118–19). Moreover, men and women lived in separate quarters and could only visit each other (Barrett 1974: 25), and children were taken from their parents when they reached school age (Barrett 1974: 24–5, 31–3, 65). Twice in its history, the commune even went so far as to abolish marriage completely, bringing about a situation where lovers could be chosen freely. This did not continue for more than one and three years respectively, however, and the group returned to strict monogamy thereafter (Barrett 1974: 23–4).

Yet in Aiyetoro as well, the years of decline from 1966 to 1972 were accompanied by a backslide into conventional patterns – conventional to the specific cultural background. Married couples started to live together again, children returned to their parents, and it was not monogamy that was most sought after now but the polygynous marriages of high-status Yoruba (Barrett 1977: 65, 80, 137).

## Conclusions

While uncommon marriage, family and kinship practices clearly do work in communes, 'philoprogenitiveness' in those cases that have done nothing to suppress it has not subverted, but, rather, supported an active long-term survival. Moreover, it is the three most stable and durable present-day communes that display the strongest sense of family and kinship.

Since no systematic empirical research about the effects of family and kinship on communes has been undertaken – not even for the best-studied cases ('ethnographic study of kibbutz kinship is lacking' (Bowes 1989: 155)) – one can only speculate about the reasons for their resilience. It appears that marriage and the family fulfil certain emotional, affective and sexual needs efficiently while, at the same time, the loyalty conflicts expected by Noyes's and Kanter's zero-sum logic do not occur. Rather, it seems likely that members who are allowed some degree of intimacy within the smaller social unit of a family can become all the more committed to the commune, maybe precisely because the family allows them to find occasional relief from the wider unit. Moreover, communal property sharing frees families from the burden of economic responsibility, including the care for children. This should make communal families more carefree than those in conventional society. In any event, family and kinship have proven to be building blocks for communal longevity rather than obstacles, and they are not easily done away with even by the most determined attempts.

This result might be seen as evidence for a general nepotistic tendency of humans, leading us to the insight that – by virtue of being the kinship animal – we had better avoid any practices that contradict our 'nature'. The examples of Twin Oaks, Riverside and Aiyetoro, however, lead me to a more careful conclusion. I suppose that, within the emotionally charged field of marriage, family and kinship, large deviations from what is considered as appropriate in a commune's society of origin – or 'peer segments' therein, such as alternative culture for Twin Oaks and Riverside – are very difficult to accomplish, even more so since members remain in contact with ordinary society and are continually challenged by its orthodoxy. Therefore, in terms of long-term functionality it seems to pay off for Utopian communes to remain non-Utopian with regard to marriage, family and kinship, staying close to what members are anyway familiar with. A commune may then focus on realising other goals while saving the energy that is necessary to struggle successfully with the heavy cultural baggage that members have brought along.

## Notes

1   Communes are also often termed 'communal groups', 'communitarian groups' (Hostetler 1974b) or 'intentional communities' (Andelson 1996), although the use of these words is not always restricted to cases that share their property. I consider it sound to draw such a boundary line here, however, since fully communal groups are especially interesting from a social theoretical point of view. Being one of the most extreme forms of egalitarian co-operation, they should be particularly prone to what has been called the 'tragedy of the commons' (Hardin 1968), i.e. the devastating consequences of widespread freeriding in the absence of effective controls. While state control or private property arrangements are often seen as the only way out of the commons dilemma, a number of theoretical contributions have argued that egalitarian co-operation and sustainable resource management can arise voluntarily (e.g. Hechter 1987; Ostrom 1990; Taylor 1982), drawing support for this argumentation also from game theoretical models (Axelrod 1984; Schüßler 1989, 1990: 61–95; Taylor 1987: 82–108). Traditional societies all over the world provide

empirical evidence for the validity of this assumption (cf., for example, McCay and Acheson 1987).

Research on communes and intentional communities – both in the strict and loose sense – has a surprisingly large number of *aficionados* in all of the social sciences and thrived especially in the 1970s when thousands of communes were founded in Europe, North America and Japan. There is a Communal Studies Association (CSA) in the United States and an International Communal Studies Association (ICSA), which is presently based in Israel (Yad Tabenkin, PO Ramat-Efal 52960). Both associations organise conferences and publish newsletters; CSA also publishes the academic journal, *Communal Societies*, and has a website (http://www.well.com/user/cmty/csa) from which further interesting links can be pursued. The University of Indiana houses a Center for Communal Studies that has recently started a master's programme. Dare (1990) and T. Miller (1990) have provided useful guides to the literature on what makes up the lion's share of the total, namely American communes. See also the more comprehensive bibliography compiled by John Goodin for CSA (cf. its newsletter and website) and the cited references of Brumann (1998).

2    According to several fragmentary data (Peter 1987: 226, note 1; Hartse 1994a: 70; Shenker 1986: 159), the permanent defection rate should not exceed 10 per cent. The fertility decline has been caused by a higher marriage age (Peter 1987: 155–6), but also by the practice of Hutterite women to have themselves sterilised after a number of births. Hutterite men either do not object, or find themselves unable to interfere when the outside physicians that the Hutterites consult recommend surgery for health reasons (Peter 1987: 150, 170, 201).

3    The dissident's viewpoint is expressed by Bohlken-Zumpe (1993), Pleil (1994) and at the website of the Peregrine Foundation at http://www.pere-found.org. The latter also offers a scholarly article on the conflicts (T. Miller 1993).

4    One is tempted to interpret this outcome as the victory of patrilineality over primogeniture as the legitimate succession principle, since it was the (unfaithful) husband of Eberhard Arnold's oldest child that was demoted. The commune, however, interprets the struggle as one over religious issues. My brief sketch hardly does justice to the complexity of events. For one, the Arnold patrilineage itself has not remained free from internal divisions. One brother of Heinrich Arnold has been excluded for many years (Bohlken-Zumpe 1993: 146–7), and other Arnold descendants have also become dissidents (Bohlken-Zumpe 1993: 179–80, 212), so that about half of Eberhard Arnold's many grandchildren live outside the commune now, with Heinrich being the only child of five whose children have all stayed (Bohlken-Zumpe 1993: unnumbered page, opposite 1). Moreover, resentment against the Arnold family has been felt repeatedly within the Bruderhof, a fact that one official historical account does nothing to hide (Mow 1989: 130, 142, 149, 174, 304–5). The Arnold family's predominance has been termed 'a problem which needs to be addressed' even in one text that the group itself has offered on the Internet (Goeringer 1995). Obviously, members' feelings about this issue are ambivalent. The Arnolds' central position as such, however, is not even questioned by the dissidents.

One of their spokespersons, Elizabeth Bohlken-Zumpe, is a daughter of the expelled son-in-law of Eberhard Arnold. In her highly critical account of Bruderhof history, she deems it appropriate to start with a genealogical tree of the Arnold family (Bohlken-Zumpe 1993: unnumbered page, opposite 1), which the reader of her book could well do without. Before being expelled herself, she reports of having become the victim of an oppositional, yet kinship-orientated – and Arnold-fixated – discourse, when being accused in the following way: 'Peter replied that, "Religious exaggeration and highly-strung spiritual awareness" was all too common among the Arnolds, and, after all, I was one too' (Bohlken-Zumpe 1993: 161). 'Margarethe was to stay with me because "I was an Arnold," after all, and with "our emotional inheritance of unbalanced feelings," I might try to commit suicide' (Bohlken-Zumpe 1993: 163). 'Arno and Peter came and stood next to my bed, saying how this was typical Zumpe or Arnold ... behavior to try and get attention through their physical ailments' (Bohlken-Zumpe 1993: 167).

5    Hereditary succession of a commune's charismatic founder/leader may also have benefited a few other cases. Of five Japanese Utopian communes, where the charismatic leader had died, two nominated a descendant as successor: in Fukuzato Tetsugaku Jikkenjô (founded in 1970) the daughter took over when her mother died, and in Ittô-en (founded in 1913) the founder was succeeded by his grandson. While the problem of transcending the charismatic leader has not been entirely solved in either case, both communes are in a comparatively better state than two others, Atarashiki mura (founded in 1918) and Shinkyô (founded in 1939), where no successor has been named and the symptoms of decline are more perceptible. Yamagishi-kai (founded in 1958) has also failed to name a successor, but in this case this seems to have worked well because the dead founder is hardly ever mentioned, in contrast to the other four communes, whose identity and public self-image – as is usually the case in communes formed around a charismatic leader (Brumann 1998) – heavily depends on the founder figure (Brumann 1996, forthcoming). Harmony might also have profited from dynastic succession. Frederick, the adopted son of the leader George Rapp, co-operated closely and, most of the time, fruitfully with his father during his lifetime but died before him (Arndt 1965: 313–14, 315, 319, 425–33, 530–1).

6    The seventeen orthodox Jewish kibbutzim (Liegle and Bergmann 1994: 45, note) amount to 6 per cent of the total number.

7    These single members may be permitted to work outside the kibbutz (Bowes 1989: 40), to go on holiday trips for singles that the kibbutz federations arrange or to consult their match-making offices (Spiro 1972: 274; Tiger and Shepher 1975: 39).

8    It seems that large kin groups, although now a common feature, are still a somewhat 'foreign' idea to a society that never thought of building itself on kinship in the first place.

9    Neither does another kind of extension of family-orientated behaviour towards the wider communal unit occur with the certainty that has been assumed. For the kibbutzim, it has been noted by a number of observers that members who had been reared within the same peer group of six to

eight same-aged children occupying one children's house reported sibling-like feelings towards one another. Although there was no prohibition, they rarely if ever married or even had sexual intercourse in their adult life. Shepher takes this finding as evidence to back up an older theory of Westermarck (1891), explaining incest avoidance by the sexual uninterest or even aversion that arises when the prospective mates grow up together. Since it is normally siblings that will do so, they avoid each other for this reason and not predominantly because of their relatedness (Shepher 1971, 1983: 51–62).

Hutterites and Amana, however, show that closeness in childhood alone need not prevent mutual attraction and the forging of marriages. Peters found one Hutterite colony where more than one-third of all marriages were within the colony (Peters 1965: 92), and, according to Stephenson, this was true for no less than 42 per cent of all marriages among the *Lehrerleut* branch in 1971, with the *Dariusleut* branch being hardly any different (Stephenson 1991: 126). (These two branches add up to more than one-half of all Hutterites since there is only one more traditional branch, the *Schmiedeleut*.) These figures are all the more significant since first-cousin marriage is avoided, so that the choice of marriageable members within the same settlement – in any event comprising rarely more than 160 to 170 members (Olsen 1987: 828) – is rather restricted. In the seven Amana villages, the proportion of intra-village marriages lay continually above 60 per cent until 1909, and it never fell below 40 per cent afterwards (Andelson 1974: 451). At their peak, Amana villages had on average about 260 inhabitants (Andelson 1974: 326), so that here again the number of children within any one age group was clearly limited. Since in both cases children are cared for collectively during daytime after the first two or three years (Hostetler 1974a: 208–14; Andelson 1974: 82), more than enough closeness should be able to develop between same-aged children. Nonetheless, there is no indication that intra-settlement marriages are less happy or produce less children than those between settlements, contrary to what would be predicted by Shepher's theory (1983: 62–7). And in the case that any systematic and marked age gaps in Hutterite and Amana couples are responsible, these have not been reported in the literature.

Thus, other factors must explain the kibbutz observations. The key difference between the kibbutzim on the one hand, and the Hutterites and Amana on the other, seems to be that, first, children in the latter cases sleep in their family's apartment rather than in children's houses, and that, second, both Hutterites and Amana boys and girls are segregated in many ways from the beginning of collective education, starting with distinct dress. Moreover, this dress covers a great deal of body and hair, especially in the case of girls (Hostetler 1974a: 174; Shambaugh 1976: 143–4). In contrast, there was no gender separation in kibbutz education. On the contrary, nakedness in front of one another and sexual play were not repressed in any way during childhood. It was only after puberty that sexual shame set in and adolescents started to sexually avoid each other (Spiro 1982: 152–3). Moreover, a later study found that after single-sex bedrooms were introduced, love affairs within peer groups became much more common (Spiro 1982: 155–6). Therefore, it seems to be the intensity of exposure rather than mere closeness alone that leads to sexual aversion. Whether the latter is subconsciously acquired, as argued by Shepher and Westermarck, or rather must be seen as the result of a self-directed and conscious repression of desires in the face of sexual tensions, as argued by Spiro (1982: 153–7), is still a different question. In any event, the Hutterite and Amana cases deserve further scrutiny and a systematic comparison of intra- and inter-settlement marriages. Such a study should be simplified by the fact that solid demographic data are available for both groups.

10 Even strictly celibate Harmony profited from the four to seven children born per year in the first two decades when infringements still occurred (Arndt 1965: 418); these stayed on and kept the group alive in the end (Arndt 1971: 105), although on a lesser scale than in Zoar and Amana. Bethel and Aurora, another Protestant German commune similar to the aforementioned ones, was never celibate, although Kanter implicitly claims the contrary when including it among the successful cases (see above). There are hints that the charismatic leader, Wilhelm Keil – himself married and the father of many children (Hendricks 1933: 3–4, 127) – regarded the celibacy of some of the younger members with some sympathy and that the overall proportion of singles was higher than among the commune's neighbours (Heming 1990: 34). Most members, however, lived in monogamous families that were not subject to centralised control or restrictions.

## References

Andelson, J.G. (1974) 'Communalism and change in the Amana Society, 1855–1932', unpublished Ph.D. dissertation, University of Michigan.
—— (1996) 'Intentional communities', in D. Levinson and M. Ember (eds) *Encyclopedia of Cultural Anthropology: Volume 2*, New York: Henry Holt.
Anonymous (1982) 'Kibbutzstatuten der Vereinigten Kibbutzbewegungen', in G. Heinsohn (ed.) *Das Kibbutz-Modell: Bestandsaufnahme einer alternativen Wirtschafts- und Lebensform nach sieben Jahrzehnten*, Frankfurt: Suhrkamp.
Arndt, K.J.R. (1965) *George Rapp's Harmony Society, 1785–1847*, Philadelphia: University of Pennsylvania Press.
—— (1971) *George Rapp's Successors and Material Heirs, 1847–1916*, Rutherford, NJ: Fairleigh Dickinson University Press.
Axelrod, R. (1984) *The Evolution of Cooperation*, New York: Basic Books.
Barrett, S.R. (1974) *Two Villages on Stilts*, New York: Chandler.
—— (1977) *The Rise and Fall of an African Utopia: A Wealthy Theocracy in Comparative Perspective*, Waterloo, ON: Wilfrid Laurier University Press.
—— (1978) 'Communalism, capitalism and stratification in an African utopia', *Journal of Asian and African Studies* 13: 112–29.
Barthel, D.L. (1984) *Amana: From Pietist Sect to American Community*, Lincoln: University of Nebraska Press.

Bennett, J.W. (1967) *Hutterian Brethren: The Agricultural Economy and Social Organization of a Communal People*, Stanford, CA: Stanford University Press.

Ben-Rafael, E. (1988) *Status, Power and Conflict in the Kibbutz*, Aldershot: Avebury.

Blasi, J. (1986) *The Communal Experience of the Kibbutz*, New Brunswick, NJ: Transaction.

Bohlken-Zumpe, E. (1993) *Torches Extinguished: Memories of a Communal Bruderhof Childhood in Paraguay, Europe and the USA*, San Francisco, CA: Carrier Pigeon Press.

Bowes, A.M. (1980) 'Strangers in the kibbutz: Volunteer workers in an Israeli community', *Man* 15: 665–81.

—— (1989) *Kibbutz Goshen: An Israeli Commune*, Prospect Heights, IL: Waveland Press.

Brewer, P.J. (1986) *Shaker Communities, Shaker Lives*, Hanover, NH: University Press of New England.

Brumann, C. (1992) 'Kommunitäre Gruppen in Japan: Alternative Mikrogesellschaften als kultureller Spiegel', *Zeitschrift für Ethnologie* 117: 119–38.

—— (1996) 'Strong leaders: The charismatic founders of Japanese utopian communities', in I. Neary (ed.) *Leaders and Leadership in Japan*, Richmond, Va.: Curzon Press.

—— (1998) *Die Kunst des Teilens: Eine vergleichende Untersuchung zu den Überlebensbedingungen kommunitärer Gruppen*, Hamburg: Lit.

—— (forthcoming) 'Dynamik und Stillstand in drei utopischen Bewegungen: Ittô-en, Atarashiki mura und Yamagishi-kai', in C. Derichs and A. Osiander (eds) *Soziale Bewegungen in Japan*, Hamburg: Mitteilungen der Gesellschaft für Natur- und Völkerkunde Ostasiens.

Carden, M.L. (1969) *Oneida: Utopian Community to Modern Corporation*, Baltimore, Md.: Johns Hopkins University Press.

Carpenter, D. (1975 [1972]) *The Radical Pietists: Celibate Communal Societies Established in the United States before 1820*, New York: AMS Press.

Coser, L.A. (1974) *Greedy Institutions: Patterns of Undivided Commitment*, New York: Free Press.

Dalsimer, M.H. (1975) 'Women and family in the Oneida Community: 1837–1881', unpublished Ph.D. dissertation, New York University.

Dare, P. (1990) *American Communes to 1860: A Bibliography*, New York: Garland.

Day, L.J. (1990) 'Koinonia Partners: An intentional community since 1942', *Communal Societies* 10: 114–23.

Eggers, U. (1985) *Gemeinschaft – lebenslänglich: Deutsche Hutterer in den USA*, Witten: Bundes-Verlag.

Federation of Egalitarian Communities (no date) *Sharing the dream*, information brochure, no place of publication given.

Fellowship for Intentional Community (1995) *Communities Directory: A Guide to Cooperative Living*, second edn, Langley, WA: Fellowship for Intentional Community.

Fogarty, R.S. (1981) *The Righteous Remnant: The House of David*, Kent, OH: Kent State University Press.

Fölling-Albers, M. (1988) 'Erziehung und Frauenfrage im Kibbutz', in W. Melzer and G. Neubauer (eds) *Der Kibbutz als Utopie*, Weinheim: Beltz.

Goeringer, H. (1995) 'A Letter to John A. Hostetler', offered at http://www.bruderhof.org in 1996 but no longer available there.

Hardin, G. (1968) 'The tragedy of the commons', *Science* 162: 1,243–8.

Hartse, C.M. (1994a) 'The emotional acculturation of Hutterite defectors', *Journal of Anthropological Research* 50: 69–85.

—— (1994b) 'Social and religious change among contemporary Hutterites', *Folk* 36: 109–30.

Hechter, M. (1987) *Principles of Group Solidarity*, Berkeley: University of California Press.

Heming, C.P. (1990) ' "Temples stand, temples fall": The utopian vision of Wilhelm Keil', *Missouri Historical Review* 85: 21–39.

Hendricks, R.J. (1933) *Bethel and Aurora: An Experiment in Communism as Practical Christianity with Some Account of Past and Present Ventures in Collective Living*, New York: Press of the Pioneers.

Holzach, M. (1982 [1980]) *Das vergessene Volk: Ein Jahr bei den deutschen Hutterern in Kanada*, Munich: dtv.

Hostetler, J.A. (1974a) *Hutterite Society*, Baltimore, Md.: Johns Hopkins University Press.

—— (1974b) *Communitarian Societies*, New York: Holt, Rinehart & Winston.

Kanter, R.M. (1972) *Commitment and Community: Communes and Utopia in Sociological Perspective*, Cambridge, MA: Harvard University Press.

Kern, L.J. (1981) *An Ordered Love: Sex Roles and Sexuality in Victorian Utopias – The Shakers, the Mormons, and the Oneida Community*, Chapel Hill: University of North Carolina Press.

Kinkade, K. (1973) *A Walden Two Experiment: The First Five Years of Twin Oaks Community*, New York: William Morrow.

—— (1994) *Is it Utopia Yet? An Insider's View of Twin Oaks Community in Its 26th Year*, Louisa, VA: Twin Oaks.

Kitch, S.L. (1993) *This Strange Society of Women: Reading the Letters and Lives of the Woman's Commonwealth*, Columbus: Ohio State University Press.

Komar, I. (1983) *Living the Dream: A Documentary Study of Twin Oaks Community*, Norwood, PA: Norwood Press.

Kruse, U. (1991) 'Diesseits von Eden', *Zeit-Magazin* 25 (14 June): 12–22.

Landing, J.E. (1981) 'Cyrus R. Teed, Koreshanity and cellular cosmogeny', *Communal Societies* 1: 1–18.

Lanza del Vasto (1978) *L'Arche avait pour voilure une vigne*, Paris: Editions Denoël.

Lauer, R.H. and Lauer, J.C. (1983) *The Spirit and the Flesh: Sex in Utopian Communities*, Metuchen, NJ: Scarecrow Press.

*Leaves of Twin Oaks*, Twin Oaks community journal, published irregularly.

Lee, D. (1971) *The Cotton Patch Evidence: The Story of Clarence Jordan and the Koinonia Farm Experiment*, New York: Harper & Row.

Liegle, L. and Bergmann, T. (1994) *Krise und Zukunft im Kibbutz: Vom Wandel einer genossenschaftlichen Wirtschafts- und Lebensform*, Weinheim: Juventa.

McCay, B.M. and Acheson, J.M. (eds) (1987) *The Question of the Commons: The Culture and Ecology of Communal Resources*, Tucson: University of Arizona Press.

McCormick, D. (1965 [1962]) *Temple of Love*, New York: Citadell Press.

McLaughlin, C. and Davidson, G. (1985) *Builders of the Dawn: Community Lifestyles in a Changing World*, Walpole, NH: Stillpoint.

Malan, J.S. (1994) 'Ideological and structural reform in the kibbutz system', *South African Journal of Ethnology* 17: 121–6.

Maron, S. (1988) 'Der Kibbutz im Jahr 2000', in W. Melzer and G. Neubauer (eds) *Der Kibbutz als Utopie*, Weinheim: Beltz.

Melzer, W. and Neubauer, G. (eds) (1988a) *Der Kibbutz als Utopie*, Weinheim: Beltz.

—— (1988b) 'Was ist ein Kibbutz? Theoretischer Anspruch und Wirklichkeit – erfahren im Kibbutz Ayeleth Hashahar', in W. Melzer and G. Neubauer (eds) *Der Kibbutz als Utopie*, Weinheim: Beltz.

Miller, M.R. (1972) 'Education in the Harmony Society', unpublished Ph.D. dissertation, University of Pittsburgh.

Miller, T. (1990) *American Communes, 1860–1960: A Bibliography*, New York: Garland.

—— (1993) 'Stress and conflict in an international religious movement: The case of the Bruderhof', paper prepared for CESNUR/INFORM/ISAR conference, London 1993, http://www.perefound.org/tm_arch.html.

Mow, D.M. (1989) *Torches Rekindled: The Bruderhof's Struggle for Renewal*, Ulster Park, NY: Plough.

Muncy, R.L. (1973) *Sex and Marriage in Utopian Communities: Nineteenth Century America*, Bloomington: Indiana University Press.

Nonaka, K., Miura, T. and Peter, K. (1994) 'Recent fertility decline in Dariusleut Hutterites: An extension of Eaton and Mayer's Hutterite fertility study', *Human Biology* 66: 411–20.

Nordhoff, C. (1960 [1875]) *The Communistic Societies of the United States: From Personal Visit and Observation*, New York: Hillary House.

Noyes, J.H. (1961 [1870]) *History of American Socialisms*, New York: Hillary House.

Olsen, C.L. (1987) 'The demography of colony fission from 1878–1970 among the Hutterites of North America', *American Anthropologist* 89: 823–37.

Ostrom, E. (1990) *Governing the Commons: The Evolution of Institutions for Collective Action*, Cambridge, UK: Cambridge University Press.

Oved, Y. (1988) *Two Hundred Years of American Communes*, New Brunswick, NJ: Transaction.

Parker, R.A. (1973 [1935]) *A Yankee Saint: John Humphrey Noyes and the Oneida Community*, Hamden, CT: Shoe String Press.

Paterwic, S. (1991) 'From individual to community: Becoming a Shaker at New Lebanon', *Communal Societies* 11: 18–33.

Peter, K. (1987) *The Dynamics of Hutterite Society: An Analytical Approach*, Edmonton: University of Alberta Press.

Peters, V.J. (1965) *All Things Common: The Hutterian Way of Life*, Minneapolis: University of Minnesota Press.

Pleil, N.M. (1994) *Free from Bondage: After Forty Years in Bruderhof Communities on Three Continents*, San Francisco: Carrier Pigeon Press.

Popenoe, C. and Popenoe, O. (1984) *Seeds of Tomorrow: New Age Communities That Work*, New York: Harper & Row.

Rain, L. (1991) *Community: The Story of Riverside, 1941–1991*, Lower Moutere, New Zealand: Riverside Community.

Randall, E.O. (1971 [1899]) *History of the Zoar Society, from its Commencement to its Conclusion: A Sociological Study in Communism*, New York: AMS Press.

Rayman, P. (1981) *The Kibbutz Community and Nation-Building*, Princeton, NJ: Princeton University Press.

Robertson, C.N. (ed.) (1972) *Oneida Community: The Breakup, 1876–1881*, Syracuse, NY: Syracuse University Press.

—— (1977) *Oneida Community Profiles*, Syracuse, NY: Syracuse University Press.

—— (1981 [1970]) *Oneida Community: An Autobiography, 1851–1876*, Syracuse, NY: Syracuse University Press.

Sato, T., Nonaka, K., Miura, T. and Peter, K. (1994) 'Trends in cohort fertility of the Dariusleut Hutterite population', *Human Biology* 66: 421–31.

Schlothauer, A. (1992) *Die Diktatur der freien Sexualität: AAO, Mühl-Kommune, Friedrichshof*, Vienna: Verlag für Gesellschaftskritik.

Schüßler, R. (1989) 'Exit threats and cooperation under anonymity', *Journal of Conflict Resolution* 33: 729–49.

—— (1990) *Kooperation unter Egoisten: Vier Dilemmata*, Munich: Oldenbourg.

Sender Barayán, R. (1995) 'The heart will find a way: Creating a network of reunion', *Communities* 88: 61–4.

Shambaugh, B.H.M. (1976 [1932]) *Amana That Was and Amana That Is*, New York: Arno Press.

Shenker, B. (1986) *Intentional Communities: Ideology and Alienation in Communal Societies*, London: Routledge & Kegan Paul.

Shepher, J. (1971) 'Mate selection among second-generation kibbutz adolescents and adults: Incest avoidance and negative imprinting', *Archives of Sexual Behaviour* 1: 293–307.

—— (1983) *Incest: A Biosocial View*, New York: Academic Press.

Spiro, M.E. (1972) *Kibbutz: Venture in Utopia*, revised, augmented edition, New York: Schocken.

—— (1982) *Oedipus in the Trobriands*, Chicago: Chicago University Press.

Stein, S.J. (1992) *The Shaker Experience in America: A History of the United Society of Believers*, New Haven, CT: Yale University Press.

Stephenson, P.H. (1991) *The Hutterian People: Ritual and Rebirth in the Evolution of Communal Life*, Lanham, MD: University Press of America.

Taylor, M. (1982) *Community, Anarchy and Liberty*, Cambridge, UK: Cambridge University Press.

—— (1987) *The Possibility of Cooperation*, Cambridge, UK: Cambridge University Press.

Thomas, R.D. (1977) *The Man Who Would Be Perfect*, Philadelphia: University of Pennsylvania Press.

Tiger, L. and Shepher, J. (1975) *Women in the Kibbutz*, New York: Harcourt Brace Jovanovich.

Treher, C.M. (1968) *Snow Hill Cloister*, Allentown, PA: The Pennsylvania German Society.

Van den Berghe, P.L. and Peter, K. (1988) 'Hutterites and kibbutzniks: A tale of nepotistic communities', *Man (N.S.)* 23: 522–39.

Wagner, J. (1986) 'Sexuality and gender roles in utopian communities: A critical survey of scholarly work', *Communal Societies* 6: 172–88.

Wayland-Smith, E. (1988) 'The status and self-perception of women in the Oneida Community', *Communal Societies* 8: 18–53.

Westermarck, E.A. (1891) *The History of Human Marriage*, London: Macmillan.

Yambura, B.S. with Bodine, E.W. (1961) *A Change and a Parting: My Story of Amana*, Ames: Iowa State University Press.

Zablocki, B.D. (1973) *The Joyful Community: An Account of the Bruderhof, a Communal Movement now in its Third Generation*, Baltimore, Md.: Penguin.

# Chapter 8

# Concluding remarks

*Peter P. Schweitzer*

One conclusion that emerges, almost by necessity, from the case studies assembled in this volume is that kinship comes in a variety of packages and with a multitude of meanings attached. This statement not only is self-evident, but was to be expected. Following the characterisation of 'kinship at large' set up in Chapter 1 anything else would be a surprise. Instead of insisting on universal characteristics as a precondition for the analytical validity of kinship, variation is viewed as a practical necessity resulting from detailed fieldwork and observation of social reality that does not a priori privilege certain aspects of social relatedness over others. However, the celebration of diversity of ethnographic detail carries a variety of potential pitfalls and dangers. First, it is obviously of little interest to the non-regional specialist if a particular case study speaks only to itself (and the few other studies conducted in the area). Second, if we are too content with ethnographic diversity, the legitimate question arises: where does this leave the anthropology of kinship (or of any other aspect, for that matter)? Some might argue that the deconstruction of concepts such as kinship – triggered by the seeming non-uniformness of the subject – is a noble goal in itself. Without denying the usefulness of periodically interrogating the conceptual tool kit of anthropology and of getting rid of concepts and terms that hide more than they reveal, it seems to me that to probe for structural and processual similarities and differences is one of the legitimate (and necessary) endeavours of the discipline.[1]

If we look beyond the local meanings of the portrayed individual cases we see a limited number of social constellations in which these culture-specific concepts of relatedness are employed. The structural constraints of how people engage kinship bring us back to the 'functional' aspects mentioned in Chapter 1. People from Greenland to Amazonia to Upper Austria use 'their' constructs and interpretations of kinship in a variety of everyday settings, in conscious and unconscious practices of social life. From the case studies presented, it appears that kinship strategies are employed predominantly within two major fields of power: relations between people and people; and relations between people and things. At first glance these relations seem to superficially coincide with 'politics' and 'economy', two concepts that not only are problematic because of their familiarity, but also because they tend to narrow our understanding of the relations in question. Several of the case studies in this volume address functions of kinship that can not be labelled 'political' or 'economic': from issues of health and personhood among the Inuit to vision quests of the Amazon region to Portuguese and Turkish notions of honour. Still, the more fundamental objection to be raised does not concern the fitness of Western labels, but the definitional content of these labels. 'Politics' and 'economy', as understood conventionally, have such narrowly defined boundaries that many of the relations referred to above – those between people and people; and those between people and things – will fall through the terminological filter.

## Two strategies: inclusion and exclusion

If we momentarily disregard the domains in which kinship becomes effective, it might be useful to take a closer look at the basic characteristics of the diverse functions that kinship can fulfil. One way of classifying these functions is to introduce a basic distinction between inclusive and exclusive. Inclusive, thereby, refers to a given kinship system whose functional characteristic is to maximise the number of individuals who can be 'made into relatives', if strategically advantageous; exclusive refers to a kinship system that keeps the definition of 'relatives' narrow and provides few, if any, venues to 'create' kinship. Evidently, Inuit kinship is a prime example of inclusiveness – the strategies (as described by Nuttall in Chapter 2) are all geared towards extending the range of relatives. Similarly, the Shuar and Achuar (Chapter 3 by Mader and Gippelhauser) use the possibilities of genealogical kinship, of affinal ties and of trade partnerships to build political networks and alliances: since more is better, inclusion prevails over exclusion. Alternatively, the peasants of Upper Austria (as described by Seiser in Chapter 4) seem to engage much more in exclusion than in inclusion: since kinship entails rights to inheritance, the exclusion of potential contenders becomes understandable. The female pieceworkers from Istanbul (Chapter 5 by White) obviously use the idiom of kinship to include non-related individuals in an imaginary network of reciprocity. The élite families of Lisbon (portrayed by Pedroso de Lima in Chapter 6), however, have little use for inclusive strategies: at crucial moments of the business cycle, kinship boundaries are kept narrow and profit maximisation becomes the ultimate goal. Even the Utopian communities (discussed by Brumann in Chapter 7) seem to demonstrate this dichotomy, despite their diverse social backgrounds: the majority of these communities displayed obvious inclusive tendencies at the beginning of their existence (by substituting the family for the community), while most of them showed signs of exclusiveness during later stages of their existence (by creating core families or quasi-lineages within the communities). As these brief remarks demonstrate, inclusive and exclusive functions can and do co-occur within the same society or within a range of similar social situations; as will be discussed below, group- and context-specific factors provide the rationale for such seemingly contradictory practices.

The way in which I have presented this assignment of inclusive and exclusive labels to individual case studies could suggest the notion of an evolutionary sequence from 'kinship functioning as a way of including people' to 'kinship functioning as a way of excluding people'. One might be tempted to suggest that hunter-gatherer and horticultural societies use kinship primarily in the first sense,[2] while in agricultural and industrial societies the latter function prevails. This could easily be extended to a model assigning inclusion to classless societies and exclusion to class societies. Furthermore, Collier's (1988) distinction between brideservice and bridewealth societies – although entirely situated within the classless category – could be used in correlating inclusiveness with brideservice societies (bridewealth societies would straddle the proposed dividing line between inclusion and exclusion). However, I argue that such correlations are, at best, 'an evolutionary optical illusion' (Godelier 1978). Not only has the assignment of inclusive and exclusive values to individual cases already violated the construction of an overtly neat evolutionary model (Chapter 5, in particular, does not conform at all to such a developmental logic), but the question of how inclusive or exclusive functions of kinship ought to be causally related to particular classes of societies has not even been touched upon.

Before entirely abandoning this attempt at classification, it is worthwhile to further inquire into what inclusiveness and exclusiveness actually refer to. From the short description provided above it is evident that these labels refer, first and foremost, to the amount of people who can be made into relatives. They refer to social relations – to relations among people. However, at the same time these social relations entail modes of relating to what Western terminology calls 'things', 'goods', 'animals', etc. In this context it is beneficial to compare what Marilyn Strathern (1985) had to say when probing the relations between 'kinship' and 'economy' and between gender and social inequality. Strathern has argued that the question of whether a society allows the substitution of people and things is decisive in this respect. According to her argument, societies in which items can not stand for persons (nor for their labour) correspond to Collier's 'brideservice' societies and Woodburn's (1980) 'immediate-return' systems: thus, gender and social inequality, as well as kinship and economic relations, are constitutive of one another (Strathern 1985: 197, 202). Where things can stand for persons (and for women in particular) – that is, in 'bridewealth' societies – the relations between kinship and economy become reversed, since relationships between persons are represented as relationships between things (Strathern 1985: 198, 203). In returning to the classificatory pair inclusion and exclusion, one obvious connection with Strathern's model arises. In societies where access to resources is primarily determined through access to services by others, inclusive functions of kinship can be expected to prevail. Exclusion, alternatively, is a function of kinship relations in contexts where access to resources is reified in property relations, which make social relations into relations between things and privilege the access to things over access to persons (or services).

In passing, Strathern (1985: 204) indicates that under conditions of capitalism a third variant appears: while 'things' and 'persons' are seemingly kept conceptually separate (and thus things cannot replace persons or vice versa), the social labour necessary to produce commodities becomes detached from the product, thus treating persons as things, or not-persons. While the heuristic benefit of the latter scenario (distinguishing bridewealth from capitalist societies) is evident, it is less clear how this variant can be deduced from the one-dimensional typology (substitution of persons and things; yes or no) used by Strathern. The introduction of a second dimension seems necessary to account for this case. If we split the issue of substitution into two separate questions – can people be equated with things? and can things be equated with people? – four logical possibilities arise:

1    People can not be equated with things, nor can things be equated with people.

2 While people can be equated with things, things can not be equated with people.

3 People can not be equated with things, but things can be equated with people.

4 People can be equated with things and things can be equated with people.

Put in this way, the two previously developed categories of inclusion (or brideservice) and exclusion (or bridewealth) appear as the two extreme points of a continuum (possibilities 1 and 4).

According to the model, the two logical possibilities situated in-between should display a mixture of inclusive and exclusive tendencies. Possibility 3 (which is neither very widespread ethnographically nor represented in this volume) is probably best exemplified by the institution of slavery, in which certain categories of person are not defined as such but as alienable things, while these 'things' are often reincorporated into household and kinship networks. Possibility 2, on the other hand, can be correlated straightforwardly with capitalist societies, given the fact that commodity production turns human labour into a 'thing'. Our sample of case studies (Chapters 4–7) confirms the expected ambiguous character of capitalist societies in regard to inclusive and exclusive functions of kinship. However, while all of the four relevant case studies are undeniably situated in a capitalist context, it is questionable whether their kinship notions and strategies can be causally linked to capitalism. As a matter of fact, the examples of Chapters 4 and 5 (Upper Austria and Turkey) seem to be best understood in relation to a pre-capitalist agricultural society. Possibility 4, or exclusion, would be the expected outcome in such a case. While the Austrian case fits this expectation, the situation in Istanbul is contrary to this prediction. However, it should be recalled that the Turkish context of female pieceworkers representing wage relations as kinship relations is characterised by the double marginalisation of poverty and gender inequality in a patriarchal society.

This leads to the important realisation that the strategies in question do not necessarily apply to entire societies, but to segments of those; or, to put it more succinctly, in societies where gender, class or other factors give rise to social divisions, the functions of kinship within those divisions can be expected to differ. It can, of course, be argued that there are even more fine-grained nuances: certain exclusive and inclusive strategies are purely individual and situational. Again, the ethnographies provided in Chapters 2–7 give ample testimony of idiosyncratic responses to particular constraints. However, individual strategies are never independent from larger structuring contexts: idiosyncrasies can only be perceived as such against a background of expected modes of conduct.

This point can be best illustrated by a classic case study: Carol Stack argues in her book, *All Our Kin* (1974), that poor black families in 'the Flats' have developed a set of successful survival strategies in response to harsh economic conditions, which include (among others): the extension of kinship ties to non-kin; patterns of co-residence; exchange networks; and elastic household boundaries (Stack 1974: 124). These strategies, which are obviously inclusive, are portrayed by the author as standing in stark contrast to how kinship is used in mainstream American society. However, as Rapp (1982) has pointed out, Stack tends to romanticise these strategies (by not problematising the costs of inclusive kinship patterns) and never really specifies how the 'mainstream' supposedly functions. Nevertheless, Stack's case study provides a powerful example of how inclusive strategies can flourish within an overall exclusive setting.[3] A reverse situation seems to be presented by the case study in this volume on Portuguese élite families. While the wider society is characterised by certain inclusive tendencies regarding the functions of kinship, the élite families discussed in Chapter 6 seem to be most concerned with narrowing the circle of kin, thereby excluding potential rivals from claims to succession and inheritance.

Returning to the female pieceworkers of Istanbul, their inclusive use of kinship notions seems to be in direct correlation with the fact that they 'own' nothing. If we understand 'ownership' as a particular set of social relations *vis-à-vis* persons and things, the question arises whether kin relations can constitute ownership relations. Notwithstanding the fact that hierarchies are a common feature of kinship systems, kin relations never seem to be entirely void of, at least minimal, notions of reciprocity. Conversely, ownership relations are best characterised as uni-directional relations.[4] With the above-mentioned exception of slavery, kin and ownership relations seem to be mutually exclusive. Furthermore, kin relations threaten the uni-directional aspect of ownership, while relations of ownership negate the reciprocity of kinship.

The proposed typology of kinship functions into inclusive and exclusive categories can be summarised in the following way:

1   Inclusion and exclusion are broad labels useful in categorising particular kinship strategies in regard to the mobilisation of people beyond categories of 'close' or binding kin relations.

2   Inclusive strategies are associated with 'flexible' kinship systems in which there is an emphasis on extending kinship and regarding relatives as allies; exclusive strategies are associated with kinship systems in which there is little room for choice and which contain an element of competition.

3   By understanding inclusion and exclusion as extreme points of a continuum it is possible to characterise entire societies, or even types of societies, with such labels. However, these labels are ideal-types at best and should not be mistaken for descriptions of actual practices.

4   Social groups within particular societies can use different strategies if these groups have differential access to limited resources. Generally speaking, the more access a particular group has to limited resources the more likely it is that exclusion will predominate; the reverse situation applies likewise.

5   Inclusion and exclusion can be used to designate a wide variety of distinct strategies. While this discussion, as well as the case studies it is based upon, has primarily made reference to relations often referred to as 'economic' or 'political', there is no compelling reason to believe that it could not be applied to relations in other domains.

6   Finally, the various strategies in question have been noticed by a variety of anthropologists over the years: indications range from Edmund Leach's (1954) analytical distinction between *gumsa* and *gumlao* systems in Highland Burma to Pierre Bonte's (1994)[5] statement that 'close marriages' (and other 'complex system of alliance and kinship') are related to strategies of closing or opening up social groups. My typology merely systematises and labels these earlier observations.

## The road ahead

Finally, what does all this mean for the future of kinship studies? Will the deconstruction of the field, as seemed to occur during the 1970s and 1980s, finally prevail in relegating kinship to the conceptual dumping ground where it will join 'totemism', 'arctic hysteria' and 'culture circles'? Will the anthropological profession reintegrate kinship into its mainstream vocabulary and continue to use pre-1960s reifications of the subject? Or, will kinship become the new key term for a generation of anthropologists seeking new stamping grounds? My rhetorical phrasing of these questions indicates that I neither believe, nor hope, that any of the mentioned possibilities will come true. However, all three scenarios contain elements of attraction beyond their obvious negative implications. It has become obvious throughout the case studies of this volume that a careful ethnographic description of kinship is the necessary starting point. This includes investigations into local meanings as well as into local functions of the phenomena labelled kinship. This could, and should, lead to further 'deconstructions' of kinship by expanding the ethnographic record of what people do, think and feel when they refer to relations we term kin. However, contrary to Schneider's dictum that the comparative study of kinship must be abandoned (1984: 177), I believe that our increased understanding of varying notions and practices of kinship provides a fruitful challenge, not an end, to our attempts.[6] So far, *nobody* has been able to argue convincingly that a particular society is able to do without social relations that we conveniently call kin relations.

The prospect of bringing the topic of kinship back to the centre of anthropological discourse should sound attractive to people who are adventurous enough to read the present book. However, even as a seemingly self-interested proponent of such a view I do not necessarily rejoice at such a prospect. The real problem is not the 'outdated' nature of pre-Schneiderian kinship studies. After all, it should be acknowledged that learning to read and draw genealogical diagrams or to ponder over the intricacies of the 'Murngin system' does not 'spoil' the fledgling anthropologist any more than do other professional requirements (despite the fact that we know about the ethnocentric roots of the 'family tree' model (Bouquet 1996) and about the illusionary facets of classic Murngin ethnography). The real problem with 'classic' kinship studies is that they privilege the domain of kinship and, thus, separate it from the totality of social relations. Schneider's critique and subsequent feminist and Marxist interventions have made us more fully aware of the inseparable links among the social fields of gender, kinship, religion, economy, etc. Kinship in its narrow sense deserves to be marginalised; 'kinship at large', however, which can be referred to by a variety of other terms, can not be neglected unless anthropology abandons all claims to understanding social life. What remains of 'classic' studies in the field of kinship is the sincere (albeit sometimes naïve) attempt to make the phenomena under consideration accessible to comparative investigations.

As was discussed in Chapter 1, a plethora of contemporary kinship studies deal with topics, regions and domains that were not part of the 'kinship canon' several decades ago. From 'new reproductive technologies' (NRT) to gay and lesbian families to 'transnational adoption', there has been a 'repatriation of kinship studies' (Peletz 1995: 362). In contrast to previous studies – when kinship seemed to be an almost exclusively non-European affair vastly relevant to Nuer, Aranda or Iroquois but not to Austrians or Englishmen – these recent studies have demonstrated how relevant the subject 'close to home' is. However, the potential danger of this laudable reorientation is obvious. If kinship were to become synonymous with 'NRT' or 'gay marriage' (as it once was with 'lineage' and 'marriage payments'), the exclusion of large segments of social reality would be a necessary consequence. The old dichotomy between the 'West and the rest' would be resurrected in a different form. Consequently, I hope that the current interest in kinship will extend beyond what seem to be 'hot topics' in contemporary Western culture, in order to cover the various forms in which different peoples construct relatedness.

The 'ideal image' of kinship studies I have been sketching is taking on more and more unlikely shapes. It would contain culturalist investigations into the idiosyncrasies of local kinship models, as well as comparative concepts and analytical tools with which to move beyond the celebration of these idiosyncrasies. It would contain a particular emphasis on kinship in industrialised societies (and in other contexts previously little studied), as well as a continuing focus on the 'traditional' loci of kinship. Although this might sound as a theoretical and practical impossibility, the inherent challenge of this conundrum would keep kinship studies vital and productive.

## Acknowledgements

I want to thank Janet Carsten, Andre Gingrich, Nelson Graburn and Michael Peletz for comments on an earlier draft of this chapter. Stacie McIntosh provided valuable editorial assistance.

## Notes

1    There are signs that comparative research, after years of neglect, is about to return to anthropological centre stage. Among those signs is the international symposium 'Comparative Dimensions in Social and Cultural Anthropology' – supported by the Socrates Intensive Programme and the Wenner-Gren

Foundation – held in September 1998 in Vienna; a publication stemming from this important exchange is forthcoming.

2    Alan Barnard's suggestion that 'universal kin classification' or 'universal kinship' is typical for hunter-gatherer societies (Barnard 1992: 280) clearly reinforces the idea that inclusive functions prevail in such societies. Barnard distinguishes between 'empirically universal systems' – those 'in which a person associates only with "kin"' – and 'ideologically universal systems' – those in which 'a person must classify as members of some kin category all those with whom he or she associates' (Barnard 1992: 266).

3    Rapp's 1982 essay provides some interesting clues as to how US American middle-class kinship patterns privilege more restricted (or exclusive) strategies than their working-class counterparts. By shifting the emphasis from lateral to lineal connections (in terms of inter-generational investments and resource pooling) and by using friendship (which entails fewer obligations than kinship bonds) as a primary social nexus, the kinship strategies of middle-class households are 'consistent with resource accumulation rather than dispersal' (Rapp 1982: 181).

4    This is a very narrow definition of 'ownership'. For a much broader and more detailed discussion of cultural variations of ownership and property relations see Hann (1998).

5    Since Bonte's volume is not at hand at the time of writing, I quote from Gingrich's (1995: 169) excellent review article on the subject.

6    Despite the obviously strong impact of *A Critique of the Study of Kinship* (Schneider 1984), it ought to be noted that the book provides an extremely one-sided and oversimplified portrait of kinship studies. Schneider's goal was to denounce the field and, thus, he had no use for nuances and shades. It remains for future biographers of Schneider to comment on why the major expert on kinship in American anthropology felt obliged to 'crown' his life-long studies with a complete revocation of their subject matter and, indirectly, of his own career achievements.

# References

Barnard, A. (1992) *Hunters and Herders of South Africa: A Comparative Ethnography of the Khoisan Peoples*, Cambridge, UK: Cambridge University Press.

Bonte, P. (ed.) (1994) *Épouser au plus proche: Inceste, prohibitions et stratégies matrimoniales autour de la Méditerranée*, Paris: Éditions de l'EHESS.

Bouquet, M. (1996) 'Family trees and their affinities: The visual imperative of the genealogical diagram', *The Journal of the Royal Anthropological Institute (N.S.)* 2: 43–66.

Collier, J.F. (1988) *Marriage and Inequality in Classless Societies*, Stanford, CA: Stanford University Press.

Gingrich, A. (1995) 'Review article: The prophet's smile and other puzzles. Studying Arab tribes and comparing close marriages', *Social Anthropology* 3: 147–70.

Godelier, M. (1978) 'Economy and religion: An evolutionary optical illusion', in J. Friedman and M.J. Rowlands (eds) *The Evolution of Social Systems*, Pittsburgh, PA: University of Pittsburgh Press.

Hann, C.M. (ed.) (1998) *Property Relations: Renewing the Anthropological Tradition*, Cambridge, UK: Cambridge University Press.

Leach, E.R. (1954) *Political Systems of Highland Burma: A Study of Kachin Social Structure*, London: Athlone Press.

Peletz, M.G. (1995) 'Kinship studies in late twentieth-century anthropology', *Annual Review of Anthropology* 24: 343–72.

Rapp, R. (1982) 'Family and class in contemporary America: Notes toward an understanding of ideology', in B. Thorne (ed.) *Rethinking the Family: Some Feminist Questions*, New York: Longman.

Schneider, D.M. (1984) *A Critique of the Study of Kinship*, Ann Arbor: University of Michigan Press.

Stack, C.B. (1974) *All Our Kin: Strategies for Survival in a Black Community*, New York: Harper & Row.

Strathern, M. (1985) 'Kinship and economy: Constitutive orders of a provisional kind', *American Ethnologist* 12: 191–209.

Woodburn, J. (1980) 'Hunters and gatherers today and reconstruction of the past', in E. Gellner (ed.) *Soviet and Western Anthropology*, London: Duckworth.

# Index